RIE SANI
BOUCHERIE
SANI
IA VAIMA NO
TA TATOU MAT

Also by Jean-Georges Vongerichten

SIMPLE TO SPECTACULAR
(with Mark Bittman)

JEAN-GEORGES
(with Mark Bittman)

Asian Flavors of Jean-Georges

Jean-Georges Vongerichten

FOOD PHOTOGRAPHY BY SANG AN

TRAVEL PHOTOGRAPHY BY DANIEL DEL VECCHIO

BROADWAY BOOKS / New York

BROADWAY

PUBLISHED BY BROADWAY BOOKS

Published in the United States by Broadway Books, an imprint of
The Doubleday Broadway Publishing Group, a division of Random House, Inc., New York.
www.broadwaybooks.com

Book design by Maria Carella

Library of Congress Cataloging-in-Publication Data
Vongerichten, Jean-Georges.
Asian flavors of Jean-Georges / Jean-Georges Vongerichten.—1st ed.
p. cm.
Includes index.
1. Cookery, Asian. I. Title.
TX724. 5. A1V67 2007
641.595—dc22 2007001757

ISBN: 978-0-7679-1273-0

PRINTED IN CHINA

10 9 8 7 6 5 4 3 2 1

First Edition

TO MY WIFE,

MARJA;

MY CHILDREN,

CEDRIC, LOUISE, AND CHLOE;

AND TO ALL MY

DEDICATED RESTAURANT STAFF

AROUND THE WORLD

Contents

Acknowledgments x

Introduction 2

APPETIZERS 13

SOUPS 71

SALADS 85

FISH 107

SHELLFISH 145

POULTRY 165

MEAT 191

VEGETABLES 211

RICE & NOODLES 223

DESSERTS 243

Sources 280

Index 282

Acknowledgments

First and foremost to my family—my wife Marja, my daughters Chloe and Louise, and my son Cedric. To Angela Miller, my agent. To Jennifer Josephy and Steve Rubin for their patience: The Spice Market road was a long one. To Sang An for capturing my Asian cuisine through his eyes. To all my staff worldwide for keeping up with me and my standards and for their loyalty and hard work day in and day out.

I must give very special acknowledgment to Daniel Del Vecchio, Gregory Brainin, and Phil Suarez. This is the team that makes it all happen. Daniel helps to organize every detail of every restaurant, and not only from a culinary perspective. He was the chef at Vong London and helps me develop all of our new concepts from kitchen design to music levels to the bowls we serve our soups in. He is absolutely critical to the day-to-day operations, as well as being a driving force behind this book. Gregory Brainin is the mind behind most of the 66 and Spice Market recipes and does most of our new recipe development with me. His range is so vast that if I even mention an idea, he'll present four dishes the next day! Lois Freedman pulls it all together with the magnificent waitstaff. She has been with me for twenty years and knows exactly what I want when it comes to service. She has an eagle eye for detail. Phil Suarez is simply the best deal maker I know. Without him, I would never have been able to realize so many of my dreams.

I would also like to thank Pichet Ong for his witty and delicious Asian desserts and Joseph Murphy for his delectable creations, such as the Caramelized Banana Cake with Crunchy Praline and Caramel Ice Cream.

Genevieve Ko did a great job of capturing the magic as I cooked for this book, and getting it down on paper. This book simply would not have been possible without her.

To Mark Bittman for being a part of making this book happen.

Asian Flavors of Jean-Georges

Introduction

When I was twenty-three, I was fortunate enough to be sent to Bangkok to be the chef de cuisine for my mentor, Louis Outhier, at his restaurant in the Oriental Hotel. I can still remember the first time I went to the Aw Taw Kaw market and saw ginger, lemongrass, galangal, and fifty kinds of rice for the first time. I can still smell the durian and remember the warm feeling it gave me after eating it.

As chef de cuisine for Outhier, my job was to execute his recipes for an international clientele. This proved to be more difficult than expected, as many products commonly available in France were either very hard or impossible to find. One day, I went to the market to buy apples for our signature foie gras dish and there were none. Instead, I bought some ginger and Thai mangoes—one of ten kinds that were available! I went back to my kitchen and seared a piece of foie gras, caramelized a piece of mango, and reduced an intense vegetable broth with some ginger. When I ate this combination, I had a true eureka moment and fusion was born for me.

I went back to that market the next day and bought lemongrass, galangal, black rice, sweet rice, spices, curry pastes and powders, and fruits and vegetables I couldn't even pronounce. I took them to my kitchen and began to experiment, to taste, to seek to understand the nuances and complexity of a whole new world of ingredients. I began an obsession that lasts to this day, an obsession that has helped define my career and my life. I spent the next four years traveling for Outhier opening restaurants in Hong Kong, Singapore, and Tokyo.

I then found myself in Boston for about a year and subsequently landed in New York at the Lafayette restaurant in the Drake Hotel. After my success at Lafayette, I opened my first restaurant, which I named JoJo's, my mother's nickname for me. Owning a restaurant and running a restaurant are very different jobs, and I quickly fell in love with all the details of opening and operating my own restaurant. I immediately saw the potential to transform people's moods by creating transporting experiences. I knew after leaving Bangkok that one day I would open a restaurant that would showcase the flavors I fell in love with in Thailand by using local ingredients and the French techniques that I had worked to master. That restaurant became Vong.

In 1992, nobody was cooking the flavors of Thailand with the precision of French technique and I felt New York would welcome it with open mouths. It was a blast! I created a decor that evoked the mood I was after—an exotic place far from midtown Manhattan. With the help of Pierre Schutz, who cooked with me at Lafayette, I created a menu really pushing the boundaries of French and Thai cuisines. It was great fun and people were extremely excited about it. For twelve years now, Pierre has been manning the kitchen at Vong, every day re-creating the magic of when we first opened. My success there is as much his as it is mine.

In 1997, I took the Vong concept to Hong Kong, and every year thereafter I traveled to Hong Kong at least four times. This opened up a whole new palette of flavors for me. Chinese food is so many things: it can be extremely subtle, almost ghostlike, in the layering of multiple flavors, and it also can be intense, powerful, and robust. Every meal in Hong Kong contained a thousand flavors. Needless to say, I fell in love. From crab claws cooked in egg whites with Hue Dew wine, to the elusive complexity of "Beggar's" Chicken, I knew I needed to explore Chinese cuisine.

In 2003, I opened 66 in Tribeca. I wanted to offer a menu that showcased some of the dishes I had fallen in love with in Hong Kong, as well as some inspired reinterpretations of my favorite New York Chinatown dishes. So often, Chinese food in New York can be heavy, a little greasy, and made with less-than-green-market quality produce. I really wanted to apply my standard of freshness and lightness to Chinese food. I also wanted to have fun with the flavors. The Cold Sesame Noodles 66 are a perfect example of this new kind of Chinese cuisine. As I travel more and more to China, I will continue to transform the dishes I cook to reflect the amazing foods I come across. It will always be a terrific work in progress for me!

Way before I dreamed of 66, however, I fantasized about Spice Market, a place to explore the marvelous street food of Southeast Asia. In 2001, my partner, Phil Suarez, and I signed the lease for Spice Market in the meat-packing district. At that time, there were only two restaurants in the neighborhood, Pastis and Florent—and a lot of meat! Now, it is crowded with great restaurants and clubs. It had taken almost five years of research and conceptualization before we were able to breathe life into Spice Market. In fact, it wasn't until we took a spice-route trip through Southeast Asia in 2003 that the flavors became clear enough to inspire an entire new cuisine. I traveled with my chefs, Daniel Del Vecchio and Gregory Brainin, through India, Burma, Malaysia, Vietnam, Thailand, Indonesia, and Singapore. We ate from seven in the morning to two the following morning for three weeks. We absorbed so many flavors, techniques, aromas, cultures, and products that it took four months just to process our experiences there. And then, just two weeks before opening, we transformed our favorite flavors from the trip into the unique dishes that define Spice Market.

It has been quite a journey! Every time I travel to Asia I discover some new flavor, some new ingredient, some new technique. I am constantly trying to bring new tastes to my clientele, so that in some way I can help to transport them, the way I love so much to be transported.

I hope the recipes in this book will take you to exotic places and titillate your senses. Have fun on *your* journey.

PANTRY

Almond flour, also known as almond meal, is finely ground whole raw almonds, available in many supermarkets and in natural food and gourmet markets. You can also make your own almond flour by grinding whole almonds in a food processor; freeze the almonds first or the powder will turn into a paste.

Ammonia powder, also known as hartshorn, is ammonium bicarbonate and was the leavening agent of choice before the advent of baking powder and baking soda. Although it produces a strong smell while being cooked, it leaves no aroma or flavor when the dish is finished. You can find it in specialty baking shops or online at www.kingarthurflour.com.

Bamboo shoots are harvested from bamboo; as soon as they are cut, they develop a bitter flavor and must be treated immediately to preserve their fresh sweetness. For this reason, canned bamboo shoots are not much inferior to fresh bamboo shoots because they have all been processed to maintain their flavor and crunch. Canned bamboo shoots are available in most major supermarkets and in Asian markets.

Café du Monde coffee comes from New Orleans and is a special blend of ground coffee beans and chicory, which is the root of the endive plant. The chicory adds body and a faint chocolate flavor to the brew. Café du Monde is available in most Asian markets or online at www.cafedumonde.com. French roast coffee is a good substitute.

Chili sauce in soybean oil, sometimes called chili paste with soybean, is a thick chili sauce stored in soybean oil. You can substitute "hot bean pastes," which are chili sauces generously flavored with soybeans. You can find these sauces in Asian markets and in some major grocery stores.

Chinese long beans are like long green beans, pale to dark green and about 18 inches long. They have a mild, grassy flavor and a lot of crunch, though they do not "snap" as regular green beans do. You can find these beans in large bunches in most Asian markets. You can substitute green beans, though they are quite different in both taste and texture.

Coconut juice—not to be confused with coconut milk—is the slightly sweet, floral juice from the inside of a coconut. It is almost as clear and thin as water. I like the Bangkok Market brand, which is sold in the freezer section of well-stocked Asian markets, because it contains large chunks of fresh coconut meat. Other canned brands on the shelf often contain additional preservatives and sweeteners that alter the subtle, fresh taste of coconut juice.

Crystallized tamarind candy is similar to candied ginger or candied orange peel, though slightly softer in texture and with a distinctive tart tamarind flavor. There are Mexican varieties available, but for the purposes of this book, the Southeast Asian varieties are best. It is available in most Southeast Asian markets or online at www.importfood.com and www.indomerchant.com. (Note: The U.S. government recently found very high levels of lead in the wrappers of the Mexican tamarind candies.)

Curry pastes (red, green, and yellow) are mixtures of fresh and dried vegetables, herbs, and spices. The red pastes are made from red chiles, the green from green; yellow contains turmeric. Curry pastes taste best when they are made fresh (page 200), but store-bought pastes work fine if you are short on time.

Dried shrimp are pinkish orange and tiny, about a half inch long. They have a strong fish odor and flavor and add a rich saltiness to dishes. Though dried, they do not keep indefinitely, so avoid any that are beginning to brown and store them in an airtight container in the refrigerator. Larger dried shrimp, which are about an inch long, are highly prized and have a more delicate flavor, but the difference in cost is only worth it if you really love the taste. Dried shrimp are available in most Asian markets.

Elderflower syrup is made from wild elderflowers, lemon juice, sugar, and water. Elderflower syrups and drinks are most popular in the United Kingdom and can be found in specialty or gourmet British markets. You can also buy elderflower syrup online at www.germandeli.com.

Gai lan, also known as Chinese broccoli, is a leafy green vegetable, with long, smooth, round stems and tiny white flowers. It is available year-round in some major supermarkets and in Asian markets. Look for bright green and firm stems and avoid any with wilted leaves.

Galangal is a relative of ginger and looks similar, but has distinctive thin yellow stripes and pink shoots. It has a stronger, more fiery bite than ginger and is the root of choice in Thailand and other Southeast Asian countries. You can find fresh galangal in many Asian markets, but you can always substitute fresh ginger.

Glutinous rice flour, also known as sweet rice flour, is made by finely grinding glutinous rice kernels. It is used primarily in pastries and gives the resulting products a very sticky, chewy texture and a faint, sweet rice flavor. It can be found in Asian markets or online at www.importfood.com.

Green papayas are unripe, with green skin, firm white flesh, and small white seeds. They range from oblong to round in shape and are about the size of summer melons. The fruit should be rock hard and uniformly green. Green papayas can be found in most Asian markets and in some natural food stores. You can substitute European cucumbers, jicama, or Granny Smith apples for a similar texture.

Hazelnut oil, a flavorful, aromatic oil, tastes much like the roasted hazelnuts from which it is pressed. It can become rancid easily and is best stored in the refrigerator. The best hazelnut oils are imported from France and can be found in most gourmet markets or online at www.amazon.com.

Licorice powder is made from grinding dried licorice root. It comes in plain, sweetened, or salted varieties and has a very strong, distinctly licorice flavor. Licorice powder can be found in gourmet or professional pastry stores, or you can grind it yourself, starting with a small piece of licorice root and using a coffee or spice grinder.

Lily buds, also known as tiger lily buds, flowers, stems, or golden needles, are the dried unopened flowers of yellow and orange daylilies. They have a subtle floral aroma and flavor and are pleasantly chewy. Look for lily buds that are pale golden and pliable and avoid any browned or brittle buds. Lily buds are available in most Asian markets or online at www.amazon.com.

Lime leaves have a wonderful floral and citrus aroma. Each leaf has two lobes, one smaller than the other. They are available fresh and dried in most Asian markets. The fresh are far preferable since their fragrance is more pronounced.

Lotus root is a long, cylindrical root that has pores inside running along the length of the root. The skin is thin and pale brown and the tan-colored flesh is fibrous and crisp when cooked. It has a wonderful earthy flavor and looks beautiful when sliced crosswise. You can find fresh lotus roots in some major supermarkets and in Asian markets. Look for roots that are not bruised and still have the tough root ends, which keep them fresh.

Mali syrup, also known as Jasmine syrup, is a sweetener made with jasmine flowers for a heady floral aroma. The best brand available is the Hale's Blue Boy brand from Thailand. Mali syrup is available in most Asian markets or online at www.grocerythai.com.

Matcha is a Japanese green tea powder made from *gyokuro* tea leaves that have been steamed, dried, and finely ground. The resulting powder is mixed with hot water and easily dissolves to become a cup of green tea. Matcha is available in Asian and gourmet markets and tea shops or online at www.amazon.com and www.japanesegreentea.com.

Nam pla, known in English as fish sauce and in Vietnamese as nuoc mam, is the primary seasoning in much of Southeast Asian cooking. Made by fermenting anchovies in brine, it has a pungent aroma and distinctive sea-saltiness. Viet Huong's Three Crabs Brand is a high-quality variety and can be found in most Asian markets. Fish sauce is now available in most well-stocked major supermarkets and in all Asian markets. Soy sauce can be substituted in a pinch.

Nori, also known as laver, is a variety of seaweed that is dried into thin sheets and is most commonly used as the wrapping around sushi. It can range from purple to dark green and comes in squares or rectangles of various dimensions. It is best to toast nori before use to refresh its flavor.

Palm sugar is a rich, caramel-like sugar made from the sap of sugar palm trees. Ranging from light to dark brown in color, palm sugar comes in jars in a single mass, soft enough to spoon out, or in hard, small blocks that must be crushed into smaller pieces before use. Since palm sugar is not highly processed, its sweetness can range slightly from batch to batch. Use regular brown sugar or, if you can find it, coconut sugar as a substitute.

Passion fruit purée is concentrated, blended passion fruit and has an aromatic sweet and tart tropical flavor. It is much stronger in flavor and thicker in texture than passion fruit juice. It can be found fresh or frozen in some gourmet markets or online at www.amazon.com.

Ponzu is a light and tart Japanese dipping sauce. You can buy it in specialty markets and in most Asian markets; Ajipon is the most famous brand produced in Japan.

Red finger chiles, also known as long red chiles or cayenne peppers, are about 6 inches in length and curved like a finger. They are quite hot and have a relatively thick flesh. They can be found in many supermarkets, and especially in Korean and Chinese markets.

Rice paper, known as *banh trang* in Vietnamese, are paper-thin sheets made from rice flour, water, and salt. They come in circles, squares, or triangles and in various dimensions. Sold dried, the rice paper sheets are brittle and crack easily and must be softened in hot water before they can be used as a wrapper. Rice paper is sold in some major supermarkets and in most Asian markets or online at www.importfood.com.

Rice vinegar, traditionally made through a long fermentation process with just rice, water, and yeast, now commonly starts from rice wine and other alcohol. Though less complex in flavor than its predecessors, rice vinegars today still have a pleasant, tart-sweet flavor, and relatively low acidity. Different countries produce slightly different varieties to best suit their cuisines. A good Japanese rice vinegar is your best bet for an all-purpose variety. Rice vinegar is available in most major supermarkets.

Shaoxing wine, also known as Hue Dew or Hua Diao wine, originates from Shaoxing in China's Zhejiang province. It is made from glutinous rice, rice millet, yeast, and local mineral and spring waters and most closely resembles dry sherry in taste. The best is aged for at least ten years in earthenware pottery in underground cellars and those labeled Hue Dew or Hua Diao have generally been aged for at least fifty years. Drunk warm, but more commonly used in cooking, Shaoxing wine is available in Asian markets or online at www.ethnicgrocer.com. The best variety is the Pagoda brand made in Zhejiang. Be sure to avoid Shaoxing "cooking" wine, which is heavily salted and lacks the bouquet of the drinkable wine. You can substitute a good dry sherry for Shaoxing wine.

Shrimp paste, called *gkapbi* in Thai and *belacan* in Malay, is made from dried, fermented ground shrimp and is sold in jars or plastic-wrapped bricks. Its color ranges from dark pink to dark brown and it is the texture of soft clay. It has a strong fermented shrimp odor and an equally strong salty shrimp flavor. For most people, its smell and taste are acquired ones, though small amounts mixed into cooked dishes add a wonderful sea-saltiness. Shrimp paste is available in most Asian markets or online at www.importfood.com.

Star anise comes from a small evergreen that grows in China and Vietnam. Though it tastes similar to aniseed, it is not related to it. The small eight-pronged star is hard and dry and is a deep reddish brown in color. It is available in Asian and gourmet markets or online at www.amazon.com and www.penzeys.com.

Sticky rice, sometimes also known as glutinous rice or sweet rice, is an opaque white grain that is short and stubby in the Chinese and Japanese varieties and long or "broken" in the Thai Jasmine varieties. The whole grains are soaked, then steamed (usually in cheesecloth; see page 224) until sticky and chewy. High-quality brands from Thailand are available in most Asian markets, but Koda Farms in California also makes a good sticky rice that is available in most major supermarkets.

Sumac comes from the bright, red berries of an evergreen that grows in the Mediterranean (and in the U.S.) and tastes intensely sour and fruity, like a strong lemon. The berries are dried and ground into brick red sumac powder. Commonly used in Middle Eastern cuisine, sumac adds a refreshing tartness to dishes. It is available in Middle Eastern and gourmet markets or online at www.amazon.com and www.penzeys.com.

Tamarind paste has a distinctive, prunelike sour flavor and is derived from the pods of large tropical trees. The fruit in the pods is soaked in hot water, then strained to form a thick paste. You can make your own with fresh or dried tamarind or buy prepared tamarind paste in most Asian and Latino markets. Though the flavor is quite different, you can substitute lime juice to achieve the desired tartness.

Taro, also known as taro root, is a thick hairy brown cylinder, with faint rings around the surface. The flesh inside is creamy white, often with lavender spots and lines throughout. Taro is available in many major supermarkets and in Asian and Latino markets. Look for firm taro and use it within a week.

Thai basil is slightly spicy, with a hint of anise flavor. The plant has small green leaves and purple stems and flowers. The leaves can be used fresh or cooked and are very common in Southeast Asian cuisine. Fresh Thai basil is available in most Asian markets and can be grown in any garden in warm weather. Micro Thai basil leaves are the tiny baby leaves of young plants and have a subtle spiciness.

Thai chiles (fresh), sometimes also called bird peppers or Thai bird chiles, are small, thin chiles, about 2 inches long, and have a lot of heat. Green chiles are not fully ripe and have a brighter flavor, while the ripened red ones have a richer spiciness. You can find Thai chiles in almost any Asian market, or you can substitute fresh chiles de Arbol.

Tofu skins, also known as bean curd skins or sheets, are made from the skin that forms over warm soybean milk that is then dried. These skins are sold fresh, frozen, or dried; the dried ones must be reconstituted in warm water to make them soft enough to use as a wrapper. They have a subtle soybean flavor and are often used in vegetarian cooking. You can find the sheets at most Asian markets and some natural food stores.

Turmeric (fresh) is a gnarly little root, smaller than ginger, with both orange skin and flesh. It is a defining flavor in many curry powders and turns almost everything it touches a rich orange-yellow color. Fresh turmeric should be hard when purchased and is best stored in the refrigerator. You can find fresh turmeric in most Asian markets, particularly those specializing in Southeast Asian and South Asian food.

Water chestnuts (fresh), slightly sweet, crisp, and refreshing, are small balls about 2 inches in diameter and have a thin brown skin. They should be rock hard and the skin should have a slight sheen. They are available in most Asian markets and in some natural food stores.

White port is made in exactly the same way as red port but from white grapes. White port ranges from very dry to very sweet and is generally drunk chilled as an aperitif. You can find white port in a well-stocked liquor store.

Yuzu juice comes from the yuzu citrus fruit, which looks like a tangerine. It has a very strong and distinct citrus tartness. Yuzu juice is available at Japanese markets or online at www.amazon.com. If you cannot find yuzu juice, you can substitute lemon juice, but the flavor will not be as pronounced.

Green papaya salad stall at the weekend food market, Aw Taw Kaw, in Bangkok →

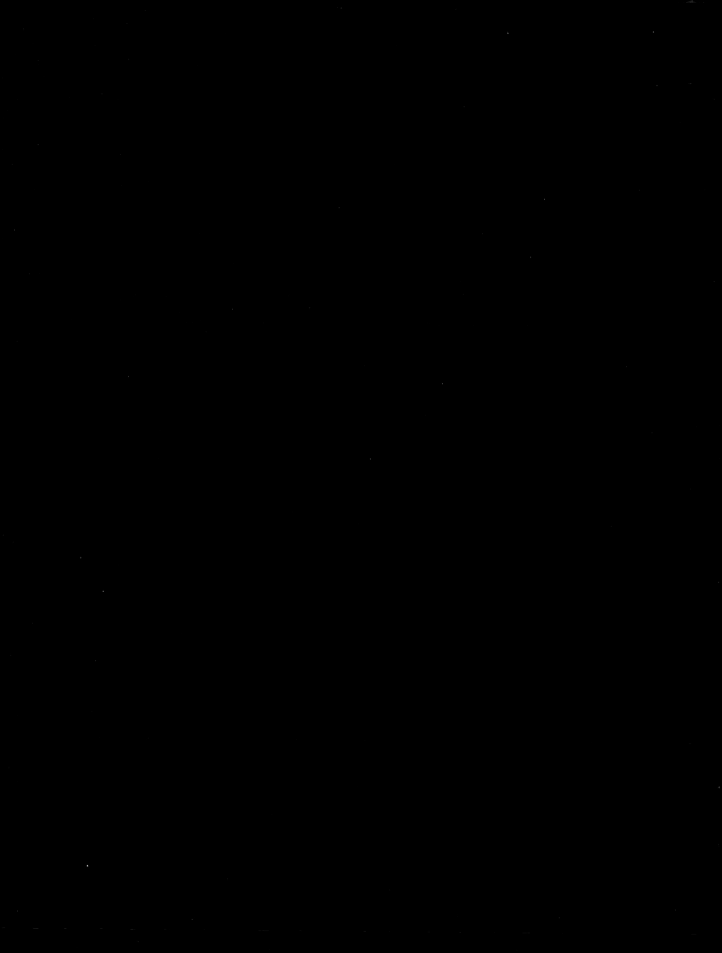

APPETIZERS

Cold Sesame Noodles 66

Makes 4 servings

SESAME PEANUT PASTE

¼ cup plus 2 teaspoons unsalted peanuts
3 tablespoons white sesame seeds
½ teaspoon grated fresh ginger
½ teaspoon minced garlic
½ fresh red Thai chile, seeded and minced
1½ teaspoons sugar
2 tablespoons chopped crystallized ginger
2 tablespoons sesame oil
2 tablespoons peanut oil
Salt and cayenne pepper

⅓ cup soy sauce
3 tablespoons black rice vinegar
3 tablespoons rice vinegar
3 tablespoons Shaoxing wine
1 cup sugar
½ cup chopped fresh cilantro
½ fresh red Thai chile
1 cinnamon stick, crushed
1 tablespoon coriander seeds
5 ounces dried cellophane noodles
¼ cup wasabi powder
½ cup peeled and julienned apple, preferably Granny Smith
½ cup peeled and julienned cucumber
½ cup trimmed and thinly sliced scallion
½ cup trimmed bean sprouts
¼ cup diced crystallized ginger
3 tablespoons peanuts, toasted (see below) and crushed
2 tablespoons white sesame seeds, toasted (see below)

Far from traditional heavy sesame noodles, this is a light and refreshing appetizer that is half noodles, half garnish. There are many different intriguing flavors in this dish; my intention was to make each bite different from the one before and after. It's more like a kind of chopped salad, really, than a typical goopy noodle dish.

I'm especially happy with the wasabi paste, because the sugar gives it a little crunch—you may find yourself using it all the time.

1. **To make the paste:** Put the peanuts in a large skillet and set over medium heat. Toast, shaking the pan occasionally, until lightly browned and fragrant. Remove from the heat and cool.

2. Put the sesame seeds in a medium skillet and set over medium heat. Toast, shaking the pan occasionally, until golden brown and fragrant. The sesame seeds will start to pop out of the pan. Remove from the heat and cool.

(continued)

3. Put the ginger, garlic, chile, and sugar in a blender. Purée, adding water as necessary (about ½ cup), until smooth.

4. Add the crystallized ginger and reserved peanuts and sesame seeds and purée. With the machine running, add the oils and blend until smooth. Season to taste with salt and cayenne.

5. **To make the broth and noodles:** Put the soy sauce, vinegars, wine, and ⅓ cup of the sugar in a small saucepan. Bring to a boil, whisking until the sugar dissolves; then add the cilantro, chile, cinnamon, and coriander seeds. Remove from the heat, cover, and let steep for 45 minutes.

6. Meanwhile, bring 4 cups water to a boil. Pour over the noodles and let sit until softened, about 30 minutes; drain. Stir together the wasabi powder and remaining ⅔ cup sugar with just enough water to make a paste, about 2½ tablespoons. Reserve the wasabi paste.

7. Strain the broth, ladle it into four serving bowls, and top with a mound of the noodles. Put a heaping tablespoon of the Sesame Peanut Paste on the mound, then portion the remaining ingredients over all. Top with a small dollop of the reserved wasabi paste and serve.

Local ladies in Bangkok buying vegetables on the street

Lobster Summer Rolls

Makes 4 servings

CHILI MAYONNAISE

1 egg yolk
2½ tablespoons Sriracha chili sauce
1½ tablespoons fresh lime juice
½ teaspoon salt
½ cup grape seed, corn, or other neutral oil

VINEGAR GELÉE

2 tablespoons white vinegar
2 tablespoons fresh lemon juice
2 tablespoons fresh lime juice
1 tablespoon elderflower syrup
1 tablespoon sugar
½ fresh green Thai chile, halved lengthwise
1 small bunch (½ ounce) fresh dill
1½ gelatin sheets soaked in cold water until softened, or 1¼ teaspoons powdered gelatin dissolved in 1 tablespoon cold water until softened

LOBSTER ROLLS

1 tablespoon salt
Two 1-pound lobsters
1 small bundle rice vermicelli, soaked in hot water for 30 minutes, drained, and chopped
Four 12-inch round rice paper wrappers
4 leaves red leaf lettuce
4 sprigs fresh dill, plus more for garnish
1 cup trimmed bean sprouts
½ cup thinly sliced carrots

This is as indulgent as a summer roll can get. Lobster, a rich substitute for the usual shrimp, is encased with fresh herbs and vegetables and a sweet-and-sour gelée. Each Southeast Asian flavor—hot, sour, salty, and sweet—has its own distinct texture here. The combination of chewy, crunchy, soft, and smooth is amazing. While one roll per person may seem like a generous serving size, your guests will be clamoring for more.

1. **To make the chili mayonnaise:** Put the first 4 ingredients and 1½ teaspoons water in a blender and blend until smooth. With the machine running, add the oil in a slow, steady stream. Blend until completely emulsified and set aside.

2. **To make the vinegar gelée:** Put the vinegar, lemon juice, lime juice, syrup, sugar, and chile in a small saucepan. Bring the mixture to a boil, stirring occasionally, and remove from the heat. Let the mixture cool for 10 minutes, then add the dill. Cool the mixture to room temperature.

3. Strain the mixture through a fine-mesh sieve, discard the solids, and return the liquid to the saucepan. Bring

to a boil and remove from the heat. Stir in the softened gelatin until completely dissolved and transfer to an 8½ x 4½-inch loaf pan. Refrigerate until set, about 2 hours.

4. Run a knife around the edge of the pan and unmold. Cut the gelée lengthwise into 4 even strips, so that you have four 8½ x 1-inch strips. Set aside.

5. **To make the lobster rolls:** Bring a large pot of water to a rolling boil. Prepare an ice water bath by filling a large bowl with ice and water and set aside. Add the salt and lobsters to the pot of boiling water and cook for 10 minutes. Remove the lobsters and plunge them into the ice water. Break off the tails and claws, shell, and remove the meat. Cut the meat into 1-inch chunks.

6. Bring a small pot of water to a boil. Add the rice vermicelli and cook for 3 minutes. Drain, rinse under cold running water, and drain again. Chop coarsely.

7. Have all the filling ingredients in one place; you'll also need a bowl of hot water (110°F to 120°F) and a clean kitchen towel. Soak a sheet of rice paper in the water just until soft, about 20 seconds. (Don't let it become too soft; it will continue to soften as you work). Lay it on the towel.

8. In the middle of the rice paper, lay a lettuce leaf and top with a strip of vinegar gelée and about a quarter each of the dill sprigs, bean sprouts, lobster, carrots, and vermicelli. Working quickly, fold in the sides and roll tightly. Repeat with the remaining rice paper sheets and filling.

9. Cut each roll into 6 even pieces and decoratively arrange on four serving plates. Garnish with dill sprigs and serve with the chili mayonnaise on the side.

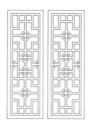

Crispy Vegetable Rolls

Makes 8 rolls

ASIAN-STYLE PICKLES

1 cup rice vinegar
2 tablespoons sugar
½ teaspoon salt
½ carrot, thinly sliced
¼ cup sliced daikon radish
¼ cup julienned red radish
¼ cup julienned black radish

NAM PRIK

¼ cup nam pla (Thai fish sauce)
2 tablespoons fresh lime juice
¼ cup rice vinegar
2 garlic cloves, minced
1 fresh red Thai chile, seeded and minced
2 tablespoons sugar

VEGETABLE ROLLS

½ cup sugar
¼ cup peeled and finely chopped jicama, fresh water chestnuts, daikon radish, or turnip
¼ cup chopped asparagus or haricots verts
¼ cup shredded carrot
¼ cup julienned leeks
1 small bundle rice vermicelli, soaked in hot water for 30 minutes, drained, and chopped
¼ cup sliced fresh shiitake mushroom caps
¼ cup trimmed bean sprouts
¼ cup diced firm tofu
¼ teaspoon minced garlic
½ teaspoon minced fresh red Thai chile
1 large egg
2 tablespoons nam pla (Thai fish sauce)
¼ teaspoon freshly ground black pepper
Eight 5-inch round rice paper wrappers
½ cup corn or vegetable oil for frying
8 Boston or Bibb lettuce leaves
¼ cup fresh mint leaves
¼ cup fresh cilantro leaves

This is basically a spring roll, Vietnamese in character. In typical fashion, we fill it with so many fresh vegetables and herbs that the result is extraordinary, the perfect starter for a vegetarian meal. And if you're short on time, you can omit the frying; these are almost as good fresh as fried.

The basic idea is to have a variety of ingredients here, but you can do it with two vegetables or ten. (In the restaurant, we often use ten; at home, I'd use just a few.) In the winter, rely more on root vegetables; in the summer, think about asparagus, peas, and sugar snap peas.

1. **To make the pickles:** Put the vinegar, sugar, salt, and 1 cup water in a saucepan and bring to a boil. Remove from the heat.

(continued)

2. Put each of the vegetables in individual bowls and pour the pickling liquid over each. Cover and refrigerate overnight.

3. **To make the nam prik:** Whisk together all the ingredients in a small bowl until the sugar dissolves. Use within a couple of hours.

4. **To make the vegetable rolls:** Put 4 cups water and the sugar in a saucepan and bring to a boil. Remove from the heat and cool to warm. Meanwhile, combine the next 13 ingredients.

5. Soak a sheet of rice paper briefly in the warm sugar water and put 2 heaping tablespoons of the vegetable filling in a line in the center. Fold in the sides and roll tightly. Repeat with the remaining rice paper sheets and filling.

6. Heat the oil in a deep skillet to about 350°F. Put the rolls in the pan, working in batches to avoid overcrowding, and fry, turning occasionally, until golden brown all around, just a couple of minutes per side.

7. To serve: Place each roll in the center of a lettuce leaf and top with the mint and cilantro. Serve with the pickles and the nam prik on the side.

Spring rolls on the streets of Bangkok

APPETIZERS

Chicken and Shrimp Egg Rolls

Makes 12 rolls

DUCK MUSTARD

2 tablespoons mustard powder
1 cup apricot jam
2 tablespoons rice vinegar, preferably Japanese
2 tablespoons nam pla (Thai fish sauce)
One 9-inch piece fresh ginger, peeled and roughly chopped
Salt

EGG ROLLS

1 teaspoon potato flour
¾ teaspoon salt, plus more as needed
½ teaspoon sugar
2 tablespoons light soy sauce
¾ teaspoon freshly ground black pepper
1½ teaspoons Shaoxing wine
2 teaspoons sesame oil
4 ounces boneless, skinless chicken breasts or thighs, diced
2 small carrots, peeled and julienned
4 ounces medium shrimp, peeled, deveined, and chopped
2 tablespoons peanut oil, plus more for frying (or use vegetable oil for frying)
1 garlic clove, minced
One ¼-inch piece fresh ginger, peeled and minced
1 scallion, trimmed and thinly sliced
2 tablespoons trimmed and julienned fresh shiitake mushrooms
¾ ounce julienned bamboo shoots
1 ounce julienned sugar snap peas
¾ ounce dried cellophane noodles, soaked in hot water for 30 minutes, drained, and chopped
Twelve 5-inch square egg roll wrappers
2 egg yolks, beaten, plus more as needed
2 tablespoons thinly sliced fresh mint
12 Napa cabbage leaves for serving

If ever there was a truly substantial egg roll, this is it. Chicken, shrimp, and a heap of vegetables make these rolls lovely and thick. The proportions here are perfect—the way egg rolls should be—lots of fresh filling with a little crunch of the thin wrapping in each bite.

1. **To make the mustard:** Mix the mustard powder with 1 tablespoon water in a small bowl to make a smooth paste; let sit for 10 minutes. Reserve.

2. Meanwhile, put the jam, vinegar, nam pla, and ginger in a food processor or blender and process until smooth, scraping down the sides as necessary. Mix in the mustard paste and season to taste with salt.

3. **To make the egg rolls:** Put the potato flour, ½ teaspoon of the salt, ¼ teaspoon of the sugar, 2 teaspoons of the soy sauce, ½ teaspoon of the black pepper, 1 teaspoon of the wine, 1 teaspoon of the sesame oil, and 1½

Cooked shrimp and crab at the Aw Taw Kaw weekend market in Bangkok →

tablespoons water in a medium mixing bowl. Stir until the sugar dissolves, then add the chicken and stir well to coat. Set aside for 30 minutes.

4. Put the carrots in a colander and sprinkle with salt. Let sit for 30 minutes to draw out the moisture; then rinse, drain, and dry.

5. Put 2 teaspoons of the soy sauce and the remaining ¼ teaspoon salt, ¼ teaspoon sugar, ¼ teaspoon black pepper, and 1 teaspoon sesame oil in another medium bowl. Stir, then add the shrimp and toss well to coat. Set aside for 15 minutes.

6. Heat half the peanut oil in a wok or large skillet over medium-high heat. Add the garlic, half the ginger, and half the scallion and stir-fry until golden, about 30 seconds. Add the chicken with its marinade and cook, stirring continuously, for 30 seconds, then add the shrimp with its marinade. Cook, stirring continuously, until the shrimp turns pink, about 1 minute.

7. Stir in the mushrooms and bamboo shoots and cook just until lightly browned and softened, about 2 minutes, then add the remaining ½ teaspoon wine. After most of the liquid has evaporated, remove everything from the wok and cool.

8. Heat the remaining tablespoon peanut oil in the wok over medium-high heat. Add the remaining ginger and scallion and cook until fragrant, then add the sugar snap peas and cook, stirring occasionally, for 1 minute. Stir in the carrots and noodles and cook just until heated through. Season with the remaining 2 teaspoons soy sauce and salt to taste. Remove from the heat and cool.

9. Lay out a wrapper on your work surface. Put 2 tablespoons of the sugar snap pea–carrot filling and 2 tablespoons of the chicken-shrimp filling diagonally across the wrapper. Fold in the sides, brush the upper triangle edges with egg yolk, then roll tightly. Repeat with remaining wrappers and filling.

10. Pour oil to a depth of 3 inches in a heavy, deep saucepan and heat to 350°F. Carefully add the rolls and cook, turning occasionally, until golden brown and crisp. Do not overcrowd; work in batches if necessary. Remove from the oil, drain on paper towels, and cut in half diagonally.

11. Stir the mint into the reserved duck mustard. Sprinkle the egg rolls with a little salt, place on cabbage leaves, and serve with the duck mustard on the side.

Mushroom Spring Rolls with Galangal Emulsion

Makes 4 servings

GALANGAL EMULSION

One 2-inch piece fresh galangal or ginger, peeled and chopped
¼ cup fresh lime juice
¼ cup plus 2 tablespoons rice vinegar
2 large egg yolks
1 tablespoon salt
1 cup grape seed, corn, or other neutral oil
¼ cup fresh tarragon leaves

SPRING ROLLS

6½ tablespoons unsalted butter
2 cups fresh shiitake mushrooms, stemmed and cut into ½-inch slices
2 cups fresh oyster mushrooms, stemmed and cut into ½-inch slices
2 cups fresh cremini mushrooms, stemmed and cut into ½-inch slices
¼ cup Shaoxing wine
1 tablespoon soy sauce
2 teaspoons extra virgin olive oil
1 garlic clove, sliced
1 teaspoon minced fresh ginger
1 tablespoon thinly sliced shallots
1 teaspoon minced fresh lemongrass
½ dried red Thai chile, minced
1 teaspoon minced lemon zest
⅛ teaspoon salt, plus more to taste
2 large egg yolks
Ten 5-inch square spring roll wrappers
Corn or vegetable oil for frying
20 Boston lettuce leaves

Crisp and light, these are a perfect starter. Tarragon, a distinctly French herb, works perfectly with the earthy mushrooms here. Use any assortment of mushrooms you like (as we do), but those listed here are among the easiest to find.

1. **To make the emulsion:** Put the galangal, lime juice, and vinegar in a blender and blend until smooth. Add the egg yolks and salt and blend well; then, with the machine running, add the oil in a slow, steady stream. Add the tarragon leaves and purée until smooth and green. Strain through a fine-mesh sieve into a container, then cover and refrigerate until ready to use.

2. **To make the spring rolls:** Melt the butter in a large deep skillet with a tightly fitting lid over medium-high heat until foamy, then add the mushrooms, wine, and soy sauce. Cover, turn the heat to low, and cook until the mushrooms have released their juices and are tender, about 20 minutes. Remove the lid and cook, stirring occasionally, until most of the liquid has evaporated and the mushrooms are lightly glazed, about 10 minutes. Transfer to a shallow baking dish, spreading in an even layer, and refrigerate until cool.

3. Heat the olive oil in a large skillet over medium heat and add the garlic, ginger, shallots, lemongrass, and chile. Cook, stirring, until golden brown, 30 seconds, then add the lemon peel and ⅛ teaspoon salt and stir well. Cool, then add to the mushroom mixture and mix well. Taste and add more salt to taste.

4. Beat the egg yolks in a bowl; lay one of the wrappers on your work surface. Put 3 heaping tablespoons of the mushroom filling diagonally across the wrapper. Fold in the sides, brush the upper triangle edges with the egg yolks, then roll tightly. Repeat with remaining wrappers and filling.

5. Pour oil to a depth of 3 inches in a heavy, deep saucepan and heat to 350°F. Carefully add the rolls and cook, turning occasionally, until golden brown and crisp. Do not overcrowd; work in batches if necessary. Remove from the oil, drain on paper towels, and cut in half diagonally. Serve each piece on a lettuce leaf with the galangal emulsion as a dipping sauce.

Local girl in Yangon traditionally dressed. The makeup on her cheeks is a powder made from stone.

Duck Sticks

Makes 4 servings

DUCK MEAT FILLING

1 small carrot, chopped

½ onion, quartered

¼ cup peeled and chopped daikon radish

2 garlic cloves

2 duck legs

Salt

1 tablespoon five-spice powder

¼ cup grape seed, corn, or other neutral oil, plus more for frying

2 scallions, trimmed and minced

2 tablespoons pickled ginger, minced

2 teaspoons soy sauce, plus more to taste

Four 8-inch square egg roll wrappers, cut in half

2 egg yolks, lightly beaten with 2 tablespoons water

Think of this as Gascony meets Shanghai: these juicy, crispy duck egg rolls can be served as part of Duck "Oriental" (page 181) but are also amazing on their own. The fork-tender duck confit and aromatic vegetables are brightened with fresh scallions and pickled ginger. Wrapped in paper-thin egg roll wrappers and fried to a crisp, they are best eaten immediately.

1. Put the carrot, onion, daikon, and garlic in a food processor. Pulse until diced small. In a large bowl, season the duck legs with salt, then cover with the vegetable mixture and five-spice powder. Cover and marinate in the refrigerator overnight.

2. Preheat the oven to 200°F. Put the duck legs in a roasting pan, skin side up, and cook for 8 hours, or until very soft. Remove from the oven, cool slightly, then remove the skin and bones, reserving the rendered fat. Mix ¼ cup of the reserved fat with the oil, duck meat, scallions, pickled ginger, and soy sauce.

3. Put an eighth of the duck meat mixture in a line lengthwise in the center of an egg roll wrapper. Brush a little egg wash around the edges of the wrapper. Fold in the sides; then, starting from one end, roll up tightly. Repeat with remaining wrappers and filling.

4. Pour oil to a depth of at least 1 inch in a heavy, deep saucepan and heat to 350°F. Add the duck sticks and cook until golden brown and crisp, turning occasionally for even browning. Do not overcrowd; work in batches if necessary. Drain on paper towels and serve.

Chicken Samosas with Cilantro-Yogurt Dip

Makes 4 servings

CILANTRO-YOGURT DIP

1½ tablespoons whole cumin seeds
1 cup fresh cilantro leaves
1 small fresh green Thai chile, sliced
¾ cup plain whole-milk yogurt
1 tablespoon fresh lemon juice
1 teaspoon sugar, plus more to taste
Salt and freshly ground black pepper

SAMOSAS

2 tablespoons grape seed, corn, or other neutral oil, plus more for deep-frying
1 cup diced onion
1 tablespoon peeled and minced fresh ginger
1 tablespoon minced garlic
2 tablespoons whole coriander seeds, finely ground
½ teaspoon turmeric powder
½ teaspoon cayenne pepper
½ cup diced tomatoes
1 tablespoon tamarind paste
1 pound boneless, skinless chicken breasts, finely minced
Salt and freshly ground pepper
Four 8-inch square spring roll wrappers

We use spring roll wrappers here, not only because they're easy but also because they make a perfectly light and flaky shell. Tightly wrapping these samosas into perfect triangles may take some practice, but the results are well worth the effort, and the highly spiced filling pairs perfectly with the cooling cilantro-yogurt dip.

You can buy ground chicken or mince it yourself in the food processor, but don't purée it.

1. Put the whole cumin seeds in a small skillet and set over medium heat. Toast, shaking the pan occasionally, until fragrant and browned. The seeds will start to pop. Remove from the heat, cool completely, and grind to a fine powder in a spice grinder.

2. **To make the dip:** Put the cilantro leaves and chile in a food processor and process until coarsely chopped. Transfer to a mixing bowl and add the yogurt, lemon juice, sugar, and ½ teaspoon of the finely ground cumin. Stir well, season with salt, pepper, and more sugar to taste, and set aside.

3. **To make the samosas:** Put the oil in a large deep skillet and set over medium heat. Add the onion and cook, stirring, until translucent and softened, about 5 minutes. Add the ginger and garlic and cook until fragrant, 1 minute, then add the coriander, turmeric, cayenne, and remaining ground cumin and cook, stirring, for 3 minutes. Add the tomatoes and cook until they begin to

break down, 5 minutes, and stir in the tamarind paste. Add the chicken and cook, stirring, until the meat is completely cooked through, about 5 minutes. Season to taste with salt and pepper, remove from the heat, and cool to room temperature.

4. Put one of the spring roll wrapper rectangles on your work surface so that the short side is facing you. Put 2 tablespoons of the filling ¼ inch from the bottom of the rectangle, then fold the bottom left corner over the filling so that the bottom edge meets the right edge to form a triangle. Press the edges to seal, then fold the triangle over the top edge and continue to fold along the edges to create a triangle. Seal the end of the spring roll wrapper with a little water. Repeat with the remaining wrappers and filling.

5. Pour oil to a depth of 3 inches in a heavy, deep saucepan and heat to 350°F. Carefully add the samosas and cook, turning occasionally, until golden brown and crisp. Do not overcrowd; work in batches if necessary. Remove from the oil and drain on paper towels. Serve immediately with the cilantro-yogurt dip.

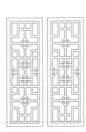

Chicken Buns

Makes 4 servings

DOUGH

1 tablespoon sugar

1 teaspoon active dry yeast

1 teaspoon baking powder

2 cups all-purpose flour, plus more as needed

2 teaspoons grape seed, corn, or other neutral oil, plus more for greasing

FILLING

1 pound boneless, skinless chicken breasts or thighs, diced

1 tablespoon cornstarch

1 tablespoon Shaoxing wine

1 teaspoon salt

⅓ cup grape seed, corn, or other neutral oil

1 tablespoon chopped scallions

1 tablespoon minced fresh ginger

½ cup fresh button mushrooms, trimmed and diced

6 fresh shiitake mushroom caps, trimmed and diced

1 tablespoon soy sauce

1 teaspoon sesame oil

1 tablespoon sugar

1 teaspoon freshly ground black pepper

Here, a traditional Chinese bun meets a savory stir-fry. We do away with the usual dense filling and substitute a light mixture that is generously flavored with fresh shiitakes. There is both labor and time involved here, but they are well worth the effort. You can use good pork or veal instead of chicken, but in any case, you want an ingredient you can taste and see.

Street cart in Bangkok

1. **To make the dough:** Dissolve the sugar in ¾ cup warm water, then add the yeast and baking powder. Let the mixture sit until it becomes foamy, about 10 minutes. Sift the flour into a large mixing bowl, then stir in 2 teaspoons oil and the yeast mixture until the liquid is absorbed.

2. Turn the dough out onto a floured board and knead until smooth and elastic, about 7 minutes. Place the dough in a large oiled bowl, cover with a towel or plastic wrap, and let it rise until at least doubled in bulk, about 2 hours.

3. **Meanwhile, make the filling:** Mix the chicken with the cornstarch, wine, and salt in a bowl and let the mixture sit for 20 minutes. Heat 2 tablespoons of the oil in a skillet over medium-high heat and add the chicken mixture. Cook, stirring, until the chicken changes color, then remove from the heat.

4. Heat the remaining 3 tablespoons oil in a large skillet over medium-high heat and add the scallions and ginger. Cook, stirring occasionally, until softened, about 1 minute. Add the mushrooms and cook until softened, about 2 minutes. Add the chicken mixture and the remaining ingredients and bring to a boil. After most of the liquid has evaporated, about 5 minutes, remove from the heat and cool.

5. Punch down the dough and divide it in half. Form each piece of dough into 2 long rolls and then cut each roll evenly into 6 pieces. Roll the pieces into balls and flatten each ball into a 6-inch disk.

6. Put about 3 tablespoons of the chicken mixture in the center of each disk of dough. Pleat together the edges of the dough and enclose the filling. Let the buns sit for about 20 minutes while you prepare a steamer. Lightly grease the bottom of the steamer. Transfer the buns to the steamer, cover, and cook until the dough and filling are cooked through, about 15 minutes. Serve hot or warm.

Crab Fritters with Three Dipping Sauces

Makes 4 servings

GREEN PAPAYA RÉMOULADE

½ cup diced green papaya
2 tablespoons fresh lime juice
½ cup mayonnaise
¼ cup crème fraîche
Salt and freshly ground black pepper

SOY AND CHILE MIGNONETTE

¼ cup soy sauce
1½ tablespoons rice vinegar
½ teaspoon hazelnut oil
1 teaspoon minced fresh red Thai chile

TAMARIND KETCHUP

One ½-pound package tamarind paste
1 garlic clove, very finely minced, almost to a purée
1 fresh red Thai chile, finely minced
1 tablespoon sugar
1 tablespoon nam pla (Thai fish sauce)

FRITTERS

8 ounces crabmeat, picked over for shells and cartilage
⅛ teaspoon celery seed
½ teaspoon salt, plus more as needed
Cayenne pepper
1½ tablespoons unsalted butter
½ cup all-purpose flour
2 large eggs
Grape seed, corn, or other neutral oil for frying
Fleur de sel, celery salt, or coarse salt

Forget crab cakes; these fritters, made with a choux paste (similar to the base you'd use for cream puffs, éclairs, or gougères), are light and airy rather than heavy. But don't expect to serve them at a sit-down dinner; in fact, they shouldn't even make it out of your kitchen. You'll want to eat them immediately.

You can make these with chopped shrimp, chopped scallops, or chopped fish, as well. At the restaurants, we serve these with three sauces. Do what you like at home; they're great with just a squeeze of lemon juice. (If I had to pick one sauce to serve with these, it would be the green papaya rémoulade.)

1. **To make the rémoulade:** Toss the papaya with the lime juice in a small container, cover, and refrigerate overnight.

2. Add the remaining ingredients to the papaya and mix well. Season to taste with salt and pepper.

3. **To make the mignonette:** Mix all the ingredients together in a small bowl with 2½ tablespoons water until very well blended.

4. **To make the ketchup:** Put the tamarind paste in a saucepan with ½ cup water and turn the heat to medium. Cook, whisking lightly to break up the lumps, and add more water whenever the mixture becomes dry until you've added a total of about 1 cup. The process will take about 10 minutes and the result should still be quite thick, but fairly smooth.

5. Pass the tamarind through a food mill into a bowl or purée in a blender; you will have about ½ cup of smooth pulp. Add the remaining ingredients and set aside for an hour; the flavor will grow during that period. Taste and adjust the seasoning as necessary.

6. **To make the fritters:** In a bowl, season the crab with the celery seed, salt, and cayenne to taste. Stir lightly, then set aside.

7. Put the butter and ¼ cup plus 2 tablespoons water in a small saucepan over medium-low heat. As soon as the butter completely melts and the mixture simmers, stir in the flour. Cook, stirring constantly, until the flour forms a ball around the spoon and no longer sticks to the bottom of the pan. Transfer to the bowl of an electric mixer fitted with the paddle attachment and beat on medium-low speed until the mixture cools. Add the eggs, one at a time, with the machine running. Continue mixing until the dough is well combined and thickened. Fold in the crab mixture until well incorporated.

8. Pour oil to a depth of ½ inch in a large skillet and set over medium heat. When the oil is hot, about 350°F, scoop a spoonful of the crab mixture and carefully push it off with your finger into the skillet. Do not try to press the mixture together; it should have a shreddy consistency. Cook the fritter until nicely browned and crisp, then turn and cook the other side until golden and crisp. Remove it from the oil and drain on paper towels. Repeat this process with the remaining crab. You can make more than one fritter at a time, but do not overcrowd the skillet; work in batches if necessary.

9. Season the fritters with fleur de sel and serve with the green papaya rémoulade, soy and chile mignonette, and tamarind ketchup.

Black Pepper Crab Dumplings

Makes 4 servings

BLACK PEPPER OIL

2 teaspoons whole black peppercorns
1 whole clove
1 whole allspice berry
1 whole star anise
2 tablespoons grape seed, corn, or other neutral oil
⅛ teaspoon salt
1¼ teaspoons extra virgin olive oil

SOY REDUCTION

2 tablespoons soy sauce
¼ cup kecap manis (sweet soy sauce)
1 teaspoon cardamom seeds

DUMPLINGS

2½ tablespoons unsalted butter
1 teaspoon minced onion
1½ teaspoons all-purpose flour
⅛ teaspoon salt, plus more to taste
¼ cup whole milk, warmed
4 ounces crabmeat, preferably Peekytoe, picked over for shells and cartilage
Sixteen 4-inch round white dumpling wrappers
4 ounces sugar snap peas, trimmed, strings removed, and split lengthwise in half
¼ cup fresh mint leaves

This is unlike any dumpling you've had before. While the rich béchamel folded into the crab makes the filling incredibly luscious, the black pepper oil cuts through the butter nicely. This dish would be an elegant beginning to any meal, but serves as a stunning entrée as well.

1. **To make the black pepper oil:** Put the spices in a small skillet set over medium heat. Toast, shaking the pan occasionally, until fragrant, about 2 minutes. Remove from the heat, cool completely, and transfer to a spice grinder. Grind to a fine powder.

2. Return the spice powder to the skillet with the grape seed oil and salt. Set over medium heat and warm for 3 minutes. Remove from the heat, stir in the olive oil, and cool to room temperature. Set aside.

3. **To make the soy reduction:** Put the soy sauces and cardamom seeds in a small saucepan and bring to a steady simmer over medium-low heat. Cook until reduced to a syrupy consistency. Strain through a fine-mesh sieve and set aside.

4. **To make the dumplings:** Melt ½ tablespoon of the butter in a small saucepan over medium heat. Add the onion and cook, stirring, until softened, about 1 minute. Add the flour and salt and cook, stirring, until the mixture is thick and pasty and sticks to the bottom of the

A variety of dim sum in Shanghai →

pan, about 1 minute. Add the milk in a slow, steady stream, stirring constantly. Continue to stir until the mixture boils and cook for about 1 minute. Strain through a fine-mesh sieve into a bowl, pressing on the solids to extract as much of the béchamel as possible. Set aside to cool.

5. When the béchamel is cool, add the crab and fold gently. Taste and add salt if necessary. Put 1 tablespoon of the crab mixture in the center of a dumpling wrapper. Wet the edges of the wrapper with water, then fold the wrapper in half, pressing the edges tightly to seal, to form a half-moon. Repeat with the remaining wrappers and filling.

6. Bring a large pot of water to a boil and add a pinch of salt. Add the dumplings and cook, stirring gently, until they float to the surface and are tender. Remove carefully with a slotted spoon and set aside.

7. Fill a large bowl with water and ice and set aside. Bring a small pot of water to a boil and add the sugar snap peas and a generous pinch of salt. Cook until bright green and tender, but still crisp, about 4 minutes. Drain and transfer to the ice water. When cold, drain again. Set aside.

8. Microwave the mint leaves in 20-second increments until they are dry and brittle, about 2 minutes total. Cool and then grind in a spice grinder to a fine powder. Set aside.

9. Melt 1 tablespoon of the butter in a large skillet over medium heat. Add the dumplings and toss gently until well coated and heated through. Transfer to 4 serving plates and drizzle the black pepper oil and soy reduction over the dumplings.

10. Melt the remaining 1 tablespoon butter in a large skillet over medium heat; when foamy, add the sugar snap peas and toss until well coated and warm. Top the dumplings with the sugar snap peas. Sprinkle the mint dust over the whole dish and serve.

Shrimp and Pork Dumplings

Makes 24 dumplings

PINEAPPLE NAM PRIK

8 ounces fresh pineapple, peeled, cored, and chopped
2 anchovy fillets
2 garlic cloves, peeled
One ½-inch piece fresh ginger, peeled and sliced
1 fresh red Thai chile, stemmed, seeded, and chopped
1 tablespoon sugar
2 tablespoons fresh lime juice
2 tablespoons rice or white vinegar
¼ teaspoon ground turmeric

DUMPLINGS

8 ounces shrimp, peeled, deveined, and chopped or ground
4 ounces pork shoulder or butt, chopped or ground
½ teaspoon minced fresh red Thai chile, crushed red pepper flakes, or freshly ground black pepper
4 fresh water chestnuts, peeled and chopped, or ⅓ cup peeled and chopped jicama
3 scallions, trimmed and minced
¼ teaspoon sugar
2 tablespoons nam pla (Thai fish sauce)
4 garlic cloves, minced
¼ cup plus 1 tablespoon grape seed, corn, or other neutral oil, plus more as needed
1 shallot, minced
3 ounces fresh shiitake mushroom caps, trimmed and finely chopped
Twenty-four 4-inch round dumpling wrappers
Nuoc Cham (page 117)

This is a classic dumpling, stuffed with shrimp and pork, though probably better than most you've eaten because all the ingredients are fresh. Our twist is the combination of Southeast Asian sauces with traditional dumpling ingredients and technique. This is how you'd see "Chinese" food in Malaysia: hotter and spicier.

Like all dumplings, these are easy and fun to make, and can be prepared ahead of time and frozen before steaming. You can even put them in the steamer without defrosting; some people insist they're best that way.

1. **To make the pineapple nam prik:** Put all the ingredients in a blender with ½ cup water. Blend until smooth. Reserve.

2. **To make the dumplings:** Put the first 7 ingredients in a mixing bowl with three-quarters of the minced garlic and 3 tablespoons of the oil. Mix just until everything is well combined.

3. Heat the remaining 2 tablespoons oil in a large skillet over medium heat. Add the shallot and remaining garlic and cook just until softened, about 1 minute. Add the

mushrooms and cook until softened, about 2 minutes. Remove from the heat and stir in the shrimp-pork mixture.

4. Brush a little oil on the bottom of a steamer and set over at least 2 inches of simmering water in a covered pot.

5. Put a heaping teaspoon of the filling in the center of each dumpling wrapper. You can bunch the wrappers around the filling, leaving the dumpling open-faced, or you can seal the edges with water and fold the dumplings into half-moons. Put the finished dumplings on a lightly floured surface; do not allow them to touch one another.

6. Transfer the dumplings to the steamer, putting them about 1 inch apart, and cook until the wrappers are soft and the fillings cooked through, about 12 minutes for fresh dumplings, 20 minutes for frozen dumplings. Serve immediately with nuoc cham and pineapple nam prik.

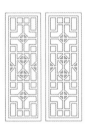

Shrimp Cakes with Cucumber-Peanut Relish

Makes 4 servings

CUCUMBER-PEANUT RELISH

2 tablespoons rice vinegar
1 tablespoon fresh lime juice
1 tablespoon sugar or honey
1 garlic clove, minced
2 tablespoons nam pla (Thai fish sauce)
1 medium cucumber, peeled, seeded, and diced
2 tablespoons chopped peanuts
2 teaspoons chopped fresh mint leaves, optional
2 teaspoons chopped fresh cilantro leaves, optional

SHRIMP CAKES

1 pound shrimp, peeled, deveined, and chopped
1 tablespoon rice flour
2 large eggs, beaten
2 tablespoons red curry paste, store-bought is fine
⅔ cup finely chopped scallions
2½ cups finely chopped Chinese long beans
2 teaspoons nam pla (Thai fish sauce)
Grape seed, corn, or other neutral oil for frying
1 fresh green Thai chile, seeded and minced

Shrimp's gelatinous texture and subtle flavor make it the best choice for seafood cakes—certainly it's among the classic choices. The curry paste provides a foundation of rich heat, the long beans add a nice crunch, and the cucumber-peanut relish is a refreshing counterpoint.

1. **To make the relish:** In a medium-size bowl, whisk together the first 5 ingredients until the sugar dissolves. Toss with the cucumber, peanuts, and, if you like, mint and cilantro. Serve within a half hour.

2. **To make the shrimp cakes:** Put the shrimp in a food processor and process until smooth. Transfer to a large mixing bowl, add the next 6 ingredients, and mix everything together until well combined.

3. Wet your hands and then form the shrimp mixture into round cakes that are 2 inches in diameter and ½ inch thick. Put the finished cakes on a rack or a sheet of wax paper.

4. Cover the bottom of a large skillet with oil to a depth of ⅛ inch. Heat over medium-high heat for 3 or 4 minutes, then put the cakes in the skillet. Do not overcrowd; work in batches as needed. Adjust the heat so the cakes do not burn, and move them around in the pan so they brown evenly. Turn after about 3 minutes. When the cakes are brown and crisp all around, they are done.

5. Mound the cucumber-peanut relish in the center of each serving plate. Put the shrimp cakes on top of the relish, garnish with the chile, and serve.

Chili Prawns with Sweet Sesame Walnuts

Makes 4 servings

SWEET SESAME WALNUTS

1 ½ teaspoons baking soda
2 ¼ cups walnut halves
⅔ cup sugar
Grape seed, corn, or other neutral oil for deep-frying
3 tablespoons white sesame seeds

CHILI PRAWNS

½ teaspoon baking soda
1 pound large shrimp, peeled and deveined
1 large egg white
2 tablespoons plus ½ teaspoon potato starch
3 tablespoons grape seed, corn, or other neutral oil
1 ½ teaspoons salt
7 dried red Thai chiles
4 garlic cloves, sliced
½ onion, diced
4 scallions, trimmed and julienned
¼ cup chicken stock, preferably homemade or canned low-sodium broth
2 teaspoons garlic chili sauce, preferably Maggi brand
1 teaspoon chili bean sauce
½ teaspoon oyster sauce
¼ teaspoon sesame oil
¼ teaspoon chili oil, preferably homemade (page 51)
½ teaspoon sugar
⅓ cup fresh lily buds, trimmed

This is my version of the classic Cantonese shrimp and candied walnut stir-fry. I add a bit of heat here and lily buds for freshness. All the parboiling may seem unnecessary, but it is the key to this dish. Boiling and drying the ingredients before frying make the walnuts light and crisp and the shrimp amazingly crunchy.

1. **To make the walnuts:** Bring 4 ¼ cups water to a boil in a large saucepan. Add the baking soda and walnuts and cook until the water returns to a boil. Drain and dry the walnuts in a colander.

2. Put the sugar in a large saucepan with ¼ cup water. Bring the mixture to a boil over medium-high heat, shaking the pan occasionally to evenly dissolve the sugar. Add the walnuts and cook, stirring, until they are well coated and the caramel returns to a boil. Strain the walnuts through a colander and cool and dry completely. Stir the walnuts occasionally to prevent them from sticking to one another.

3. Pour oil to a depth of 2 inches in a medium saucepan and heat to 350°F. Add the walnuts and cook, stirring constantly, until deep brown and crisp, about 5 minutes. Remove the walnuts with a slotted spoon and drain in a colander. Toss with the sesame seeds and set aside.

4. **To make the chili prawns:** Mix the baking soda with 4 1/4 cups water in a large mixing bowl. Add the shrimp, stir well, and let sit for 30 minutes. Drain the shrimp through a colander, wash well with cold water, and drain again. Blot the shrimp dry with paper towels.

5. Put the egg white, 2 tablespoons of the potato starch, 1 tablespoon of the oil, and 1 teaspoon of the salt in a large mixing bowl and mix until well combined. Add the shrimp and mix well. Bring a large saucepan of water to a boil. Add the shrimp, shaking off any excess marinade, and cook, stirring, for 5 seconds. Drain.

6. Stir the remaining 1/2 teaspoon potato starch with 1 teaspoon water until dissolved. Set aside. Heat the remaining 2 tablespoons oil in a wok or large skillet over high heat until almost smoking. Add the chiles, garlic, onion, and scallions and cook, stirring, until fragrant and softened, about 1 minute. Stir in the shrimp, chicken stock, garlic chili sauce, and chili bean sauce. Continue stirring and add the oyster sauce, sesame oil, chili oil, sugar, and remaining 1/2 teaspoon salt. Pour in the potato starch mixture and cook, stirring, until the sauce thickens. Toss the lily buds and walnuts into the mixture, transfer to a serving plate, and serve immediately.

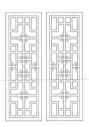

Shrimp Toasts with Water Chestnuts

Makes 12 toasts

15 ounces shrimp, peeled and deveined
¼ cup unsalted butter, softened
2 teaspoons salt
¼ cup sliced scallions
¼ cup Shaoxing wine
1 tablespoon plus 1 teaspoon light soy sauce
1 tablespoon sesame oil
6 water chestnuts, preferably fresh, peeled and diced, or ½ cup peeled and diced jicama
1 teaspoon sugar
6 slices white bread, preferably Arnold or Pepperidge Farm
2 tablespoons sesame seeds, toasted (see page 15), plus more as needed
Peanut oil or clarified unsalted butter for frying
3 tablespoons snipped chives
Duck Mustard (page 21) or Chinese mustard, store-bought is fine

The popularity of shrimp toasts peaked in the '60s and has since largely faded into oblivion. But I love these crisp triangles of white toast topped with the sweet, savory spread, rich with shrimp and crunchy with water chestnuts. When beautifully browned, it's irresistible. And the addition of butter to my version certainly doesn't hurt. To me, this is Chinese-American food at its best.

1. Put 5 ounces of the shrimp in a food processor and grind. Chop the remaining shrimp into ½-inch pieces and set aside. Add the butter and 1 teaspoon salt to the food processor and purée until smooth. Transfer the mixture to a mixing bowl and add the chopped shrimp, scallions, wine, soy sauce, sesame oil, water chestnuts, sugar, and remaining teaspoon salt. Mix until well combined.

2. Cut the crusts off the bread and cut each slice of bread in half diagonally. Put the shrimp mixture on each slice of bread, patting it down to secure it. Sprinkle generously with sesame seeds. At this point, you can brown the toasts or refrigerate, covered, until ready to serve.

3. Pour oil or clarified butter to a depth of ⅛ inch in a large skillet and set over medium heat. Add the shrimp toasts, shrimp side down, and cook until browned and crisp, then turn and brown the other side. Do not overcrowd the skillet; work in batches if necessary. Drain on paper towels, then transfer to a serving plate. Garnish with chives and serve with Duck Mustard or Chinese mustard.

Seared Shrimp with Gingered Butternut Squash

Makes 4 servings

PUMPKIN SEEDS

½ cup shelled pumpkin seeds

1½ teaspoons extra virgin olive oil

¼ teaspoon salt

GINGER SYRUP

1 cup fresh lemon juice

1 cup sugar

1 cup peeled and grated fresh ginger

½ fresh red Thai chile

½ butternut squash, seeded

Salt and freshly ground white pepper

5 tablespoons unsalted butter

3 tablespoons whole star anise

1½ teaspoons crushed red pepper flakes

2 tablespoons grape seed, corn, or other neutral oil

1 pound large shrimp, peeled and deveined

2 tablespoons fresh micro Thai basil or chopped fresh regular Thai basil

The silky butternut squash purée adds a spiced sweetness to the crisp shrimp. This is an ideal starter for a fall dinner.

1. **To make the pumpkin seeds:** Preheat the oven to 350°F. Line a rimmed baking sheet with some parchment paper.

2. Toss the pumpkin seeds with the oil and salt. Spread in a single layer on the baking sheet. Bake, stirring once, until golden and fragrant, about 7 minutes. Set aside to cool. Leave the oven on.

3. **To make the ginger syrup:** Put all the ingredients in a small saucepan and bring to a boil. Remove from the heat and squeeze the ginger juice into the saucepan. Return the squeezed ginger pulp back to the saucepan and stir well. Cool to room temperature, then strain through a fine-mesh sieve. Set aside.

4. Season the squash generously with salt and white pepper and dot with 3 tablespoons of the butter. Wrap in foil and bake on a rimmed baking sheet until completely tender, about 1 hour. Unwrap, cool slightly, and scoop out the flesh into a blender.

5. Add the reserved ginger syrup and 2 teaspoons salt to the blender and purée until smooth. Set aside.

(continued)

6. Grind the star anise and chile flakes in a spice grinder until the mixture becomes a fine powder. Set aside.

7. Heat the oil in a large skillet over high heat until hot but not smoking. Season the shrimp with the spice mixture and add to the skillet. Cook on one side until nicely browned and crisp, about 2 minutes, then flip the shrimp over and cook until cooked through and nicely browned, about 2 more minutes. Remove from the heat.

8. Divide the squash purée among four shallow serving dishes. Decoratively arrange the shrimp next to it.

9. Melt the remaining 2 tablespoons butter in a medium skillet over medium-high heat. When the butter becomes foamy, add the pumpkin seeds and cook, tossing, until warm and fragrant, about 1 minute. Sprinkle the pumpkin seeds over the shrimp and drizzle the pumpkin seed butter on top. Garnish with the basil and serve.

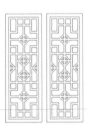

Mussels Steamed with Lemongrass, Thai Basil, Dried Chile, and Coconut Juice

Makes 8 servings

- Two 10½-ounce cans coconut juice, preferably Bangkok Market brand
- 2 tablespoons chopped fresh galangal or ginger
- 4 lemongrass stalks, trimmed, smashed, and chopped
- 1 fresh green Thai chile, halved lengthwise
- ½ tablespoon finely grated fresh lemon zest
- ¼ cup plus 1 tablespoon fresh lemon juice
- ½ teaspoon salt, plus more to taste
- ¼ cup grape seed, corn, or other neutral oil
- 3 tablespoons minced garlic
- 3 tablespoons minced shallots
- 3 tablespoons minced fresh red Thai chiles
- 6 pounds mussels, washed well and beards removed
- 8 cups loosely packed fresh Thai basil leaves, roughly sliced

This is based on a casserole you find in Thailand, a combination of coconut, lemongrass, and shellfish; it's like *moules marinière,* Thai style. The broth is so delicious you will need a ton of good white rice to take advantage of it. (Use either Sticky Rice on page 213 or steamed white rice.)

Coconut juice can now be found in most Asian or specialty markets, either canned or frozen. (Frozen usually comes in 10½-ounce plastic bottles and must be thawed before using.) We use the Bangkok Market brand because it contains the most pieces of coconut meat.

1. Put the coconut juice with its meat, galangal, lemongrass, and chile in a large saucepan and bring to a boil over high heat. Add the lemon zest, lower the heat, and simmer for 15 minutes. Remove from the heat and strain, pressing down on the mixture. Cool to room temperature, uncovered, then add the lemon juice and salt. Stir to combine and set aside.

2. Put the oil in a large deep saucepan that can later be covered and set over medium-high heat. Add the garlic and shallots and cook until lightly browned. Stir in the chiles, then add the mussels and the lemongrass infusion. Shake the pan vigorously, then add two-thirds of the basil and season to taste with salt. Cover and cook just until the mussels open, about 3 minutes.

3. Transfer the mussels to serving bowls with the cooking liquid. Garnish with the remaining basil leaves and serve immediately.

Seared Tuna with Sichuan Pepper and Soy-Mustard Sauce

Makes 4 servings

2 tablespoons Dijon mustard
2 tablespoons soy sauce
1 tablespoon minced fresh ginger
1 tablespoon minced shallots
2 tablespoons fresh lime juice
¼ cup plus 1 tablespoon grape seed, corn, or other neutral oil, plus more as needed
2 cups mesclun or other mix of greens
¼ cup alfalfa sprouts
Freshly ground black pepper

½ cup Sichuan peppercorns, husks only, cracked
Salt
Four 3-ounce pieces sushi-grade tuna, each about 1 inch in diameter
A few cooked fresh soybeans, optional

A lightning-quick and very impressive appetizer, one we've been serving for nearly twenty years and one that has remained enormously popular. Sichuan peppercorns add their wonderful, smoky overtones, and finishing the dish with my soy-and-mustard "vinaigrette" is just perfect.

1. In a small bowl, whisk together the first 4 ingredients and 1 tablespoon of the lime juice. Continue whisking and slowly drizzle in ¼ cup of the oil. Set aside.

2. Toss the mesclun and sprouts with the remaining 1 tablespoon lime juice and 1 tablespoon oil in a medium-size bowl. Add freshly ground black pepper to taste.

3. Press the cracked Sichuan pepper and a little salt on all sides of the tuna. Heat a pan over high heat and lightly coat it with oil right before the pan starts smoking. Sear the tuna on each side for 30 seconds.

4. Slice the tuna into ½-inch slices with a serrated knife and arrange on a plate. Garnish with the salad, soy-mustard sauce, and soybeans, if you like.

Rice Cracker-Crusted Tuna with Spicy Citrus Sauce

Makes 4 servings

2 tablespoons bonito flakes
1 large egg yolk
2 tablespoons fresh lime juice
1 tablespoon fresh orange juice
2 teaspoons Sriracha chili sauce
¾ teaspoon salt
½ cup plus 3 tablespoons grape seed, corn, or other neutral oil, plus more for deep-frying
3 large egg whites
2 tablespoons cornstarch
One 12-ounce piece sushi-grade tuna, cut into four 4 x 1½-inch pieces
Seven 4-inch round rice crackers, ground to small crumbs
2 scallions, white parts only, thinly sliced

Searing tuna isn't the only way to get a crisp exterior and rare center on this delicious fish. A quick dip in the deep fryer works well too and the rice cracker crumbs here give this dish an amazing crunch.

1. Put the bonito flakes in a medium bowl and cover with 3 tablespoons hot water. Let sit for 10 minutes, then strain through a fine-mesh sieve, squeezing as much liquid as possible out of the bonito flakes.

2. Transfer the liquid to a blender and add the egg yolk, lime juice, orange juice, Sriracha, and salt and purée. With the machine running, add the oil in a slow, steady stream. Transfer to a small bowl, cover with plastic wrap, and refrigerate until ready to serve.

3. Pour oil to a depth of 3 inches in a heavy, deep saucepan and heat to 400°F.

4. Whisk the egg whites and cornstarch together in a shallow dish until the mixture is smooth. Coat the tuna pieces with the mixture, then dredge in the rice cracker crumbs, making sure the entire surface is covered.

5. Carefully transfer the tuna to the hot oil and cook, turning once, until deep golden brown, about 30 seconds total; the tuna should remain rare in the middle. Remove carefully and drain on paper towels. Cut the tuna crosswise into 1-inch slices and arrange decoratively on serving plates. Stir the scallions into the chilled sauce and spoon onto the plates. Serve immediately.

Ribbons of Tuna with Ginger Marinade

Makes 4 servings

CHILI OIL

1 dried ancho chile, stemmed and seeded
1½ dried chipotle peppers, stemmed and seeded
1 whole allspice berry
1 whole clove
¾ teaspoon fennel seeds
1 small piece mace or nutmeg, cracked
1 whole star anise
½ cinnamon stick
½ teaspoon salt
½ cup grape seed, corn, or other neutral oil

GINGER MARINADE

2 tablespoons sugar
⅛ ounce kaffir lime leaves, roughly chopped
2 tablespoons fresh lime juice
½ cup peeled and chopped fresh ginger
2½ tablespoons extra virgin olive oil
¼ cup champagne or other wine vinegar
¼ cup soy sauce

One 4-inch square, 1-inch-thick piece sushi-grade tuna
Salt
1 fresh red Thai chile, seeded and minced
2 shallots, minced
2 tablespoons extra virgin olive oil
1 ripe avocado, seeded, peeled, and diced
1 teaspoon fresh lime juice
4 small red bunch radishes, stemmed, scrubbed, and cut into ¼-inch slices
½ small daikon radish, stemmed, peeled, and cut into ¼-inch slices
½ small icicle radish, stemmed, peeled, and cut into ¼-inch slices

Did you ever think you'd see the day when tuna imitated pasta? Here, the wonderful taste and texture of tuna cut into linguine-like strands is sauced by a refreshing ginger marinade. The natural spiciness of radishes is heightened by the addition of homemade chili oil and tempered by cool avocado. The explosion of flavors in your mouth is really exciting; people love this.

1. **To make the oil:** Put the chiles, allspice, clove, fennel, mace, anise, and cinnamon in a large dry skillet and set over medium heat. Cook, stirring occasionally, until fragrant and toasted, 2 minutes. Transfer the toasted ingredients to a blender or spice grinder with the salt and blend until finely ground.

2. Transfer the mixture to a small saucepan and cover with the oil. Set over medium-low heat until very warm, then remove from the heat and cool completely. Strain the oil through a fine-mesh sieve into a container and set aside at room temperature to use immediately, or cover and refrigerate until ready to use.

(continued)

3. **To make the marinade:** Put the sugar, lime leaves, and lime juice in a small saucepan. Set over medium-high heat and bring to a boil, stirring occasionally. Remove from the heat and cool to room temperature, then strain the lime syrup through a fine-mesh sieve and set aside.

4. Put the ginger in a blender and blend, adding the olive oil in a slow, steady stream through the feed tube, until the mixture becomes a smooth purée. Transfer to a medium mixing bowl and stir in the vinegar, soy sauce, and reserved lime syrup and set aside.

5. Cut the tuna into strands lengthwise, ¼ inch thick, so that the cut pieces resemble thick linguine. Place in a bowl. Season lightly with salt, then gently toss with the chile, shallots, and 1 tablespoon of the olive oil. In a small bowl season the avocado lightly with salt, then toss gently with the lime juice and the remaining 1 tablespoon olive oil. Season the radishes lightly with salt, then toss gently with half the reserved chili oil.

6. Divide the avocado among four serving bowls and decoratively arrange half the radish slices, then half the tuna strands on top. Stack the remaining radishes and tuna on top, and spoon the ginger marinade around the dish and drizzle the remaining chili oil all around. Serve immediately.

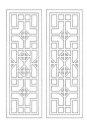

Shaved Tuna, Chile Tapioca, Asian Pear, and Lime

Makes 4 servings

LIME-COCONUT BROTH

1 cup coconut juice, preferably Bangkok Market brand
1/4 cup coconut milk
1/3 fresh green finger chile, chopped
1/4 cup sugar
1/2 teaspoon salt
1/4 cup plus 2 tablespoons fresh lime juice
2 lemongrass stalks, trimmed, smashed, and finely chopped
14 kaffir lime leaves, chopped

CHILE TAPIOCA

1 dried ancho chile
1 1/2 cinnamon sticks
1 teaspoon whole cloves, cracked
1 tablespoon sugar
1 teaspoon salt, plus more to taste
1/4 cup plus 2 tablespoons large tapioca pearls
1 tablespoon chili oil, preferably homemade (page 51)

One 10-ounce, 1/2-inch-thick piece sushi-grade tuna
1/4 cup diced jicama
1/4 cup diced Asian pear
1/4 cup sliced scallion greens
1/4 cup diced roasted red bell pepper

This playful dish of tiny orange rounds—actually tapioca cooked in an intense chile-spiced broth—might make you think you're about to experience the salty burst of juice from salmon roe. The wonderfully intense chewy pearls are complemented by the subtle sweetness of tuna and the refreshing crunch of jicama and Asian pear.

Red and green Thai chiles at the weekend food market, Aw Taw Kaw, in Bangkok

(continued)

1. **To make the broth:** Put the coconut juice, coconut milk, chile, sugar, salt, and ¼ cup of the lime juice in a medium saucepan. Stir well and bring to a boil. Stir in the lemongrass and lime leaves, remove from the heat, and cool, uncovered.

2. When the mixture has cooled, strain through a fine-mesh sieve. Stir in the remaining 2 tablespoons lime juice and set aside.

3. **To make the chile tapioca:** Put the chile and cinnamon in a small skillet set over medium heat. Toast, turning the chile and cinnamon occasionally, until dark brown and fragrant. Remove from the skillet, cool completely, and cut the chile into ½-inch pieces and crack the cinnamon into small pieces. Transfer to a piece of cheesecloth, add the cloves, and wrap tightly.

4. Put the sachet in a small saucepan with the sugar, salt, and 2½ cups water. Bring the mixture to a boil and add the tapioca. Turn the heat to low and cook, stirring, until the tapioca is almost clear, about 15 minutes. The tapioca should be tender, but still chewy. Drain, rinse under cold running water until cool, and drain again.

5. Transfer the tapioca to a mixing bowl and remove the sachet. Season lightly with salt and stir in the chili oil until well mixed. Set aside.

6. Cut the tuna lengthwise into 1-inch-wide strips. Cut each strip crosswise into ⅛-inch-thick slices. Divide the tuna slices among four serving bowls and arrange decoratively on the bottom. Season the tuna lightly with salt, then scatter the chile tapioca on top. Garnish with the jicama, pear, scallions, and bell pepper. Pour enough broth into the bowls so that it comes halfway up the sides. Serve immediately.

Hamachi with Chile-Citrus Sorbet and Mango

Makes 4 servings

CHILE CITRUS SORBET

1/4 cup sugar
1/2 fresh red finger chile, chopped
1/4 cup plus 2 tablespoons fresh lemon juice
2 tablespoons elderflower syrup

10 ounces *hamachi*, the belly of sushi-grade yellowtail, cut into 1/4-inch dice
1 medium mango, preferably Champagne, cut into 1/4-inch dice
Kosher salt
2 teaspoons extra virgin olive oil, plus more for garnish
2 tablespoons torn fresh mint leaves
1 teaspoon fleur de sel

Hamachi, the fatty belly of yellowtail, has a smooth, rich sweetness incomparable to any other cut of sushi. It's great on its own, but I like it even better when topped with this sweet and spicy sorbet. The contrast between the tender fish and crunchy ice is amazing. And the lemon really brings out the freshness of the fish.

The best place to find *hamachi* is a good sushi restaurant. You can ask the sushi chef for the cut you need or just get a few orders of *hamachi sashimi*.

1. Put four serving bowls in the freezer to chill.

2. **To make the sorbet:** Put the sugar, chile, lemon juice, and elderflower syrup in a blender. Purée until smooth and very well blended. Transfer to a shallow dish and freeze, uncovered, until firm. The mixture will remain creamy and not be rock solid even when completely frozen.

3. Put the *hamachi* and mango in a large mixing bowl. Season lightly with salt and toss with the olive oil. Divide among the chilled serving bowls, forming the mixture into little mounds.

4. Use a fork to scrape the lemon juice mixture into fluffy ice shavings. Top the fish mounds with a spoonful of the shaved ice. Pour a thin line of olive oil around the base of the fish mound. Garnish with the mint leaves and fleur de sel. Serve immediately.

Soy-Cured Salmon, Asian Pear, and Cilantro Crème Fraîche

Makes 4 servings

This Asian version of gravlax uses soy sauce to cure the salmon in place of salt. The result is a rich sweet-saltiness in the fish, punctuated by the heat of the ginger and chile. The crème fraîche dipping sauce counters with a cooling effect, as does the crunchy Asian pear.

SOY-CURED SALMON

1 cup light soy sauce
1 cup fresh cilantro leaves
One 2-inch piece fresh young ginger, peeled and chopped
1 fresh green Thai chile, chopped
One 9-ounce salmon fillet, skinned, trimmed, and halved lengthwise

DIPPING SAUCE

½ cup plus 2 tablespoons crème fraîche
2 scallions, white parts only, thinly sliced
⅓ cup sliced fresh cilantro leaves
1 tablespoon fresh lime zest, plus more for garnish
¼ teaspoon minced fresh green Thai chile
2 tablespoons fresh lime juice
1 teaspoon salt

¼ cup diced Asian pear

1. **To make the salmon:** Put the soy sauce, cilantro, ginger, and chile in a blender and purée until the mixture is blended, but still chunky. Transfer to a shallow bowl, submerge the salmon completely in the brine, cover with plastic wrap, and refrigerate for 20 hours.

2. Remove the salmon from the brine and rinse thoroughly in cold water. Pat dry with paper towels and cut crosswise into ¼-inch-thick slices.

3. **To make the sauce:** Put the crème fraîche, scallions, cilantro, lime zest, and chile in a small mixing bowl and mix well. Stir in the lime juice and salt.

4. Spoon a pool of the sauce onto each serving plate. Decoratively lay the salmon slices on top of the sauce and garnish with the Asian pear and lime zest. Serve immediately.

Thai Fried Chicken Wings with Hot-and-Sour Sauce and Salted Mango

Makes 4 servings

HOT-AND-SOUR SAUCE

¼ cup grape seed, corn, or other neutral oil
½ cup thinly sliced shallots
¼ cup thinly sliced garlic
2 tablespoons chopped dried red finger chiles
½ fresh red Thai chile
One ¼-inch piece fresh galangal, peeled and cut crosswise into ¼-inch slices
⅛ teaspoon belacan (shrimp paste)
1½ tablespoons palm sugar
2 tablespoons tamarind paste
2 tablespoons red wine vinegar
2 tablespoons fresh lime juice
¾ teaspoon nam pla (Thai fish sauce)
¾ teaspoon salt

WINGS

½ cup soy sauce
½ cup fresh lime juice
2 tablespoons nam pla (Thai fish sauce)
3 garlic cloves, crushed
2 fresh red Thai chiles, thinly sliced
1 tablespoon sugar
2 pounds chicken mini drumsticks from chicken wings or chicken wings, separated at joint
1 ripe mango, cut into 1-inch slices
2 teaspoons salt
Grape seed, corn, or other neutral oil for deep-frying
½ cup cornstarch
½ cup rice flour
¼ cup chopped fresh mint leaves

Anyone who loves fried chicken will love this dish. It's sort of a Thai version of buffalo wings, coated with a sweet-and-sour sauce after being fried to a crisp. You can double this recipe to make a large batch for a party.

1. **To make the sauce:** Heat the oil in a medium saucepan over medium heat. Add the shallots and garlic and cook, stirring, until they become a deep golden brown. Add the remaining ingredients and bring the mixture to a boil.

2. Simmer, stirring, for 1 minute, then remove from the heat and transfer to a blender. Purée carefully until smooth, transfer to a large mixing bowl, and set aside until ready to use.

3. **To make the wings:** Put the soy sauce, lime juice, nam pla, garlic, chiles, and sugar in a medium saucepan and bring to a boil, stirring occasionally. Cool completely, then pour over the mini drumsticks in a shallow baking dish and toss to coat well. Cover with plastic wrap and refrigerate for at least 1 hour.

(continued)

4. Meanwhile, toss the mango cubes with the salt in a small bowl and let sit for 30 minutes.

5. When ready to cook, pour oil to a depth of 3 inches in a heavy, deep pot and heat to 375°F. Remove the drumsticks from the marinade and pat dry. Combine the cornstarch and rice flour on a shallow plate. Dredge the chicken in the mixture, then carefully put in the pot. Do not overcrowd; work in batches if necessary. Cook until crisp, brown, and cooked through, about 10 minutes. Adjust the heat as necessary to maintain the oil's temperature.

6. Drain on paper towels and transfer to the bowl of hot-and-sour sauce. Toss well to coat and transfer to the serving plates. Arrange the salted mango in a little mound next to the chicken, garnish with the mint leaves, and serve.

Thai mangoes at the weekend food market, Aw Taw Kaw, in Bangkok

Raw Beef with Five Condiments

Makes 4 servings

1 tablespoon sticky (sometimes also called glutinous) rice
8 ounces fresh lean beef tenderloin (filet mignon), cut into small dice
2 teaspoons minced fresh ginger
1½ teaspoons salt
2 teaspoons peanut oil
7 fresh mint leaves, thinly sliced
1 scallion, green parts only, thinly sliced
1 teaspoon minced fresh lemongrass, tender interior part only
1 teaspoon finely minced kaffir lime leaves
1 teaspoon chili purée (page 76)
2 lime wedges

Steak tartare, Southeast Asian style. The ginger flavors the beef to complement the contrasting flavors and textures of the dipping condiments. All the smooth and bright flavors simply explode in your mouth.

1. Put the rice in a bowl and cover with ½ cup water. Soak for 1 hour, then drain and rinse. Pat the rice dry with paper towels, then transfer to a small skillet set over medium heat. Cook the rice, shaking the skillet occasionally, until lightly browned, about 3 minutes. Cool and then grind in a spice grinder to a cornmeal consistency. Set aside.

2. Put the beef in a bowl and thoroughly mix with the ginger and salt. Add the oil and mound the beef mixture in the center of your serving plate.

3. Put the mint leaves on top of the beef. Put the remaining ingredients and the fresh toasted rice powder in little mounds around the beef.

4. Serve: instruct your diners to dip the beef in each of the condiments and to finish with a squeeze of lime juice.

Chicken Satay

Makes 4 servings

PEANUT SAUCE

1 teaspoon grape seed, corn, or other neutral oil
1 tablespoon red curry paste, store-bought is fine
1 tablespoon sugar
1½ cups coconut milk
1½ cups chopped roasted peanuts
1 tablespoon soy sauce, plus more to taste

MARINADE

1 tablespoon coriander seeds
1 teaspoon cumin seeds
3 shallots, finely chopped
¼ cup peanuts, toasted (see page 15) and chopped
½ cup coconut milk
1 teaspoon ground turmeric
1 tablespoon sweetened condensed milk
1 tablespoon palm sugar
2 tablespoons nam pla (Thai fish sauce)
1 tablespoon whiskey
¼ teaspoon salt, plus more to taste

1 pound boneless, skinless chicken breast, cut into 1-inch-cubes
Bamboo skewers, soaked in water for 1 hour
Salt and freshly ground black pepper

Simple and incredibly good, especially with the peanut sauce.

1. **To make the sauce:** Put the oil in a medium saucepan and set over high heat. When the oil is very hot and almost smoking, add the curry paste and sugar and cook, stirring, until fragrant, about 1 minute. Add the coconut milk and bring the mixture to a boil. Stir in the peanuts and soy sauce. Taste and adjust the seasoning.

2. **To make the marinade:** Put the coriander and cumin seeds in a small skillet set over medium heat. Toast, shaking the pan occasionally, until lightly browned and fragrant. Remove from the heat, cool completely, and grind to a fine powder in a spice grinder.

3. Put the shallots, peanuts, ground coriander and cumin in a blender. Blend until the mixture becomes a paste. Add the coconut milk, turmeric, sweetened condensed milk, palm sugar, nam pla, whiskey, and salt. Blend again until smooth and set the marinade aside in a shallow plate.

4. Thread the chicken cubes onto the skewers, leaving 3 inches at the end. Dip and roll each skewer in the marinade and let sit while you start a charcoal or gas grill or broiler; the fire should be medium-hot, and the grill rack should be about 4 inches from the heat source. (You can also cover the meat and refrigerate it for up to a day.) Season the skewers with salt and pepper and grill or broil for 5 minutes per side, or until lightly browned all over and cooked through. Serve immediately with the peanut sauce.

STAUB

แม่น้ำ-ลำคลอง
เป็นสมบัติของท่าน
โปรดช่วยกันดูแลรักษา

Pork Satay

Makes 4 servings

2 tablespoons oyster sauce
1 tablespoon nam pla (Thai fish sauce)
1 teaspoon caramel (page 178) or sugar
3 tablespoons grape seed, corn, or other neutral oil
2 tablespoons minced fresh lemongrass
2 tablespoons white sesame seeds, toasted (see page 15) and ground
2 shallots, minced
1 garlic clove, minced
5 ounces boneless pork butt (shoulder)
Bamboo skewers, soaked in water for 1 hour
Peanut Sauce (page 62), warmed
Asian-style Pickles (page 19)

Close to a must for the modern barbecue, this is sweet and savory, with the aromatic lemongrass bringing it all together. Freeze the pork for about 30 minutes to facilitate slicing or, better yet, ask your butcher to slice it for you.

1. Mix together the first 8 ingredients in a small bowl until well combined. Slice the pork as thinly as possible; you want strips about ⅛ inch thick, 1 inch wide, and 6 inches long. Thread the pork slices onto the bamboo skewers, as if you were sewing. The pork should be slightly bunched together on the skewer, not flat.

2. Start a charcoal or gas grill or broiler; the fire should be medium-hot, and the grill rack should be about 4 inches from the heat source. Pour the marinade onto a shallow plate and dip and roll each pork skewer in the marinade.

3. Grill just until browned and cooked through. Serve hot with the Peanut Sauce for dipping and the Asian-style Pickles on the side.

← Boat vendor grilling satay on the Klong in Bangkok

Charred Chile-Rubbed Beef Skewers with Thai Basil Dipping Sauce

Makes 4 servings

THAI BASIL OIL

2 cups fresh Thai basil leaves
½ cup grape seed, corn, or other neutral oil
1 teaspoon salt

DIPPING SAUCE

1 egg yolk
2 tablespoons fresh lime juice
1 teaspoon nam pla (Thai fish sauce)
Salt

1 pound beef sirloin, cut into ¼-inch-thick slices across the grain
Bamboo skewers, soaked in water for 1 hour
3 garlic cloves, thinly sliced
3 fresh red Thai chiles, thinly sliced
⅓ cup soy sauce
1½ teaspoons brown sugar
2 tablespoons fresh orange zest, pith removed
1 small bunch (1½ ounces) fresh cilantro, chopped
1 tablespoon plus 1 teaspoon nam pla (Thai fish sauce)
1 teaspoon grape seed, corn, or other neutral oil

Quite possibly the best beef skewers you've ever had. We rub the beef with an intense, spicy-sweet marinade, and we keep it juicy and tender by just charring it on the grill. The citrus in the Thai basil dipping sauce tempers the heat of the skewers perfectly.

1. **To make the oil:** Fill a large bowl with water and ice and set aside. Bring a small pot of water to a boil and add the basil leaves. As soon as the water returns to a boil, transfer the leaves to the ice water. When cold, remove the basil leaves from the water and squeeze all the water out of the leaves with your hands. Put the basil in a blender with the oil and salt. Purée until smooth, then strain through a fine-mesh sieve into a small bowl.

2. **To make the dipping sauce:** Put the egg yolk, lime juice, nam pla, and ¼ cup water in a blender. Blend until smooth, then add the Thai basil oil in a slow, steady stream through the feed tube with the machine running. The mixture will emulsify into a mayonnaise. Taste and add salt if necessary.

3. Thread the thin slices of beef onto the skewers, leaving 3 inches at one end. Start a charcoal or gas grill or broiler; the fire should be hot, and the grill rack should be about 4 inches from the heat source.

4. Put the garlic, chiles, soy sauce, brown sugar, orange zest, cilantro, nam pla, and oil in a blender and purée until smooth. Transfer the marinade to a large shallow

bowl. Dip the beef skewers in the marinade, evenly coating the beef, then transfer to the hot grill and cook until charred, 1 minute. Turn and char the other side, 1 minute, then serve immediately with the dipping sauce.

Woman cooking satay over a wood-burning grill at the weekend food market, Aw Taw Kaw, in Bangkok

Grilled Oyster Mushroom and Avocado Carpaccio

Makes 4 servings

8 ounces (about 4) fresh King Oyster mushrooms
20 sprigs fresh thyme, plus more for garnish
1 fresh green Thai chile, thinly sliced
¼ cup plus 1 tablespoon extra virgin olive oil
1 teaspoon salt, plus more to taste
2 jalapeño peppers
2 ripe avocados, peeled, pitted, and thinly sliced
1 lime

The delicate slices of chewy mushroom and smooth avocado provide pleasing textural contrast. While this is ideal as an appetizer, it can also serve as a light vegetarian lunch.

1. In a bowl, toss the mushrooms, thyme, chile, 2 tablespoons of the olive oil, and ¾ teaspoon of the salt together until well mixed. Cover tightly with plastic wrap and marinate in a warm place for 30 minutes.

2. Start a charcoal or gas grill or broiler; the fire should be hot, and the grill rack should be about 4 inches from the heat source.

3. Put the jalapeños on the grill and cook, turning occasionally, until completely charred. Remove from the grill and cool slightly. Remove the stems and skin, then transfer to a blender with the remaining 3 tablespoons olive oil and the remaining ¼ teaspoon salt. Purée until completely smooth and strain through a fine-mesh sieve into a bowl, pressing on the solids to extract as much oil as possible. Set aside.

4. Put the mushrooms on the grill in one layer and cook, turning occasionally, until the mushrooms are tender, about 2 minutes. Transfer to a large bowl, cover tightly with plastic wrap, and set aside for 15 minutes. Uncover the mushrooms and remove the stems. Slice each mushroom as thinly as possible.

5. Alternately layer the mushroom slices and avocado slices, overlapping them slightly. Brush with the jalapeño oil, sprinkle lightly with salt, squeeze lime juice on top, and garnish with thyme sprigs. Serve immediately.

Braised Pork Belly with Shallot

Makes 4 servings

BRAISED PORK BELLY

One 2-pound piece pork belly
3 onions, chopped
2 carrots, chopped
3 celery stalks, chopped
1 small bunch fresh thyme
1 small bunch fresh parsley stems
1½ tablespoons black peppercorns

SHALLOT CONFIT

1½ cups thinly sliced shallots
2 tablespoons thinly sliced fresh ginger
¼ cup honey
⅓ cup red wine vinegar
¼ teaspoon cracked black pepper
Salt

¼ cup honey
½ cup red wine vinegar

Think of this as an exquisite variation on sweet-and-sour pork. The honey-and-vinegar-glazed cubes of meat simply melt in your mouth. This can also serve as an entrée with crusty bread or steamed white rice.

1. Preheat the oven to 300°F.

2. **To make the braised pork:** Put all the braised pork ingredients in a Dutch oven or casserole. Add enough water to cover the pork and bring the mixture to a simmer over medium-high heat. Transfer to the oven and cook, uncovered, until the pork is tender, about 2 hours. Remove from the oven and set aside to cool.

3. **Meanwhile, make the shallot confit:** Put the shallots, ginger, and honey in a medium saucepan. Set over medium-high heat and cook, stirring occasionally, until the shallots are softened and caramelized, about 10 minutes. Add the vinegar and cook until it has evaporated. Add ½ cup water and turn the heat to low. Simmer the mixture until it is almost dry. Season with pepper and salt to taste. Set aside.

4. Remove the pork from the Dutch oven and cut into 1-inch cubes. Put the honey in a large saucepan and set over medium heat. Cook until thickened and a deep amber color, about 5 minutes. Add the vinegar and stir well. Add the pork and cook, stirring occasionally, for 10 minutes. If the mixture becomes too thick, add a tablespoon of water.

5. Divide the shallot confit among four serving plates and top with the pork. Serve warm.

SOUPS

Mushroom-Ginger Broth with Sea Scallops

Makes 4 servings

4 cups chicken stock, preferably homemade or canned low-sodium broth
½ cup julienned leeks
¼ cup julienned fresh ginger
½ teaspoon minced fresh green Thai chile, or to taste
4 ounces fresh oyster mushrooms, about 1 cup
Salt and freshly ground black pepper
2 tablespoons unsalted butter
8 ounces sea scallops, cut crosswise into slices about ¼ inch thick
2 tablespoons chopped fresh cilantro leaves

Given the minimal amount of work involved here and the incredibly quick prep time, this soup is an ideal starter for wowing your guests. It's luxurious, light, complex, and stunningly delicious. The soup and scallops come together beautifully; the broth is filled with the flavor of leeks, ginger, and mushrooms—it's almost a tea-like infusion—and, poured over the almost raw scallops, it makes for a great contrast.

1. Preheat the oven to 450°F.

2. Bring the chicken stock to a boil. Add the leeks, ginger, chile, and mushrooms and season the broth with salt and pepper. Cook until everything is soft, about 5 minutes.

3. Meanwhile, generously butter the bottoms of four ovenproof soup bowls. Distribute the scallops among them, laying them flat in a single layer. Transfer the bowls to the oven.

4. When the scallops have been in the oven for about 3 minutes and are just warm, remove them and season with salt. Sprinkle the cilantro on top of the scallops, then ladle the broth and everything in it into each bowl. Serve hot.

Tomato Egg Drop Soup

Makes 4 servings

3 tablespoons grape seed, corn, or other neutral oil
2 large shallots, thinly sliced
½ teaspoon sugar
3 large tomatoes, preferably beefsteak, cored, seeded, and cut into wedges, juices reserved
2½ cups chicken stock, preferably homemade or canned low-sodium broth
2 kaffir lime leaves
One ½-inch piece fresh galangal or ginger, sliced
1 large egg, lightly beaten
⅓ cup sliced scallions
1 fresh red Thai chile, seeded and minced
1 tablespoon nam pla (Thai fish sauce), or to taste
Salt and freshly ground black pepper
½ cup chopped fresh cilantro leaves

A terrific, modern, and unusual version of the classic—sweet and tart from tomatoes and rich from the egg. It's also heavy on the black pepper, which is characteristic of traditional Vietnamese dishes. This is a great way to start off a meal, but is also lovely at lunch.

1. Put the oil in a large saucepan and set over medium heat. Add the shallots and cook until softened and golden, about 5 minutes. Add the sugar and the tomatoes along with their reserved juices and cook, stirring occasionally, until the tomatoes break down, 10 to 15 minutes.

2. Add the chicken stock, lime leaves, and galangal and bring the mixture to a boil. Lower the heat and simmer for about 10 minutes. Remove the lime leaves and galangal. Add the egg in a slow, steady stream, whisking constantly.

3. Stir in the scallions and chile; season to taste with nam pla, salt, and pepper. Garnish with the cilantro and serve.

Hot-and-Sour Soup

Makes 4 servings

¼ pound boneless, skinless chicken breast, cut into thin shreds
1 teaspoon Shaoxing wine
½ teaspoon cornstarch
¼ teaspoon sugar
2¼ teaspoons salt, plus more to taste
2 tablespoons plus 1 teaspoon light soy sauce
2½ teaspoons sesame oil
2 ounces dried shiitake mushrooms
¼ ounce dried wood ear mushrooms
5 cups Chinese Chicken Stock (page 78)
8 ounces firm bean curd, drained well and thinly sliced
4 ounces bamboo shoots, thinly sliced
2 large eggs, beaten with 2 teaspoons sesame oil and a pinch of salt
¼ cup plus 2 tablespoons black rice vinegar
1 teaspoon freshly ground white pepper
2 teaspoons chili oil, preferably homemade (page 51)
2 tablespoons finely chopped fresh cilantro leaves

This is the popular Northern Chinese variation on egg drop soup. A far cry from the versions you've tasted at take-out joints, this one keeps the flavors vibrant by cooking everything just until hot.

1. Put the chicken, wine, cornstarch, sugar, ¼ teaspoon of the salt, 1 teaspoon of the soy sauce, and ½ teaspoon of the sesame oil in a small bowl and mix well. Set aside at room temperature for 30 minutes.

2. Meanwhile, put the mushrooms in a medium bowl and cover with very hot water. Soak until softened, 20 minutes. Drain and cut off and discard the stems. Cut the mushrooms into thin slices.

3. Bring the chicken stock to a boil in a large pot. Add the chicken with its marinade and cook, stirring, for 1 minute. Add the mushrooms, bean curd, and bamboo shoots and cook for 2 minutes.

4. While the soup is boiling, add the egg mixture in a slow, steady stream, whisking constantly. Remove from the heat and stir in the vinegar, white pepper, remaining 2 tablespoons soy sauce, and remaining 2 teaspoons salt. Stir in the chili oil, cilantro, and remaining 2 teaspoons sesame oil. Serve hot in soup bowls.

Fresh bamboo shoots at a local street market →

Corn and Crab Soup

Makes 4 servings

CHILI PURÉE

4 ounces fresh red finger chiles, chopped
1 tablespoon plus 1 teaspoon rice vinegar
1½ teaspoons sugar
1⅛ teaspoons salt

SOUP

5 cups Chinese Chicken Stock (page 78)
1½ cups fresh corn kernels (cut from 1 pound corn on the cob)
2 teaspoons peeled and finely chopped fresh ginger
1 tablespoon Shaoxing wine
1 tablespoon light soy sauce
1 tablespoon cornstarch mixed with 2 tablespoons water
1 teaspoon sugar
1 teaspoon salt
½ teaspoon freshly ground white pepper
2 large egg whites beaten with 2 teaspoons sesame oil
4 ounces crabmeat, picked over for shells and cartilage
½ cup plus 2 tablespoons fresh lime juice
2 tablespoons thinly sliced scallions
2 tablespoons chopped fresh cilantro leaves

This version of a Cantonese home-style favorite maintains the spirit of the original, but replaces the typical blandness with a clean, fresh flavor. We use fresh corn kernels and milk, in lieu of the more commonly used canned creamed corn. We also prefer crabmeat to chicken, which seems more Southeast Asian in spirit.

1. **To make the purée:** Put the chiles in a small saucepan with 2 tablespoons water, cover, and cook over medium-high heat until the chiles are soft.

2. Transfer the chiles to a blender. Add the rice vinegar, sugar, and salt and purée until smooth. Set aside.

3. **To make the soup:** Bring the chicken stock to a boil in a large pot and add the corn kernels. Turn the heat to medium-low and simmer the mixture for 5 minutes. Add the ginger, wine, soy sauce, cornstarch mixture, sugar, salt, and white pepper. Turn the heat to medium-high and bring the mixture back to a boil.

4. While the soup is boiling, add the egg white mixture in a slow, steady stream, whisking constantly.

5. Add the crabmeat, lime juice, and chili purée. Stir well, then transfer the soup to four serving bowls. Garnish with the scallions and cilantro and serve immediately.

Chicken and Coconut Milk Soup

Makes 4 servings

1 tablespoon grape seed, corn, or other neutral oil
1 medium onion, minced
1 garlic clove, minced
2 teaspoons red curry paste, store-bought is fine
1 lemongrass stalk, trimmed, smashed, and chopped
One ¾-inch piece fresh galangal or ginger, peeled and sliced
3 kaffir lime leaves
4 cups chicken stock, preferably homemade or canned low-sodium broth
1⅔ cups coconut milk
12 ounces boneless, skinless chicken breast, cut into ½-inch cubes
2 cups fresh shiitake mushroom caps, quartered
¼ cup fresh lime juice
2 tablespoons nam pla (Thai fish sauce)
3 scallions, trimmed and minced
¼ cup minced fresh cilantro leaves

Tom Yum Gai is the quintessential soup of Thai restaurants. The rich coconut milk is offset with tart lime juice and a little hot curry paste. While the resulting flavors taste complex, this soup is very easy to make at home. It's the ideal starter to any Thai meal and great as a light lunch too.

1. Put the oil, onion, and garlic in a large saucepan and set over medium heat. Cook, stirring, for 1 minute, then add the curry paste, lemongrass, galangal, and lime leaves. Cook, stirring, until browned and fragrant, about 4 minutes.

2. Add the chicken stock and bring the mixture to a boil. Turn the heat to medium and simmer vigorously for 15 minutes. Stir in the coconut milk, chicken, and mushrooms. Cook until the chicken is cooked through and the mushrooms tender, about 5 minutes.

3. Stir in the lime juice and nam pla; taste and adjust the seasonings. Garnish with the scallions and cilantro and serve. You may remove the galangal and lemongrass before serving, or leave them in; they are delicious to gnaw on at the table.

Chicken Noodle Soup with Chinese Vegetables

Makes 4 servings

CHINESE CHICKEN STOCK

One 2-pound chicken
½ onion, preferably Spanish, sliced
One 2-inch piece fresh ginger, sliced
1 fresh red Thai chile, halved lengthwise

CHINESE VEGETABLE NOODLE SOUP

6½ ounces fresh lo mein noodles, cut in thirds
1 tablespoon grape seed, corn, or other neutral oil
4 garlic cloves, minced
One 8-inch piece fresh ginger, diced
2 shallots, thinly sliced
½ fresh red Thai chile, minced
1 teaspoon salt, plus more to taste
¼ cup Shaoxing wine
3 tablespoons light soy sauce
2 tablespoons black rice vinegar
1 tablespoon sesame oil
2 scallions, trimmed and sliced, plus more for garnish
2 Napa cabbage leaves, cut into 1-inch pieces crosswise
1 Chinese celery stalk, trimmed and sliced
¼ cup chopped gai lan leaves
¼ cup chopped bok choy leaves
¼ cup chopped chive buds
2 tablespoons Chinese celery leaves
2 tablespoons fresh cilantro leaves
2 tablespoons fresh watercress leaves
1 fresh chile, preferably red finger, sliced

Chinese greens, mustardy and sweet, add a fresh crunch to this rich, aromatic soup. The flavors are light, but this soup is hearty enough to serve as a one-bowl meal.

Chinese celery bunches at a local street market

SOUPS

1. **To make the stock:** Put the chicken, onion, ginger, and chile in a large stockpot with 12 cups water. Bring the mixture to a steady gentle simmer over medium heat and cook until the chicken is cooked through and tender, about 45 minutes. Remove from the heat and transfer the chicken to a large bowl. Strain the broth through a fine-mesh sieve into another large bowl and set aside.

2. When the chicken is cool enough to handle, remove the skin and pull all the meat from the bones. Shred the chicken into bite-size pieces and set aside.

3. **To make the noodle soup:** Bring a medium saucepan of water to a boil. Add the noodles and cook, stirring, just until the water returns to a boil and the noodles are tender but firm, about 3 minutes. Drain and rinse under cold running water until the noodles are at room temperature. Drain again.

4. Put the oil, garlic, and ginger in a large pot. Set over low heat and cook, stirring occasionally, until the garlic and ginger are softened and golden. Stir in the shallots and chile and season with salt. Continue cooking until the shallots are tender.

5. Add the reserved stock, turn the heat to medium-high, and bring the mixture to a steady simmer. Stir in the wine, soy sauce, vinegar, and sesame oil. Add the scallions, Napa cabbage, Chinese celery, gai lan, bok choy, chive buds, reserved chicken, and blanched noodles. Cook just until the vegetables are tender, about 2 minutes.

6. Divide the chicken noodle soup among four serving bowls. Garnish with the celery leaves, cilantro, watercress, chile, and scallions and serve hot.

Shrimp Dumplings with Fragrant Lemongrass Broth

Makes 4 servings

FRAGRANT LEMONGRASS BROTH

½ cup grape seed, corn, or other neutral oil
5 garlic cloves, thinly sliced
3 shallots, thinly sliced
1⅔ ounces shrimp shells, from about 10 extra-large shrimp, rinsed well and dried completely
1 small fennel bulb, trimmed and thinly sliced
One ½-inch piece fresh ginger, thinly sliced and crushed
2 fresh green Thai chiles, halved lengthwise
4 strips fresh lemon zest, pith removed and chopped
1½ cups chicken stock, preferably homemade or canned low-sodium broth
2 lemongrass stalks, smashed and chopped
1 cup chopped fresh mint leaves
¾ teaspoon salt
2 tablespoons fresh lemon juice

SHRIMP DUMPLINGS

½ pound (about 10) extra-large fresh shrimp, peeled, deveined, and quartered
1 tablespoon Shaoxing wine
½ fresh red Thai chile, seeded and minced
2 teaspoons minced fresh young ginger
⅛ teaspoon salt
1 tablespoon cornstarch
16 wonton skins
2 scallions, trimmed and thinly sliced
¼ cup picked fresh dill
¼ cup fresh mint leaves

2 teaspoons extra virgin olive oil
20 fresh shiitake mushrooms, stemmed and cut into ½-inch-thick slices
4 Chinese celery stalks, cut into ½-inch-long matchsticks

This is my take on wonton soup. Loads of fresh herbs make the dumplings and broth aromatic and refreshing.

Rather than discarding the shrimp shells from the shrimp used for the dumplings, I fry them and add them to the broth for a distinctive sea-saltiness.

1. **To make the broth:** Heat the oil in a small saucepan over medium-high heat until very hot, but not smoking. Add the garlic and shallots and cook, stirring, until deep golden brown. Remove with a slotted spoon and drain on paper towels.

2. Add the shrimp shells to the oil and cook, stirring, until deep golden brown. Remove with a slotted spoon and drain on paper towels.

3. Put the fried garlic, shallots, and shrimp shells in a large saucepan with the fennel, ginger, chiles, lemon zest, chicken stock, and 2 cups water. Bring to a steady

simmer over medium heat. As soon as the mixture simmers, remove from the heat and add the lemongrass and mint. Cover and steep for 45 minutes. Strain through a fine-mesh sieve, squeezing the solids to extract as much liquid as possible. Season with salt and lemon juice.

4. **Meanwhile, make the dumplings:** Stir together the shrimp, wine, chile, ginger, salt, and cornstarch until well mixed. Put a spoonful of the shrimp mixture in the middle of one wonton wrapper. Wet the edges of the wrapper with water and fold the wrapper in half to form a triangle. Wet the two opposing corners and fold them in over the center to form a little pouch. Repeat with the remaining filling and wrappers.

5. Bring a large saucepan of water to a boil. Add the shrimp dumplings and cook, stirring gently, until they float to the surface and are cooked through, about 10 minutes. The wrapper will be tender and the shrimp will be pink. Drain and put 4 dumplings in each serving bowl. Top with the scallions, dill, and mint.

6. Heat the olive oil in a large wide saucepan over medium-high heat. Add the mushrooms and sear until nicely browned, turning once. Add the broth and celery and bring the mixture to a boil. Remove from the heat and divide the broth, mushrooms, and celery among the serving bowls. Serve immediately.

Herb bundles for soup in →
the street markets of Saigon

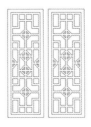

SALADS

Mixed Lettuces with Coconut-Anise Vinaigrette

Makes 4 servings

COCONUT TUILES

2 cups grated unsweetened dry coconut
1 dried Thai chile, minced, or ½ teaspoon crushed red pepper flakes
½ tablespoon sugar
½ teaspoon salt
3 large egg whites

COCONUT-ANISE VINAIGRETTE

1 tablespoon aniseed
3 tablespoons sugar
½ cup plus 1 tablespoon coconut juice, preferably Bangkok Market brand
1 dried hot chile, preferably Thai, seeds removed
1½ tablespoons white sesame seeds, toasted (see page 15)
2½ teaspoons soy sauce
1 tablespoon plus 2 teaspoons rice vinegar
1½ tablespoons fresh lime juice
2½ tablespoons grape seed, corn, or other neutral oil
1 teaspoon salt, or to taste

12 cups mixed lettuces, washed well, dried, and cut into 1-inch strips
1 carrot, peeled and julienned

Scented with anise, sweetened with coconut juice, and tart with lime, this dressing is powerful and amazing. Producing it takes a bit of work, but the greens themselves take none, of course. The coconut tuile, a savory-sweet crouton, is a great addition if you have the time.

You're looking for coconut juice here, not coconut milk; it's sold, mostly in cans, in Asian and Latin markets.

1. **To make the tuiles:** Preheat the oven to 200°F. Line a baking sheet with parchment paper or a Silpat.

2. Put the coconut and chile in a medium mixing bowl and mix well. Put the sugar, salt, and egg whites into the bowl of an electric mixer. Whisk at medium speed until soft peaks form. Gently stir in the coconut mixture.

3. Spoon a quarter of the mixture onto the baking sheet and spread into a 3-inch round. Repeat with the remaining batter, working with a quarter of the batter at a time.

4. Transfer to the oven and bake until light golden and crispy, about 30 minutes. Remove from the oven and cool on a cooling rack. The tuiles are ready when cool and dry.

5. **To make the vinaigrette:** Put the aniseed in a small skillet and set over medium heat. Toast, shaking the pan occasionally, until fragrant and browned. The seeds will start to pop. Remove from the heat, cool completely, and grind to a fine powder in a spice grinder.

6. Put the sugar in a small saucepan and add just enough water to wet it, about 1 tablespoon. Shake the pan to distribute the sugar and water and caramelize over medium-high heat, shaking the pan occasionally. The sugar will gradually liquefy and darken; when it becomes dark brown, remove from the heat and carefully add the coconut juice (it may spatter; hold the pan at arm's length), then return to the heat. Cook, stirring, until the caramel is melted and well mixed. Add the chiles, sesame seeds, and ground aniseed. Remove from the heat, transfer to a blender, and blend until smooth.

7. With the machine running, add the soy sauce, vinegar, and lime juice and blend until smooth. Then add the oil in a slow, steady stream and blend until the mixture is emulsified. Season with salt and set aside.

8. Put the lettuces in a large mixing bowl and season to taste with salt. Drizzle the dressing over the greens and toss well to coat. Divide the lettuces among four serving plates and top with the julienned carrot and coconut tuiles.

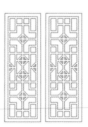

Boston Lettuce Salad with Lemon-Licorice Dressing

Makes 4 servings

¼ cup fresh lemon juice
2 tablespoons champagne or white wine vinegar
1 tablespoon soy sauce
½ teaspoon mustard powder
1½ teaspoons licorice powder
¼ cup peanut oil
Salt and freshly ground black pepper
1 cup shredded carrot
1 cup shredded daikon radish
1 cup shredded fennel
20 Boston lettuce leaves, torn
2 medium oranges, peeled and segmented between membranes
2 teaspoons white sesame seeds, toasted (see page 15)

Licorice, a powerfully flavored root, has long been a favorite of mine. But it takes time to infuse, even when ground. (You can sometimes buy ground licorice, but you may have to buy a stick and grind it in a coffee or spice grinder.) It is, therefore, best to make this dressing at least a few hours, and preferably a day, ahead. The flavor is intriguing, because the taste of the licorice is not evident at first; it comes long after the initial swallow and it lingers for awhile. Needless to say, this is not a salad for anyone who does not like licorice, though, combined as it is with citrus here, it may produce converts.

1. Put the first 6 ingredients into a blender with a pinch of salt and pepper to taste. Blend until the mixture is smooth. Place in a covered container and refrigerate overnight.

2. Put the carrot, daikon, fennel, lettuce, and oranges in a large mixing bowl. Season to taste with salt and pepper, then toss with the dressing. Transfer to a serving platter, sprinkle with sesame seeds, and serve.

Cucumber Marinated with Orange Peel

Makes 4 servings

1 medium cucumber, peeled, seeded, and cut into strips about 2 inches long and ¼ inch wide
2 teaspoons salt
1 tablespoon sugar
3 tablespoons rice vinegar
1 teaspoon sesame oil
1 fresh red Thai chile, seeded and minced
1 medium orange

This delicious little thing is nothing more than a quick Chinese-style pickle, though the orange zest makes it special. Serve it as either a side dish or starter.

1. Toss together the cucumber, salt, and sugar in a small bowl and marinate for 20 minutes. Toss in the vinegar, oil, and chile and marinate for another 30 minutes.

2. Toss the mixture again, then grate the orange zest over the top and serve.

Young ginger and mixed vegetables in the produce markets in the heart of Shanghai

Shredded Cabbage Salad

Makes 4 servings

2 fresh green Thai chiles, seeded and minced
2 garlic cloves, chopped
2 tablespoons sugar
2 tablespoons rice vinegar
3 tablespoons fresh lime juice
3 tablespoons nam pla (Thai fish sauce)
3 tablespoons grape seed, corn, or other neutral oil
4 cups shredded Napa cabbage
1 cup shredded carrot
½ cup thinly sliced red onion
¾ cup chopped fresh mint leaves
½ cup chopped fresh cilantro leaves
1 teaspoon black peppercorns, cracked
Salt, optional

This is a super-quick, Vietnamese-style salad, essentially a coleslaw with Asian overtones. It pairs well with most Asian dishes. (And, if you want to make it into a meal, toss in a couple of cups of cooked, shredded chicken.)

1. Combine the first 7 ingredients in a large mixing bowl and let stand for 30 minutes.

2. Add the cabbage, carrot, onion, mint, cilantro, and peppercorns and toss well. Add salt to taste.

Salad to go at the Aw Taw Kaw weekend market in Bangkok

Shredded Vegetable Salad

Makes 4 servings

3 tablespoons ponzu or soy sauce plus more to taste
⅓ cup mayonnaise
1 tablespoon fresh lime juice
½ teaspoon chopped fresh green Thai chile
Salt
1 cup thinly sliced red cabbage
1 cup thinly sliced Napa cabbage
1 cup julienned carrot
1 cup julienned daikon radish
1 cup julienned jicama
1 cup thinly sliced cucumber
1 cup trimmed bean sprouts
½ cup thinly sliced scallions
3 tablespoons fresh cilantro leaves

My take on chopped salad, and it doesn't get much better than this. If you have ponzu on hand (it keeps forever and, in fact, improves in the refrigerator), use it; otherwise, plain soy sauce is fine. And if you have a mandoline, this is the place to use it; it will take care of all of the slicing and julienning very quickly.

1. In a large serving bowl, whisk together the ponzu or soy and mayonnaise, stir in the lime juice and chile, and season to taste with salt.

2. Toss the dressing with the remaining ingredients until well mixed, then add additional ponzu or salt to taste. Garnish with cilantro and serve.

Mango Salad, Cherry Tomato, Long Bean, and Tamarind

Makes 4 servings

¼ cup plus 1½ teaspoons fresh lime juice
2 tablespoons finely ground palm sugar
½ teaspoon nam pla (Thai fish sauce)
1 teaspoon tamarind paste
½ teaspoon kosher salt, plus more to taste
One ½-inch piece fresh ginger, peeled and sliced
1 dried Thai chile, finely ground
1 tablespoon extra virgin olive oil

1 cup cashews
1 teaspoon grape seed, corn, or other neutral oil
4 Chinese long beans, trimmed and cut into 1-inch pieces
1 small green mango, peeled, pitted, and julienned
2 small ripe mangoes, peeled, pitted, and julienned
3 tablespoons tamarind candy, torn into small pieces
1 cup trimmed bean sprouts
24 Toy Box tomatoes, a colorful mix of cherry, pear, and other small tomatoes, halved
1 cup fresh cilantro leaves
½ head iceberg lettuce, quartered

Mango salad can be found on countless street corners in Bangkok. The first time I ate it, it knocked me out. It features all the flavors you most commonly associate with Thai cuisine: hot, sour, salty, sweet, bitter.

My super-complex version is worth the effort. In the traditional salad, everything is raw, but we char the beans for more depth. This dressing is also sensational, and any leftover can be kept, refrigerated, for a day or so (the garlic oil will keep up to a week). Tamarind candy (sold at most Asian markets) adds even more complexity.

1. Put the first 7 ingredients and 3 tablespoons water in a blender and blend until smooth. With the machine running, add the olive oil in a slow, steady stream. Blend until the mixture is completely emulsified. Set aside.

2. Put the cashews in a small skillet over medium heat. Toast, shaking the pan occasionally, until fragrant and browned. Remove from heat, cool, and roughly chop.

3. Heat the oil in a large skillet over high heat. Add the long beans and cook, stirring occasionally, until charred and wrinkled, about 7 minutes. Transfer to a large mixing bowl.

4. Add the mangoes, tamarind candy, bean sprouts, tomatoes, cilantro, and cashews. Season lightly with salt and toss in the dressing. Put the lettuce wedges and a mound of salad on the serving plates.

Asparagus Salad with Chinese Mustard

Makes 4 servings

2 tablespoons mustard powder, preferably Coleman's
2½ tablespoons soy sauce, preferably mushroom flavored
2 tablespoons rice vinegar
2 tablespoons red wine vinegar
One 2-inch piece fresh ginger, peeled and sliced
¼ cup plus 2 tablespoons white sesame seeds, toasted (see page 15)
1 tablespoon plus 1 teaspoon salt, plus more to taste
¼ cup grape seed, corn, or other neutral oil
1 large bunch asparagus (about 1½ pounds), trimmed
1 medium avocado, peeled, pitted, and sliced
½ cup trimmed bean sprouts
1 large bunch (about 2 ounces) chives, cut into 1-inch lengths
1 cup sliced fresh Thai basil

If you love the rich heat of mustard, this is the dish for you. Think ribbons of raw asparagus, and fresh bean sprouts add a nice crunch to the cooked asparagus and avocado. The assertive flavors of this "green" salad complement hearty meat dishes well.

1. Put the mustard powder in a small mixing bowl and add just enough water to make a thick paste, about 3 tablespoons. Stir well, then let stand for 10 minutes. Transfer to a blender with the soy sauce, vinegars, ginger, 2 tablespoons of the sesame seeds, and 1 teaspoon of the salt. Blend until smooth. With the machine running, add the oil in a slow, steady stream. Blend until completely emulsified and set aside.

2. Peel 5 asparagus stalks into thin ribbons by running a vegetable peeler along the length of the asparagus from the base to the tip. Set the ribbons aside. Cut the remaining asparagus into 2-inch lengths.

3. Fill a large bowl with water and ice and set aside. Bring a large pot of water to a boil and add the remaining 1 tablespoon salt and the cut asparagus. Cook just until bright green and tender, about 3 minutes. Drain and transfer to the ice water. When cold, drain again.

4. Put the cut asparagus, asparagus ribbons, avocado, bean sprouts, chives, basil, and remaining ¼ cup sesame seeds into a large mixing bowl. Season to taste with salt, toss gently with the dressing, and serve.

Avocado and Radish Salad with Onion Tempura

Makes 4 servings

ONION TEMPURA

1 medium onion, cut into ½-inch slices crosswise
¾ cup coconut juice, preferably Bangkok Market brand
¾ cup heavy cream
¼ teaspoon salt, plus more to taste
1 cup cornstarch
1 cup potato starch
2 teaspoons baking powder
Corn, or vegetable oil for deep-frying

LIME-CHILE SALT

7 kaffir lime leaves, center ribs removed
1 fresh red Thai chile, seeded and minced
¼ teaspoon salt

MUSTARD SAUCE

1½ teaspoons Chinese mustard powder
1½ teaspoons superfine or powdered sugar
1 tablespoon minced fresh ginger
1 tablespoon peeled and minced fresh galangal, or use more ginger
1½ tablespoons peanut oil
1 fresh red Thai chile, seeded and crushed
1 tablespoon fresh lime juice
1 tablespoon rice vinegar
½ teaspoon salt

CITRUS VINAIGRETTE

1½ tablespoons nam pla (Thai fish sauce)
3 tablespoons fresh grapefruit juice
1½ teaspoons mustard oil
¾ teaspoon sesame oil
1½ tablespoons fresh lime juice
¼ cup rice vinegar
1 tablespoon cornstarch

2 avocados, preferably Hass, seeded, peeled, and cut into ½-inch slices
Salt
½ cup paper-thin slices round red radishes (about 6 radishes)
½ cup paper-thin slices icicle radish (about ½ radish)
1½ cups radish sprouts

Feathery light onion tempura is the perfect counterpoint to the smooth avocado and crisp radishes in this salad, and the spiciness of Chinese mustard is offset by the citrus vinaigrette.

1. **To make the tempura:** Separate the rings of the onion slices from one another and lay them in an even layer in a shallow baking dish. Stir the coconut juice, cream, and salt together and pour over the onions. Let the onions soak in this mixture for at least 1 hour. Mix the cornstarch, potato starch, and baking powder together in a shallow dish. Drain the onions and dredge them in the dry ingredients.

(continued)

2. Pour oil to a depth of 2 inches in a heavy, deep saucepan and heat to 350°F. Carefully add the onions and cook, turning occasionally, until golden brown and crisp. Do not overcrowd; work in batches, if necessary. Remove from the oil and drain on paper towels, season lightly with salt, and set aside.

3. **To make the lime-chile salt:** Microwave the lime leaves and chile in 10-second intervals until they are dry, about 1½ minutes total. The time will vary depending on the strength of your microwave, but you will be able to see when the leaves and chiles have dried out. Cool completely and then grind in a spice grinder to a very fine powder and season with salt. Set aside until ready to use.

4. **To make the sauce:** Put the mustard powder in a small mixing bowl and add just enough water to make a thick paste, about 2 teaspoons. Stir well, then let stand for 10 minutes. Transfer to a blender with the sugar, ginger, galangal, peanut oil, chile, lime juice, vinegar, and salt and purée until smooth. Set aside until ready to use.

5. **To make the vinaigrette:** Put the nam pla, grapefruit juice, mustard oil, sesame oil, lime juice, and rice vinegar into a medium mixing bowl and whisk well. Let stand for 15 minutes, then transfer 2 tablespoons of the dressing into a small mixing bowl. Add the cornstarch to the small bowl and whisk until completely dissolved, then pour the cornstarch mixture back into the dressing. Whisk until well incorporated, then set aside until ready to use.

6. For each serving, put a little pool of mustard sauce in the center of a round serving plate and top with avocado slices. Season the avocado lightly with salt, then top with the radish slices and sprouts. Put 3 onion rings on top of the avocado so that the radishes are in the center of the rings. Sprinkle everything lightly with the reserved lime-chile salt and pour the citrus vinaigrette over the whole salad. Serve immediately.

Crunchy Fried Squid Salad

Makes 4 servings

SPICY SOUR DRESSING

1 tablespoon grape seed, corn, or other neutral oil
2 garlic cloves, thinly sliced
2 shallots, thinly sliced
½ small carrot, diced
½ small red bell pepper, cored, seeded, and diced
½ fresh red Thai chile, stemmed, seeded, and diced
2½ tablespoons fresh lime juice
3½ tablespoons rice vinegar
¾ teaspoon salt
1 tablespoon granulated sugar
1 tablespoon palm sugar
1 tablespoon chili oil, preferably homemade (page 51)

CRUNCHY SQUID SALAD

1 tablespoon soy sauce
1½ teaspoons rice vinegar
½ teaspoon sugar
1 cup rice or all-purpose flour
Corn or vegetable oil for deep-frying
10 ounces baby squid, bodies cut into ½-inch rings crosswise and tentacles separated
Salt
1 small ripe papaya, peeled, seeded, and cut into 1-inch cubes
4 fresh water chestnuts, peeled and cut into ¼-inch slices
½ cup cashews, toasted (see page 15) and slightly crushed
One 1-inch piece young ginger, minced
4 cups frisée, roughly chopped
1 tablespoon white sesame seeds, toasted (see page 15)

This variation on calamari is my new favorite way of preparing squid. The rice flour makes the batter extra crisp and slightly puffy. The spicy sour dressing accentuates the powerful salad. Everything is crispy, crunchy, and just perfect.

1. **To make the dressing:** Heat the oil in a medium saucepan over medium-low heat. Add the garlic and cook, stirring, until golden brown, about 2 minutes. Turn the heat to medium-high and add the shallots, carrot, pepper, and chile. Cook, stirring, until the vegetables are tender, about 3 minutes.

2. Add the lime juice, vinegar, salt, and sugars. Turn the heat to low and simmer, uncovered, stirring occasionally, until the mixture is syrupy, about 30 minutes. Almost all of the liquid will have evaporated. Transfer the mixture to a blender. With the blender running, add the chili oil. Blend until completely smooth. Transfer to a shallow dish to cool and set aside.

3. **To make the salad:** Mix together the soy sauce, vinegar, and sugar in a large mixing bowl. Add the rice flour and ¼ cup water and stir; then add another ¼ cup water and stir. You should have a smooth, lump-free, medium-

thick consistency of batter that runs from the spoon but is not completely liquid. Add more water if needed, and stir.

4. Pour oil to a depth of 2 inches in a heavy, deep saucepan and heat to 375°F. Dip the squid in the batter and transfer to the hot oil. Do not overcrowd the pan; work in batches if necessary. Cook until golden brown and really crisp, about 2 minutes. Drain on paper towels and season with salt.

5. Put the papaya, water chestnuts, cashews, ginger, and frisée in a large mixing bowl. Season to taste with salt and toss with the reserved dressing. When everything is well coated, transfer to the serving plates. Top with the fried squid, sprinkle on the sesame seeds, and serve immediately.

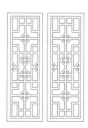

Salad of Wild Mushrooms and Steamed Spinach

Makes 4 servings

- 1 pound fresh wild mushrooms, like chanterelles or morels (or use shiitakes), trimmed and lightly rinsed
- 1 tablespoon minced fresh lemongrass
- 1 teaspoon minced fresh green Thai chile
- ½ cup fresh lime juice
- ½ cup grape seed, corn, or other neutral oil
- ¼ cup chopped shallots
- 1 tablespoon nam pla (Thai fish sauce)
- Salt and freshly ground black pepper
- 4 cups mixed baby greens, like amaranth, cress, mâche, or frisée
- 1 fresh red finger chile, seeded and thinly sliced, or to taste
- Snipped chives

This warm salad is both comforting and refined at once, an ideal starter for an elegant dinner party. It's one of the ways in which we treat wild mushrooms when we get them, because steaming really helps them retain their flavor. But even store-bought shiitakes are great treated in this manner.

1. Prepare a steamer. Wrap the mushrooms tightly in plastic wrap and steam until cooked through, about 5 minutes.

2. Remove the mushrooms from the plastic wrap, place in a bowl, and gently toss with the lemongrass, minced chile, lime juice, oil, shallots, nam pla, salt, and pepper.

3. Put the greens on a plate and top with the mushrooms. Drizzle on any of the remaining juices from the mushroom mixture, garnish with long chile and chives, and serve.

Crunchy Potato Salad

Makes 4 servings

¼ cup champagne or other white wine vinegar
¼ cup rice vinegar
2 tablespoons sugar
1 tablespoon cornstarch mixed with 1 tablespoon water
4 Yukon Gold or other all-purpose medium potatoes, peeled and julienned (preferably on a mandoline), and soaked in cold water until ready to use
3 round red radishes, trimmed and thinly sliced
1 red bell pepper, cored, seeded, and julienned
½ fresh red finger chile, seeded and thinly sliced, or to taste
Salt and freshly ground black pepper

This Sichuan-inspired creation is one of the most unusual potato dishes you will ever come across, because you cook the potatoes just long enough to take off the raw edge. They retain a great potato flavor and crunch, making for a refreshingly light salad. It is a welcome change from the heavy mayonnaise-laden potato salads we're all used to.

1. Put the vinegars and sugar in a saucepan over medium heat and bring to a boil. Add the cornstarch mixture to the saucepan 1 teaspoon at a time, stirring constantly, until the mixture is the consistency of an emulsified vinaigrette. Remove from the heat and set aside.

2. Fill a large bowl with water and ice and set aside. Bring a large pot of water to a boil and add the potatoes. Boil for 1 minute, then drain and transfer to the ice water. When cold, drain again. You want the potatoes to still be crunchy.

3. Put the potatoes, radishes, pepper, and chile in a large mixing bowl. Toss with the dressing, season to taste with salt and pepper, and serve.

Charred Lamb Salad

Makes 4 servings

- $\frac{1}{2}$ cup white vinegar
- $\frac{3}{4}$ teaspoon sugar
- $\frac{1}{2}$ garlic clove, minced
- 1 fresh red Thai chile, minced
- 1 lemongrass stalk, trimmed and $\frac{1}{2}$ minced, $\frac{1}{2}$ smashed
- 3 tablespoons grape seed, corn, or other neutral oil
- One 10-ounce boneless lamb loin, $1\frac{1}{2}$ inches thick
- Salt and freshly ground pepper
- $\frac{1}{2}$ cup jus rôti, store-bought is fine, or chicken stock, preferably homemade or canned low-sodium broth, or water
- 1 small cucumber, seeded and julienned
- 1 carrot, peeled and julienned
- $\frac{1}{4}$ jicama, peeled and diced
- 1 cup trimmed bean sprouts
- $\frac{1}{2}$ cup sliced fresh cilantro leaves, plus more for garnish
- $\frac{1}{4}$ cup sliced fresh mint leaves
- 3 tablespoons nam pla (Thai fish sauce), plus more to taste

Lamb salad is not something you eat—or even hear about—very often, but the combination of crunchy vegetables, fresh herbs, and gamy lamb is nothing short of spectacular. I was inspired to make it by my love for Thai beef salad, but lamb is perhaps an even better choice. Char the lamb—really char it—for the best flavor.

1. Put the first 3 ingredients and half the chile in a saucepan and whisk until the sugar is dissolved. Bring the mixture to a boil, then remove from the heat, cool, and set aside.

2. Put the smashed lemongrass in a small saucepan with $\frac{1}{4}$ cup cold water. Bring to a boil, then remove from the heat, cool, and set aside.

3. Heat 2 tablespoons of the oil in a large skillet over high heat. Season the lamb with salt and pepper and put in the skillet. Sear each side for 5 minutes. Remove the lamb from the skillet, then deglaze the pan with the jus, stock, or water.

4. Meanwhile, in a large bowl toss the cucumber, carrot, jicama, bean sprouts, cilantro, mint, and reserved minced lemongrass with the nam pla, reserved vinegar infusion, and lemongrass water. Add the remaining 1 tablespoon oil and the remaining chile and toss again.

5. Cut the lamb into $\frac{1}{4}$-inch slices. Put the salad on a serving plate, top with the lamb slices, and drizzle with the deglazed jus. Garnish with cilantro leaves and serve immediately.

Shrimp and Bean Sprout Salad

Makes 4 servings

½ pound white mushrooms, stems removed and caps cut into ½-inch dice
Salt and cayenne pepper
¼ cup fresh lime juice
½ cup plain whole-milk yogurt
2 tablespoons unsalted butter
¼ cup minced shallots
24 medium shrimp, peeled and deveined
¼ cup soy sauce
2 tablespoons roasted peanut, hazelnut, or sesame oil
1 cup trimmed bean sprouts
½ cup chopped peanuts

This is a wonderful, odd combination of things, sour and crunchy and hot and cool and very salty. It's almost Indian, but more Chinese, and it all works very well. And it's fast and easy enough to be a light weeknight meal.

1. Put the mushrooms in a mixing bowl and season with salt, cayenne, and the lime juice. Stir in the yogurt, cover, and refrigerate while you prepare the other ingredients.

2. Melt the butter in a large skillet over medium heat. Add the shallots and cook for 30 seconds, then season the shrimp with salt and cayenne and add to the skillet. Cook just until the shrimp turns pink, about 2 minutes, then lower the heat and add the soy sauce. As soon as the mixture comes to a boil, remove from the heat and stir in the oil, bean sprouts, and peanuts. Let the mixture cool slightly.

3. Transfer the shrimp mixture and mushroom mixture to the serving plates, arrange the two mixtures side by side, and serve.

Street food cart →
in Bangkok

PEPSI
PEPSI

FISH

Spiced Cod with Curried Artichoke

Makes 4 servings

1½ tablespoons coriander seeds
1½ teaspoons cumin seeds
3 whole star anise
1 whole nutmeg, roughly chopped
1 tablespoon crushed red pepper flakes
4 whole cloves
2 whole artichokes
2 tablespoons unsalted butter
½ teaspoon medium-hot curry powder
½ teaspoon salt, plus more to taste
Four 6-ounce cod steaks or fillets
3 tablespoons grape seed, corn, or other neutral oil
¼ pound snow peas, trimmed and strings removed, optional
2 scallions, trimmed and julienned
½ cup Tamarind Ketchup (page 32)

A long-term Vong favorite, one in which we cook the artichokes with one spice mix, a more-or-less traditional curry powder, and coat the cod with another before we quickly sear it. The artichokes become crunchy and add their distinctive sweetness to the subtle, tender cod. You can use any tender or firm white-fleshed fillet for this dish.

1. Coarsely grind the first 6 ingredients in a spice grinder or food processor until the mixture resembles cornmeal. Set aside.

2. Preheat the oven to 450°F.

3. Trim the artichokes: Cut off their pointy tops to within 1 or 1½ inches of the base; remove all but about ½ inch of the stem. Cut all around the artichoke, removing all of the hard parts. Open up the center and dig out the choke with a spoon. Trim any remaining hard parts; what's left is the artichoke bottom.

4. Julienne the artichoke bottoms. Melt the butter in a large skillet. Add the artichokes and season with the curry powder and salt. Stir over medium heat; do not allow the curry to brown. Add a tablespoon or two of water and cook the artichokes until the liquid evaporates, about 5 minutes.

5. Season the fish with salt and press a tablespoon of the reserved spice mix on top of one side. Heat the oil in a large ovenproof sauté pan. Place each piece of fish, spice

side down, in the pan and sear for about 5 minutes, then transfer to the oven and cook for another 5 minutes. Take the pan out of the oven and turn the fish over.

6. Meanwhile, fill a large bowl with water and ice and set aside. Bring a large pot of water to a boil and add the snow peas, if you like. Cook just until bright green and tender, but still crisp. Drain and transfer to the ice water. When cold, drain again.

7. Arrange a line of artichokes on each serving plate and place the cod, spice side up, beside it. Garnish with the snow peas, if desired, scallions, and Tamarind Ketchup.

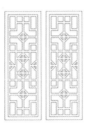

Steamed Cod with Caramelized Onion, Ginger, and Scallions

Makes 4 servings

¼ cup plus 2 tablespoons peanut oil
2 medium onions, thinly sliced
One 1-inch piece fresh ginger, julienned
Four 6-ounce thick cod fillets
Salt
Cayenne pepper
2 tablespoons sesame oil
¼ cup slivered scallions
¼ cup chopped fresh cilantro leaves
Soy sauce

This is a lovely variation on classic Cantonese steamed fish, one that uses fillets of cod—though you can use any tender or firm white-fleshed fillet for this dish—which makes it simple enough for a weeknight meal. With the caramelized onion, it has an added dimension of sweetness.

1. Heat ¼ cup of the peanut oil in a large skillet over medium-high heat until almost smoking. Add the onions and brown, but do not cook through, about 2 minutes. Toss in the ginger and remove from the heat.

2. Prepare a steamer. Season the cod with salt and cayenne, then top each piece with the onion-and-ginger mixture. Steam until a thin-bladed knife pierces through the flesh easily, about 10 minutes.

3. Meanwhile, heat the sesame oil and remaining 2 tablespoons peanut oil in the same skillet in which you cooked the onions, until the oil smokes. Transfer the cod from the steamer to the serving plates. Top each piece with some scallions, then pour on the hot sesame-peanut oil mixture. Top the fish with cilantro, season to taste with soy sauce, and serve.

Choosing seafood for →
dinner outside a
restaurant in Shanghai

Cod with Malaysian Chili Sauce

Makes 4 servings

¼ cup plus 2½ tablespoons grape seed, corn, or other neutral oil
5 garlic cloves, minced
2½ tablespoons minced fresh ginger
2½ tablespoons Guilin chili sauce
1½ tablespoons light soy sauce
2 teaspoons rice vinegar
2½ tablespoons Shaoxing wine
1½ tablespoons sugar
1 teaspoon salt, plus more to taste
5 scallions, trimmed and sliced, green and white parts separated
Four 6-ounce cod fillets, 1½ inches thick
¼ teaspoon freshly ground white pepper, plus more to taste
4 celery stalks, trimmed and diced, 4 leaves reserved for garnish
Thai Basil Oil (page 66)

The robust spicy-sweet sauce in this dish is the perfect accompaniment to the subtle flavor of cod. Crunchy bits of celery are a welcome textural addition too. The bright green Thai Basil Oil brightens up the jamlike sauce. Serve this with steamed white rice.

1. Preheat the oven to 350°F.

2. Heat the oil in a medium saucepan over medium heat. Add the garlic and ginger and cook, stirring, until golden, about 5 minutes. Add the chili sauce, soy sauce, vinegar, wine, sugar, salt, and scallion whites and turn the heat to low. Simmer, stirring occasionally, until the mixture is thick like jam, about 10 minutes. Add the scallion greens and simmer just until cooked through, about 2 minutes. Remove from the heat and set aside.

3. Put the remaining 2½ tablespoons oil in a large nonstick ovenproof skillet over medium-high heat. Season the cod fillets with salt and white pepper, then add to the skillet. Cook for 30 seconds, then transfer the fish to the oven. Cook until a thin-bladed knife pierces through the flesh easily, about 8 minutes.

4. Meanwhile, put the celery in a small saucepan and add just enough water to coat the bottom of the pan. Set over medium-high heat and cook until bright green and warmed through, about 4 minutes. Drain.

(continued)

5. If the sauce has cooled, reheat it gently over medium-low heat. Season to taste with salt, then divide the sauce among the serving plates. Put the fish fillets on top of the sauce and the celery on top of the fish. Drizzle the Thai Basil Oil around the plate, garnish with celery leaves, and serve.

Different grades of rice at the Aw Taw Kaw weekend market in Bangkok

FISH

Poached Sole with Watercress and Noodles

Makes 4 servings

FISH FUMET

½ onion, sliced
1 leek, trimmed, washed, and cut into 2-inch lengths
1 celery stalk, cut into 2-inch lengths
2 sprigs fresh thyme
1 bay leaf
1 tablespoon unsalted butter
1 pound white fish bones, cut into small pieces
1 lemongrass stalk, trimmed, smashed, and chopped
½ cup chopped fresh ginger
2 garlic cloves, chopped
1 fresh green Thai chile, seeded and minced
½ cup dry white wine
2 cups chicken stock, preferably homemade or canned low-sodium broth, or water

1 pound thin fresh egg noodles
¼ cup julienned fresh ginger
2 cups fresh oyster mushrooms, cleaned, trimmed, and julienned
1½ pounds sole or fluke fillets, skinned, deboned, and cut diagonally into 1-inch slices
Salt and cayenne pepper
¼ cup fresh lime juice, plus more to taste
1 tablespoon nam pla (Thai fish sauce), plus more to taste
1 teaspoon minced fresh green Thai chile, plus more to taste
4 cups fresh watercress, washed, trimmed, and roughly chopped
1 cup fresh cilantro leaves

This soupy fish and noodle bowl is humble in presentation, but the mushrooms and fragrant fish stock add an exquisite sophistication. We like to add mussels, shrimp, or other seafood to make this a hearty one-dish meal.

1. **To make the fumet:** Put the onion, leek, celery, thyme, and bay leaf into a large square of cheesecloth. Wrap tightly and secure the sachet with kitchen string. Set aside.

2. Melt the butter in a large saucepan over medium-high heat. Add the bones and sweat until opaque, then add the lemongrass, ginger, garlic, and chile. Cook just until fragrant, about 30 seconds, then pour in the wine.

3. Cook until most of the wine has evaporated, then add the reserved sachet and chicken stock. Bring the mixture to a boil, then lower the heat and simmer for 25 minutes. Strain through a fine-mesh sieve and return to the saucepan. Set aside.

4. Bring a medium pot of water to a boil. Add the noodles and cook until al dente, about 3 minutes, then drain and run under cold water. Set aside.

(continued)

5. Bring the fumet to a boil over medium heat, add the ginger and mushrooms, and cook for 1 minute. Season the fish with salt and cayenne, then turn the heat to low and add the fish. Cook until a thin-bladed knife pierces through the flesh easily, about 5 minutes.

6. Stir in the lime juice, nam pla, and chile, adjusting each seasoning to taste. Add the noodles and cook just until heated through. Transfer the noodles to the serving bowls and spoon the broth over the noodles. Arrange the fish and mushrooms on top of the noodles, then top with watercress and cilantro. Serve immediately.

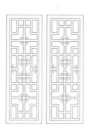

Halibut Cha Ca La Vong

Makes 4 servings

NUOC CHAM

2 garlic cloves, crushed
1 fresh red Thai chile, seeded and minced
2 tablespoons sugar
2 tablespoons fresh lime juice
¼ cup rice vinegar
¼ cup nam pla (Thai fish sauce)

2 ounces fresh turmeric, peeled and chopped (about 2 tablespoons), or 1 tablespoon ground turmeric
2 tablespoons nam pla (Thai fish sauce)
Four 8-ounce halibut fillets, each about 1 inch thick, skinned
2 tablespoons grape seed, corn, or other neutral oil
2 teaspoons unsalted butter
Salt
8 ounces dried rice vermicelli, cooked in boiling water just until softened
1 carrot, peeled and cut into thin ribbons
½ cup fresh dill leaves
¼ cup fresh Thai basil leaves
¼ cup fresh cilantro leaves
Peanut Sauce (page 62)
2 tablespoons crushed peanuts, toasted (see page 15)

Homemade *nuoc cham,* Vietnamese table sauce, really brings out the flavor of the fish and fresh vegetables in this sharp, refreshing dish. Finishing it with Peanut Sauce and crushed peanuts gives it great depth of flavor as well as crunch.

Turmeric, a gnarled root with brilliant orange flesh, can sometimes be found fresh in Chinese and other Asian markets; definitely use it if you have it. But the much more common dried and ground turmeric is fine too.

1. **To make the nuoc cham:** Put the ingredients and ¼ cup water in a blender and blend until smooth. Transfer to a mixing bowl and set aside.

2. Put the turmeric and fish sauce in a blender and blend until smooth; if you're using ground turmeric, combine it with the nam pla to create a paste.

3. Spread a thin layer of the turmeric mixture all over the fillets. Heat the oil and butter in a medium skillet over medium-high heat. When the butter has melted, season the fish lightly with salt and add to the skillet. Cook until nicely browned, about 4 minutes, then flip and cook the other side until nicely browned, another 4 minutes.

4. Meanwhile, put the noodles, carrot ribbons, and two-thirds of the nuoc cham in a medium skillet. Set over

medium heat and heat until warmed through. Toss the dill, basil, and cilantro with the remaining nuoc cham in a mixing bowl.

5. Put the Peanut Sauce in a small saucepan and set over medium heat until warmed through. Spoon some of the sauce on the side of the serving plates and put the noodle-carrot mixture next to it. Put the halibut on top of the noodles and top with the herb salad and a sprinkling of crushed peanuts. Serve immediately.

Young monks asking for rice outside the vegetable market in Bagan

Slow-Baked Halibut with Apples, Onions, and Coconut

Makes 4 servings

LEMON VERBENA OIL

2 cups lemon verbena leaves
1 cup grape seed, corn, or other neutral oil
1 teaspoon salt, plus more as needed

Unsalted butter as needed
Four 6-ounce boneless halibut steaks or fillets (or use any firm white-fleshed fish)
1 cup thinly sliced Granny Smith apples, skin on
1 cup thinly sliced new onions
One 1-inch piece fresh ginger, peeled and julienned
4 ounces fresh coconut, thinly sliced
10 fresh Thai basil leaves, thinly sliced
Salt and freshly ground black pepper
Fresh lemon juice to taste
Coarse salt and cracked black pepper to taste
⅓ cup coconut milk

Tender fish topped with crunchy, high-flavored ingredients, this might be best called a great fish salad. You can often find fresh, prepared coconut in Asian markets, but if you cannot, use dried unsweetened coconut.

If you have a mandoline, use it to shave the apples, onions, and coconut. Otherwise, use a very sharp knife and slice them as thinly as possible.

1. **To make the oil:** Put the lemon verbena leaves, oil, and salt in a blender. Blend until thoroughly combined, then set aside and infuse for 30 minutes. Strain through a fine-mesh sieve into a container and refrigerate until use.

2. Preheat the oven to 250°F.

3. Generously grease the bottom of a baking sheet or roasting pan with butter. Put the halibut steaks on the pan and bake until a thin-bladed knife pierces through the flesh easily, 20 to 25 minutes.

4. Meanwhile, toss together the apples, onions, ginger, coconut, and basil. Season to taste with salt, pepper, and lemon juice. Drizzle with lemon verbena oil, then taste and adjust the seasoning.

5. When the halibut is done, season to taste with coarse salt and cracked black pepper. Put the halibut steaks in the center of each serving plate and top with the salad. Drizzle with the coconut milk and the reserved lemon verbena oil and serve.

Coconut-Poached Halibut and Eggplant

Makes 4 servings

SPICY CRUST MIX

2 tablespoons unsalted butter
2 fresh red Thai chiles, seeded and finely chopped
½ lemongrass stalk, trimmed and finely chopped
2 garlic cloves, finely chopped
1 cup bread crumbs, preferably Japanese panko
2 tablespoons minced fresh mint leaves
2 tablespoons minced fresh cilantro leaves
2 tablespoons minced fresh Thai basil leaves

12 small Japanese eggplants, trimmed and cut into quarters lengthwise
Salt
2 tablespoons unsalted butter
4 shallots, sliced
1 fresh red Thai chile, seeded and finely chopped
¼ cup finely chopped fresh lemongrass
4 kaffir lime leaves, thinly sliced
Four 6-ounce boneless halibut steaks or fillets (or use any firm white-fleshed fish)
Cayenne pepper
1 cup dry white wine
¾ cup coconut milk
1 tablespoon plus 1 teaspoon fresh lime juice
1 teaspoon nam pla (Thai fish sauce), optional

First poached, then broiled, this halibut is tender, juicy, rich, flavorful, and crisp; it's really amazing, especially given how easy it is. The eggplant provides a lovely counterpoint.

1. **To make the crust mix:** Put half the butter in a skillet over medium heat. When the butter melts, add the chiles, lemongrass, and garlic, and cook, stirring, for 30 seconds. Add the bread crumbs and the remaining butter to the mixture and sauté until the bread crumbs are golden brown, about 4 minutes. When the mixture has cooled, mix in the mint, cilantro, and basil.

2. Preheat the oven to 450°F.

3. Rinse and drain the eggplants in a colander, then generously sprinkle them with salt. After 20 minutes, rinse and drain them again. Prepare a steamer and steam the eggplant until tender, about 7 minutes. Set aside and keep warm.

4. Meanwhile, melt 1 tablespoon of the butter in a large deep ovenproof skillet that can later be covered over medium heat. Add the shallots, chile, lemongrass, lime leaves, and salt to taste and cook, stirring occasionally. When the shallots are softened, season the halibut with salt and cayenne and add to the pan. Then add the wine and bring to a boil.

5. Cover the skillet and transfer to the oven. Poach the fish until a thin-bladed knife pierces through the flesh easily, about 10 minutes, then remove from the oven and switch the oven to broil.

6. Transfer the halibut steaks to a baking sheet and top each steak with a thick layer of the crust mix and small nuggets of the remaining tablespoon of butter. Crisp under the broiler just until the bread crumbs color, 1 to 2 minutes. Lightly season with salt to taste.

7. Meanwhile, put the skillet with the remaining liquid over medium heat and add the coconut milk. Cook until the sauce has reduced and thickened, about 5 minutes. Season with lime juice and, if you like, the nam pla. Put the eggplant on the serving plates, top with the halibut steaks, and spoon the pan sauce all around. Serve immediately.

Maa-euk (hairy eggplants) at a local street market

Steamed Skate with Tarragon and Toasted Sesame Seeds

Makes 4 servings

The skate is the star here—with a browned butter vinaigrette. But the accompanying sushi rice and bok choy make this an amazing meal. The tarragon is distinctively French and pairs perfectly with toasted sesame seeds.

SUSHI RICE

¼ cup plus 2 tablespoons rice vinegar
3 tablespoons seasoned sushi rice vinegar
One ¼-inch piece kombu (dried seaweed)
2½ teaspoons salt, plus more to taste
1¼ teaspoons sugar
1 cup sushi rice, rinsed well and drained

BROWNED BUTTER VINAIGRETTE

6 tablespoons unsalted butter
2 teaspoons sherry vinegar
2 teaspoons balsamic vinegar
1 teaspoon sesame oil

4 boneless, skinless skate wings
1 tablespoon grape seed, corn, or other neutral oil
4 heads baby bok choy, trimmed and halved lengthwise
Salt
Fleur de sel and cracked black peppercorns
2 tablespoons white sesame seeds, toasted (see page 15)
2 tablespoons chopped fresh tarragon

1. **To make the sushi rice:** Stir the vinegars, kombu, salt, and sugar together in a small bowl and set aside.

2. Put the rice and 1¼ cups water in a rice cooker and cook. Alternatively, put the rice and 1¼ cups water in a small saucepan and bring to a boil. Turn the heat to low, cover, and cook until all the water has been absorbed and the rice is tender, about 20 minutes.

3. Transfer the cooked rice to a large mixing bowl, add the reserved rice vinegar mixture, and stir well. Set aside.

4. **To make the browned butter vinaigrette:** Fill a large bowl with ice and water. Put the butter in a medium skillet and set over medium heat. Melt, stirring and scraping the pan occasionally, until the butter becomes a dark golden brown and smells nutty. Transfer to a medium mixing bowl and set over the ice water bath until cool.

5. Add the vinegars and sesame oil to the browned butter and whisk until well combined. Set aside.

6. Prepare a steamer. Add the skate and steam, covered, until a thin-bladed knife pierces through the flesh easily, about 8 minutes.

7. Heat the oil in a wok or skillet over high heat. Add the bok choy and 1 tablespoon water, season with salt, and cook, stirring, until cooked through, about 4 minutes.

8. Put the skate on the serving plates and drizzle the vinaigrette over and around the fish. Sprinkle fleur de sel, cracked black pepper, sesame seeds, and tarragon over the fish. Put 2 bok choy pieces on each plate and top with a mound of the rice. Serve immediately.

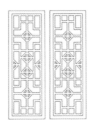

Skate Wings with Ginger-Garlic-Black Bean Crumbs

Makes 4 servings

GINGER-GARLIC-BLACK BEAN CRUMBS

½ cup grape seed, corn, or other neutral oil
2 tablespoons minced fresh ginger
2 tablespoons minced fresh garlic
Salt
2 tablespoons fermented black beans, minced
2 dried Thai chiles, minced

TEMPURA BATTER

1 cup plus 2 tablespoons rice flour
¼ teaspoon baking soda
¼ teaspoon baking powder
2 teaspoons sherry vinegar
2 teaspoons sesame oil
1½ teaspoons grape seed, corn, or other neutral oil
¾ teaspoon salt

Corn or other vegetable oil for deep-frying
4 boneless, skinless skate wings, cut into 12 even pieces
1 cup rice flour
2 teaspoons kosher salt
1 teaspoon finely ground white pepper
¼ cup thinly sliced iceberg lettuce
2 tablespoons fresh Thai basil leaves
1 fresh green finger chile, seeded and sliced
1 tablespoon fresh lime zest
2 limes, quartered

This fish tempura gets an added crunch from the fragrant ginger-garlic-black bean crumbs. Deliciously crisp and savory, this dish is best eaten right away.

1. **To make the crumbs:** Heat half the oil in a large skillet over medium heat. Add the minced ginger and garlic and season lightly with salt. Cook, stirring occasionally, until crisp and golden brown. Strain through a fine-mesh sieve, drain on paper towels, and set aside.

2. Heat the remaining ¼ cup of oil in a large skillet over medium-high heat. Mix the black beans and chiles together and add to the skillet. Cook, stirring occasionally, until crisp and very fragrant. Strain through a fine-mesh sieve, drain on paper towels, and set aside.

3. **To make the tempura batter:** Sift together the flour, baking soda, and baking powder. Mix the vinegar, oils, salt, and ¾ cup cold water together in a large mixing bowl. Add the dry ingredients to the mixing bowl and stir gently until the mixture is smooth.

4. Pour oil to a depth of 3 inches in a heavy, deep saucepan and heat to 400°F.

(continued)

จำหน่าย และ
นาฬิกา
DUNA

5. Dredge the skate well in the rice flour and shake off excess. Coat the skate in the tempura batter and shake off excess. Gently lower the coated skate into the saucepan and fry, turning occasionally, until golden and crisp. Do not crowd the pan; work in batches if necessary. Drain the skate on paper towels and immediately sprinkle with kosher salt and white pepper to taste. Transfer to serving plates.

6. Mix the ginger-garlic crumbs with the black bean crumbs and sprinkle all over the fish tempura. Garnish with the lettuce, basil, chile, and lime zest. Serve immediately with lime quarters.

← Eating on the streets of Bangkok

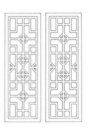

"Barbecued" Red Snapper, Thai Style

Makes 4 servings

MARINADE

1 small bunch fresh cilantro, plus leaves for garnish
1 garlic clove, peeled
1 tablespoon nam pla (Thai fish sauce)
1 tablespoon black peppercorns, cracked

Four 6-ounce snapper fillets (or use fillets of any firm white fish), skin on
2 cups canned whole tomatoes
1 tablespoon palm or brown sugar
2 shallots, sliced
1 garlic clove, chopped
1 tablespoon fresh lime juice
1 tablespoon sherry vinegar
2 teaspoons nam pla (Thai fish sauce)
Coarse salt
1 tablespoon grape seed, corn, or other neutral oil, plus more as needed
2 tablespoons julienned scallions
2 tablespoons julienned fresh red finger chiles

The Thai-inspired tomato sauce is great on the fish, which is beautifully marinated with a strong cilantro paste. Both sauce and fish can be prepared ahead of time, leaving only a quick grilling for the last minute.

1. **To make the marinade:** Fill a large bowl with water and ice. Bring a small pot of water to a boil and add the cilantro. As soon as the water returns to a boil, drain and transfer to the ice water. When cold, drain again and transfer to a blender. Blend thoroughly, then add the garlic, nam pla, and cracked black pepper and purée. With the machine running, add enough water to make a smooth purée, about ¼ cup plus 2 tablespoons.

2. Make slits in the fish and fill with the marinade. Cover and refrigerate for about 2 hours.

3. Put the tomatoes in a food processor. Process until smooth, then strain through a fine-mesh sieve into a bowl. Stir in the sugar, shallots, garlic, lime juice, vinegar, and nam pla. Salt to taste and set aside.

4. When you're ready to cook, start a charcoal or gas grill or broiler; the fire should be medium-hot, and the grill rack should be about 4 inches from the heat source. Salt the fish and coat it with the oil, then put the fish on the grill and cook, turning when nicely browned, about 4 minutes. Cook an additional 4 minutes; the fish is done when a thin-bladed knife pierces through the flesh easily.

5. Pool the tomato sauce on the serving plates and top with the fish. Garnish with scallions, chiles, and cilantro leaves and serve.

Grilled Swordfish with Sautéed Butternut Squash

Makes 4 servings

- ¼ cup Tamarind Ketchup (page 32)
- ⅓ cup honey
- 2 teaspoons thick soy sauce
- 2 teaspoons kecap manis (sweet soy sauce)
- 2 tablespoons nam pla (Thai fish sauce), plus more to taste
- 1 tablespoon chili sauce in soybean oil
- 2 tablespoons unsalted butter
- ½ small butternut squash, peeled, seeded, and cut into ½-inch cubes
- 2 garlic cloves, chopped
- 2 teaspoons sugar
- 1 cup chicken stock, preferably homemade or canned low-sodium broth
- 2 teaspoons cracked black peppercorns
- Salt
- 1 celery stalk, finely chopped and parboiled
- Four 6-ounce swordfish steaks
- Salt and freshly ground black pepper
- 1 fresh red Thai chile, seeded and julienned, optional
- Chopped fresh cilantro leaves, optional

The combination of swordfish and butternut squash makes this dish a hearty winter meal and the sweet soy sauce-based sauce adds a beautiful and rich glaze to the fish. The subtle sweetness is offset by the heat of the chili sauce and black pepper.

1. In a small bowl, mix the first 6 ingredients together and reserve.

2. Melt the butter in a large skillet over medium heat and add the squash and garlic; cook until the squash begins to brown, about 10 minutes, then add the sugar and stir. Add the chicken stock, sprinkle with pepper, and cook until the squash is very soft, but still in cubes. Season to taste with salt and nam pla and mix in the celery. Set aside.

3. Meanwhile, start both a charcoal or gas grill and a broiler; the fire should be medium-hot, and the grill racks should be about 4 inches from the heat sources.

4. Season the fish with salt and pepper, then grill until cooked through, marking with a crisscross pattern on each side. Coat each steak with 2 tablespoons of the reserved sauce and place under the broiler for a minute.

5. Mound the squash, with the sauce from the pan, in the center of each serving plate. Place the fish on top and garnish with the chile and cilantro, if desired.

Black Sea Bass with Fragrant Coconut Juice

Makes 4 servings

FRAGRANT COCONUT JUICE

1 cup plus 2 tablespoons coconut juice, preferably Bangkok Market brand
3 tablespoons coconut milk
3 tablespoons fresh lime juice
1 small jalapeño pepper, stemmed
1 lemongrass stalk, smashed and chopped
One 5-inch piece cassia, broken into small pieces
One 2-inch piece fresh, young ginger, peeled and thinly sliced
2 tablespoons sugar
⅓ teaspoon salt
12 kaffir lime leaves, finely chopped

MINT EMULSION

¾ teaspoon cornstarch
½ teaspoon plus ⅛ teaspoon salt
1½ cups fresh mint leaves
½ cup plus 1 tablespoon grape seed, corn, or other neutral oil

2 fresh poblano peppers
1 tablespoon extra virgin olive oil
1 small parsnip, peeled and cut into ¼-inch-thick slices
¼ teaspoon sugar
⅛ teaspoon salt, plus more to taste
2 tablespoons unsalted butter

Four 6-ounce black sea bass fillets
Freshly ground white pepper
1 cup fresh basil leaves
½ cup diced young coconut meat
1 lime, peeled and cut into segments between the membranes
2 teaspoons fresh lime zest

The light, clean flavors of the coconut juice and mint emulsion are complemented by the creamy parsnip purée and smoky poblano peppers in this dish. At the same time, the fresh herbs and aromatics bring out the sweetness of sea bass. Impress your guests with this elegant dish when you pour the coconut broth into the dishes at the table.

1. **To make the coconut juice:** Put all the ingredients except the lime leaves into a medium saucepan and bring to a simmer over medium-high heat. Remove from the heat and stir in the lime leaves. Set aside to cool at room temperature.

2. **To make the mint emulsion:** Fill a medium bowl with ice and water. Put the cornstarch and ⅛ teaspoon of the salt into a small saucepan with 2¼ teaspoons water. Bring to a boil over medium-high heat, whisking constantly, and continue cooking and whisking until the mixture is thick and clear. Transfer to a small bowl and set the bowl over the ice water bath.

3. Fill a large bowl with water and ice and set aside. Bring a small pot of water to a boil and add the mint

leaves. As soon as the water returns to a boil, drain the leaves and transfer to the ice water. When cold, drain again. Squeeze as much water as you can from the mint leaves, then transfer to a blender with the grape seed oil and remaining ½ teaspoon salt. Blend until very smooth, then strain through a fine-mesh sieve, squeezing on the solids to extract as much oil as possible.

4. Put the cornstarch mixture in the blender and turn the machine to the highest setting. With the machine running, add the mint oil in a slow, steady stream. Purée until the mixture has emulsified. Set aside.

5. Start a charcoal or gas grill or broiler; the fire should be hot, and the grill rack should be about 4 inches from the heat source.

6. Coat the poblano peppers with the olive oil and grill, turning occasionally, until well charred, but not black. Remove from the heat, cool, and peel. Remove the stems and seeds and dice. Set aside.

7. Put the parsnip, sugar, salt, and ½ cup water in a small saucepan and bring to a steady simmer over medium-high heat. Turn the heat to medium-low, cover, and cook about 15 minutes until the parsnip is very tender. A knife will pierce through easily. Drain well, then transfer to a blender. Purée until completely smooth.

8. While the parsnip is cooking, preheat the oven to 225°F. Generously grease a baking sheet with the butter. Season the fish fillets with salt and white pepper and put on the baking sheet, skin side down. Scatter the basil leaves around the fish and transfer to the oven. Cook about 20 minutes until the skin peels off easily and a thin-bladed knife pierces through the flesh easily.

9. Gently toss the diced poblano peppers with the coconut and lime segments. Spoon the parsnip purée on the side of shallow serving dishes. Put the fish on top of the parsnip and top the fish with the poblano pepper mixture. Spoon the mint emulsion in the corner of the plate. Immediately before serving, pour the coconut broth into the dishes. Garnish with a sprinkle of lime zest and serve.

Crispy Black Sea Bass with Sweet-and-Sour Sauce and Green Tea

Makes 4 servings

SWEET-AND-SOUR SAUCE

2 tablespoons extra virgin olive oil
2 shallots, thinly sliced
½ cup cubed fresh pineapple
2 tablespoons honey
½ cup crystallized ginger
½ fresh green Thai chile, or pinch of cayenne pepper
¼ cup red wine vinegar
2 tablespoons fresh lime juice
1 teaspoon nam pla (Thai fish sauce)
Salt
¼ cup elderflower syrup

¼ cup pine nuts
¼ teaspoon ammonia powder
1 cup cake flour
1 teaspoon baking powder
3 tablespoons grape seed, corn, or other neutral oil, plus more for frying
Four 6-ounce black sea bass fillets (or use any firm white-fleshed fish fillets)
Salt and cayenne pepper
2 tablespoons shredded fresh ginger
1 tablespoon matcha (green tea powder)

There is a tradition of using tiny amounts of powdered ammonia in Chinese cooking (see page 4) because it helps create an amazingly crisp exterior. Hearing of this, I seized the opportunity. (You can prepare this dish without it, but it won't be quite the same.) We serve the crisp fish with a well-balanced sweet-and-sour sauce, finished with a sprinkle of fragrant green tea powder.

1. **To make the sauce:** Heat the oil in a saucepan over medium heat. Add the shallots and cook until tender, about 5 minutes. Stir in the pineapple and honey and cook until caramelized, about 5 minutes. Transfer this mixture to a blender.

2. Add the remaining ingredients to the blender and blend until well mixed. Strain the sauce through a fine-mesh sieve and set aside.

3. Put the pine nuts in a small skillet and set over medium heat. Toast, shaking the pan occasionally, until fragrant and browned. Remove from the heat and set aside to cool completely.

4. Whisk together the ammonia powder, flour, baking powder, and oil, then slowly pour in water while stirring until you achieve a pancake-batter consistency (about 1½ cups). Pour this mixture onto a rimmed platter.

(continued)

5. Pour oil to a depth of ¼ inch in a large skillet and place over medium-low heat. Season the fish with salt and cayenne. When the oil is hot, dredge one side of the fish in the batter and put into the pan, batter side down. When the fish is nicely browned, turn and brown the other side.

6. Cover the bottom of the serving plates with the sauce, top with a sprinkling of the ginger and pine nuts, and put the fish in the center of the plate. Garnish with a sprinkle of matcha and serve.

Hand-strung flowers in the streets of Bangkok

Monkfish with Tandoori Spices and Tomato Chutney

Makes 4 servings

TOMATO CHUTNEY

1 tablespoon grape seed, corn, or other neutral oil
1 medium onion, sliced
1 garlic clove, sliced
1 teaspoon paprika
1 tablespoon ground coriander
2 pounds tomatoes, cored, peeled, seeded, and diced
1 cup red wine vinegar
2 cups sugar

½ cup plain whole-milk yogurt
¼ cup plus 2 tablespoons fresh lime juice
2 tablespoons tandoori spice mixture
Salt and freshly ground black pepper
1½ to 2 pounds monkfish, cut into 2-inch chunks
4 lemongrass stalks, trimmed and halved lengthwise
1 medium onion, quartered and separated
8 kaffir lime leaves or bay leaves
3 tablespoons grape seed, corn, or other neutral oil
Lemon wedges for serving

I love this straightforward dish because it packs a punch, with its aromatic tandoori spices and the accompanying chutney. The chutney can be prepared ahead of time, and the fish is best marinated for about an hour, so you can simply assemble and cook the skewers immediately before serving.

You can find tandoori spice mixes in most Indian markets.

1. **To make the tomato chutney:** Heat the oil in a large deep skillet over medium heat. Add the onion and garlic and cook until softened, about 5 minutes. Stir in the paprika and coriander and cook, stirring, until fragrant, about 2 minutes. Add the tomatoes, vinegar, and sugar and cook, stirring occasionally, until dry, 1 hour or more.

2. Meanwhile, mix together in a container big enough to hold the fish the yogurt, lime juice, tandoori spices, and a pinch of salt and pepper. Put the fish in the mixture, cover, and refrigerate for about 1 hour.

3. Remove the fish from the marinade and skewer onto the lemongrass stalks (or use regular skewers), alternating with the onion piece, and lime or bay leaves.

4. Heat the oil in a large skillet, preferably nonstick, over medium heat. Add the fish skewers and cook until nicely browned, then turn and brown the other sides. Divide the skewers among the serving plates and spoon the tomato chutney on the side. Season with lemon juice and salt to taste.

Salmon in Tofu Skin with Green Curry Lentils

Makes 4 servings

GREEN CURRY LENTILS

1 tablespoon grape seed, corn, or other neutral oil
2 ounces slab bacon, diced
1 onion, diced
1 carrot, diced
1 celery stalk, diced
1 tablespoon Green Curry Paste (page 200)
1 cup Le Puy lentils, washed and picked over
2½ cups chicken stock, preferably homemade or canned low-sodium broth
2 kaffir lime leaves
1 lemongrass stalk, trimmed and smashed
Salt
1¼ cups coconut milk
2 teaspoons nam pla (Thai fish sauce)
1 tablespoon sherry vinegar

2 large sheets fresh tofu skins, or more as needed
Four 6-ounce salmon fillets, each cut into 4 strips
Salt and cayenne pepper
¼ cup grape seed, corn, or other neutral oil
¼ cup chopped fresh cilantro leaves
¼ cup pea shoots

In this recipe, we wrap salmon. It is a technique I love because it preserves the moisture of the fish, prevents overcooking, and adds crunch—all at once. The trickiest part of this one lies in finding fresh tofu skins (also called bean curd sheets). They're sold in the Chinatowns of major cities, but not much elsewhere. (If you can't find them, wrap the salmon in soaked and softened rice paper.) Once that's done, the dish is quick and easy, but looks and tastes fabulous.

1. **To make the lentils:** Heat the oil in a Dutch oven or casserole over medium heat. Add the bacon and cook until about 2 tablespoons of fat is rendered. Remove the bacon and add the onion, carrot, and celery. Cook, stirring, for about 2 minutes, then add the Green Curry Paste and cook until fragrant, about 1 minute.

2. Add the lentils and cook, stirring occasionally, until the vegetables are softened and the lentils glistening, about 5 minutes. Add the chicken stock, lime leaves, lemongrass, and a pinch of salt and cook until the lentils are tender, about 20 minutes.

3. Stir in the coconut milk, nam pla, and vinegar, and taste and adjust seasoning. Keep warm over low heat.

4. Meanwhile, preheat the oven to 450°F. Cut the tofu skins into 16 rectangles measuring 12 inches by the length of the salmon strips. Season a salmon strip with salt and cayenne and place on the matching end of tofu skin. Roll the salmon in the tofu skin, brush water along

the end, and seal. The sides of the rolls should be open, not sealed shut. Repeat with the remaining salmon strips and tofu skins.

5. Heat the oil in a large ovenproof skillet over medium-high heat. Add the tofu-salmon rolls and cook until browned and crisp, then turn and brown the remaining sides. Transfer the skillet to the oven and cook until a thin-bladed knife pierces through the flesh easily, about 5 minutes. Remove the salmon rolls from the oven and carefully cut each roll, at an angle, into 3 medallions.

6. Stir the cilantro into the lentils and mound the lentils onto your serving plates. Put the salmon rolls, cut side up, on top. Garnish with pea shoots and serve.

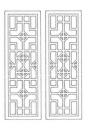

Salmon Glazed with Lime Leaf, Bok Choy, and Cinnamon

Makes 4 servings

Basic sweetened soy sauce is the foundation for this glaze, which is given a boost of tartness with the lime juice and lime leaves. The bok choy and cucumber provide a lovely contrast of color, texture, and flavor. We grind cinnamon fresh for this, but you can use pre-ground cinnamon, of course.

CINNAMON OIL

1 tablespoon ground cinnamon
2 tablespoons grape seed, corn, or other neutral oil
Salt

GLAZE

¼ cup sugar
⅓ cup fresh lime juice
¼ cup Shaoxing wine
6 kaffir lime leaves
Salt
¼ cup soy sauce

1 tablespoon unsalted butter
Four 6-ounce salmon fillets
1 cucumber, peeled, seeded, and cut into ¼-inch dice
Salt and cayenne pepper
1 tablespoon grape seed, corn, or other neutral oil
4 heads baby bok choy, trimmed and washed well

1. Preheat the oven to 450°F.

2. **To make the cinnamon oil:** Put the cinnamon and the oil in a small saucepan over medium-high heat. Once the cinnamon starts sizzling, cook for another 30 seconds, then remove from the heat, season with a pinch of salt, and set aside.

3. **To make the glaze:** Whisk together the sugar, lime juice, wine, lime leaves, and a pinch of salt in a small saucepan over medium heat and bring to a boil. As soon as the mixture boils, remove from the heat and let it steep for 5 minutes. Strain through a fine-mesh sieve, then whisk in the soy sauce and set aside.

4. Grease a baking sheet with the butter, put the salmon on it, and transfer to the oven. Roast the salmon until a thin-bladed knife pierces through the flesh easily, about 6 minutes. Meanwhile, toss the cucumber with just enough of the lime leaf glaze to moisten well, then season to taste with salt and cayenne pepper.

5. Heat the oil in a wok or large skillet over high heat.

Add the bok choy, season with salt, add 1 tablespoon water, and stir-fry just until tender, about 1 minute.

6. Transfer the bok choy to your serving plates, then put the salmon on top. Spoon the cucumber mixture on top of the salmon and drizzle the remaining lime leaf glaze and cinnamon oil all around. Serve immediately.

Beautifully displayed baby bok choy at the local vegetable market in Shanghai

Steamed Salmon in Ginger Broth

Makes 4 servings

¾ cup Shaoxing wine
½ cup light soy sauce
¼ cup Ginger Syrup (page 43)
1 teaspoon sesame oil
1 teaspoon nam pla (Thai fish sauce)
1 fresh green Thai chile, minced
Four 5-ounce salmon fillets
One 2-inch piece fresh, young ginger, peeled and thinly sliced
5 scallions, white parts only, cut into 2-inch lengths and thinly sliced lengthwise
¼ red bell pepper, cut into 2-inch lengths and thinly sliced lengthwise
3 bok choy leaves, thinly sliced crosswise
3 tablespoons sliced fresh Thai basil leaves
1 tablespoon extra virgin olive oil
½ teaspoon fleur de sel

This method of steaming is almost like poaching. The salmon absorbs all the aromatic flavors from the broth and fresh vegetables. This is easy enough to do on a weeknight and impressive enough for a dinner party. It's wonderful over steamed white rice.

1. Stir together the wine, soy sauce, syrup, sesame oil, nam pla, and chile. Set aside ½ cup of the mixture.

2. Put the remaining mixture in a large shallow dish and add the salmon. Turn to coat well and set aside for 10 minutes.

3. Meanwhile, prepare a large steamer.

4. Put the reserved broth in a large bowl. Transfer the salmon fillets to the bowl and top with the ginger, scallions, bell pepper, and bok choy. Cover the bowl tightly with plastic wrap and transfer to the steamer. Steam until the fish is cooked through, about 14 minutes.

5. Remove the bowl from the steamer and let rest for 1 minute. Remove the plastic wrap and stir in the basil until wilted.

6. Put each salmon fillet in a shallow serving dish. Spoon the vegetables all around, drizzle with olive oil, and sprinkle with the fleur de sel. Serve immediately.

"Fish" with Wok-Fried Napa Cabbage

Makes 4 servings

½ pound fresh red finger chiles, chopped
2 tablespoons sugar
⅓ cup white vinegar
2 garlic cloves
¼ cup plus 1 tablespoon nam pla (Thai fish sauce)
¼ cup peanut oil, plus more for frying
2 red onions, sliced
1 tablespoon plus 1 teaspoon coriander seeds
8 fresh water chestnuts, peeled and quartered, or 1 cup peeled and chopped jicama
8 cups Napa cabbage, cut into 1-inch pieces
Two 2-pound red snappers, sea bass, or other white-fleshed fish, gutted, scaled, and tail and fins trimmed but otherwise left whole
Salt and cayenne pepper
4 cucumbers, sliced
¼ cup sherry vinegar
¼ cup chopped fresh cilantro leaves

This has been on the menu at Vong since it opened—always in quotes—and I love it: Think instant kimchi with whatever fish is fresh. It's fiery and refreshing all at once. If you make this with fillets, it becomes a quick dish and a great addition to your weeknight repertoire. Simply cut 1½ pounds firm white-fleshed fish fillets into 2-inch pieces. Heat 3 tablespoons of oil in a large wok or skillet and brown the fish on both sides until cooked through, about 5 minutes total.

1. Put the chiles, sugar, white vinegar, garlic, and 1 tablespoon of the nam pla in a blender or food processor. Blend until the mixture is minced, but not puréed. Strain through a fine-mesh sieve and reserve the juices. Set the chile mixture aside. Bring the juices to a boil and reduce to a glaze over low heat. Remove from the heat and set aside.

2. Heat the ¼ cup oil in a large pan or wok over medium-high heat until hot. Add the onions and cook until softened and golden brown. Toss in the coriander seeds, water chestnuts, cabbage, ¼ cup of the chile mixture, and 2 tablespoons of the chile juice. Keep warm over low heat while you cook the fish.

3. Pour oil to a depth of at least 3 inches into a wok or large, deep skillet and heat over medium-high heat to 400°F. When the oil is hot, pat one fish dry and sprinkle with salt and cayenne. The fish must be completely dry or the hot oil will splatter; use a spatula or skimmer to

lower the fish carefully into the oil. Fry on both sides until browned and crisp, about 10 minutes. Drain on paper towels. Replenish and reheat the oil and repeat with the other fish.

4. Add the cucumbers and sherry vinegar to the cabbage and raise the heat a bit, then stir in the remaining nam pla. Put the fish on a plate and cover with the vegetables. Garnish with the cilantro and spoon on the remaining chile mixture and juice to taste.

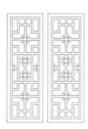

SHELLFISH

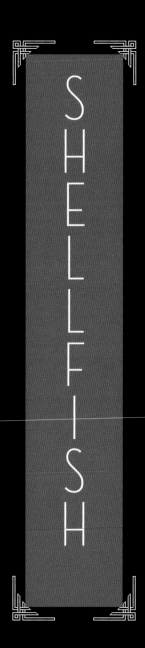

Grilled Shrimp with Papaya Mustard

Makes 4 servings

2 tablespoons mustard powder, preferably Coleman's
¼ cup Dijon mustard
2 tablespoons rice vinegar or plum wine vinegar
½ cup honey, plus more as needed
1½ pounds papaya, peeled, seeded, and cut into ½-inch chunks
Salt
2 tablespoons fresh lime juice, or to taste

24 large shrimp, peeled and deveined
2 tablespoons extra virgin olive oil, plus more as needed
Cayenne pepper
2 tablespoons chopped fresh cilantro leaves
Lime wedges for serving

Simple grilled shrimp combined with papaya mustard becomes wondrous. The fabulous dipping sauce, which combines mustard powder for heat and Dijon-style mustard for complexity, is also wonderful over tuna, crab, or scallops. I like it on hot dogs too.

1. Start a charcoal or gas grill or broiler; make sure the fire is very hot, and adjust the rack so that it is as close to the heat source as possible.

2. Meanwhile, make the papaya mustard. Whisk together the mustards and vinegar in a small bowl until the mustard powder is dissolved; let sit while you proceed. Put the honey in a small heavy saucepan over medium-high heat. Cook, stirring constantly with a rubber spatula, until the honey bubbles, thickens, and darkens slightly, about 7 minutes.

3. Turn the heat to medium and add the papaya. Cook, stirring occasionally, until the papaya water evaporates and the mixture becomes mushy, about 15 minutes. Remove from the heat and immediately stir in the mustard mixture. Season to taste with salt and lime juice and set aside.

4. Brush the shrimp with the oil, then sprinkle with salt and cayenne. Grill for 2 or 3 minutes per side, turning once. Serve the shrimp, garnished with the cilantro, with the papaya mustard and lime wedges on the side.

Shrimp with Roasted Butternut Squash

Makes 4 servings

BLACK SESAME VINAIGRETTE

2 tablespoons thinly sliced shallots
2 tablespoons mirin
2 tablespoons black sesame seeds, toasted (see page 15)
2 tablespoons rice vinegar
3 tablespoons extra virgin olive oil
1 tablespoon sesame oil
1/8 teaspoon minced fresh red Thai chile
2 1/4 teaspoons nam pla (Thai fish sauce)
Salt

1 1/2 pounds butternut squash, peeled, halved lengthwise, seeded, and cut crosswise into 1/2-inch slices
1/3 cup extra virgin olive oil
1 teaspoon crushed red pepper flakes, or to taste
Salt
16 large shrimp, peeled and deveined
Cayenne pepper
1 apple, preferably Granny Smith, peeled, cored, and julienned

This is an odd pairing that makes a wonderful autumn dish. The heat from the red pepper flakes and the rich vinaigrette (you can use any vinaigrette you like, but I really love the black sesame) bring all the flavors together.

1. **To make the vinaigrette:** Put the shallots and mirin in a small saucepan over medium-high heat. Bring to a boil, then cook for 1 minute and remove from the heat. The shallots should remain crunchy.

2. Transfer the shallots and mirin to a mixing bowl and add the sesame seeds. Whisk in the remaining ingredients for the vinaigrette and season to taste with salt. Set aside.

3. Preheat the oven to 400°F.

4. Put the squash in a roasting pan and drizzle with 1/4 cup of the oil, making sure it is well coated. Sprinkle with the red pepper flakes and salt and put in the oven. Cook until the squash is browned on the bottom, then turn and cook until the squash is tender and caramelized, about 20 more minutes. Remove from the oven and cool.

5. Heat the remaining 1 tablespoon oil in a large skillet over medium-high heat. Season the shrimp with salt and cayenne and add to the skillet. Cook, stirring occasionally, until the shrimp is cooked through, about 5 minutes.

6. Put the squash onto the serving plates with the shrimp. Scatter the apple on top, and spoon the vinaigrette all around.

Stir-Fried Shrimp with Two Flavors

Makes 4 servings

SHRIMP

1 large egg white

2 tablespoons potato starch or cornstarch

1 tablespoon grape seed, corn, or other neutral oil, plus more for frying

1 teaspoon salt, or to taste

24 large shrimp, peeled and deveined

TOMATO SAUCE

½ cup red wine vinegar, plus more to taste

½ cup sugar

1 tablespoon plus 1 teaspoon tomato paste

Cayenne pepper

MAYONNAISE SAUCE

½ cup mayonnaise

1 tablespoon sweetened condensed milk

1 tablespoon fresh lemon juice

Salt and cayenne pepper

2 teaspoons black sesame seeds, toasted (see page 15)

2 teaspoons white sesame seeds, toasted (see page 15)

We've tweaked this classic—known as "yin-yang shrimp" in Cantonese, because of the two sauces' contrasting colors—to make it easy and absolutely perfect. The crunchy shrimp with the two sauces is just irresistible. The combination of contrasting sesame seeds is a nice touch, but you can use only white if that's what you have.

1. **To make the shrimp:** In a large bowl, beat the egg white with the starch, oil, and salt. Stir in the shrimp and set aside.

2. **To make the tomato sauce:** Put the vinegar, sugar, and tomato paste in a medium saucepan over medium-high heat. Stir until the sugar dissolves and bring to a boil; lower the heat and cook until the mixture is bubbly and syrupy and has reduced a bit. Season to taste with cayenne and vinegar. Set aside and keep warm.

3. **To make the mayonnaise sauce:** In a medium bowl, mix together the mayonnaise, condensed milk, and lemon juice until well combined and smooth. Season to taste with salt and cayenne. Set aside.

4. Pour oil to a depth of ¼ inch in a large skillet and place over high heat. When the oil is very hot, add the shrimp and cook, stirring, just until done. Immediately transfer half the shrimp to the tomato sauce and half the shrimp to the mayonnaise sauce. Toss each to coat, then transfer to the serving plates in separate mounds. Garnish with the toasted sesame seeds and serve immediately.

Plates of cooked shrimp with the sauce in a bag to go at the Aw Taw Kaw weekend market in Bangkok →

Black Pepper Shrimp with "Sun-Dried" Pineapple

Makes 4 servings

½ pineapple, peeled, cored, and cut into 1-inch chunks
3 tablespoons grape seed, corn, or other neutral oil
3 scallions, trimmed and sliced
1 tablespoon peeled and minced fresh ginger
1 tablespoon minced garlic
1¾ teaspoons black peppercorns, crushed
1¾ teaspoons fermented black beans, rinsed, squeezed dry, and chopped
3 tablespoons kecap manis (sweet soy sauce)
1 tablespoon soy sauce
1 tablespoon fresh lime juice
1½ tablespoons sugar
½ teaspoon salt
12 large shrimp, peeled and deveined
½ cup diced jicama
½ cup baby pea shoots

The distinctive saltiness of black bean and black pepper stir-fries is given a twist here with the addition of chewy, sweet pineapple. Dried in the oven until the sweetness is intensified and the texture like that of candy, the pineapple is an amazing addition here. Don't skip it.

1. Preheat the oven to 200°F. Put a rack on top of a rimmed baking sheet and line the rack with a Silpat.

2. Put the pineapple pieces on the mat in a single even layer. Bake until the pineapple is dried, shriveled, and chewy, about 2 hours. Remove from the Silpat and cool completely on a rack.

3. Heat 1 tablespoon of the oil in a large saucepan over medium-high heat. Add the scallions, ginger, and garlic and cook, stirring, until softened and golden. Add the crushed peppercorns and cook until fragrant, then add the black beans, soy sauces, lime juice, sugar, and salt and bring the mixture to a boil, stirring occasionally. Reduce the heat to medium and simmer for 2 minutes. Transfer to a blender and purée until coarsely blended. Set aside.

4. Heat the remaining 2 tablespoons oil in a wok or large skillet over high heat. When the oil is just about smoking, add the shrimp and cook, turning once, until crisp and browned. Remove the oil from the wok, then add the black pepper sauce and 2 tablespoons water. Cook, stirring, until the shrimp is well coated, then stir in the dried pineapple. Arrange on a serving plate, garnish with the jicama and pea shoots, and serve.

Steamed Lobster with Garlic-Ginger-Basil Sauce

Makes 4 servings

Four 1½-pound lobsters, claws separated
½ cup clarified unsalted butter
¼ cup thinly sliced garlic
One 4-inch piece fresh ginger, julienned
1 teaspoon crushed red pepper flakes
1 teaspoon salt, plus more to taste
1 cup chopped fresh Thai basil leaves
8 cups pea shoots and leaves
4 lemon wedges for serving

Here, the classic steamed lobster is completely transformed. This quite elegant dish can be made in less than an hour, even if you must begin by clarifying the butter.

1. Fill a large bowl with water and ice and set aside. Bring a large pot of water to a rolling boil and salt it.

2. Add the lobster claws to the boiling water and cook for 5 minutes, then transfer to the ice water bath. When cool, remove the meat completely from the shells and set aside. Add the remaining lobster parts to the boiling water and cook for 1 minute. Transfer to the ice water bath. When cool, remove the heads from the bodies. Split the tails lengthwise in half, keeping the shells on. (You can remove the vein from the tail if you like.)

3. Prepare the sauce. Put the butter in a large skillet over medium-high heat. Add the garlic and simmer, shaking the skillet occasionally, until golden brown, 3 minutes. Add the ginger, red pepper flakes, and salt and cook, shaking the skillet occasionally, until fragrant. Add the basil and cook briefly, just until wilted. Remove from the heat.

4. Meanwhile, put the claws and tails in a large steamer. Top with the pea shoots and a sprinkling of salt, and cook just until the lobster is heated through and the pea shoots are wilted, about 3 minutes.

5. Mound the pea shoots in the middle of each serving plate and top with the lobster claw meat and tails. Spoon the sauce over the lobster and serve immediately, with the lemon wedges.

Lobster with Black Bean Sauce and Broccoli

Makes 4 servings

CILANTRO OIL

1 cup fresh cilantro leaves
¼ cup grape seed, corn, or other neutral oil
1 teaspoon salt, plus more to taste

BLACK BEAN SAUCE

¼ cup peanut oil
1 tablespoon plus 1 teaspoon minced fresh ginger
1 tablespoon plus 1 teaspoon minced garlic
¼ cup preserved black beans, rinsed, squeezed, and roughly chopped
1 fresh green Thai chile, seeded and minced
¼ cup oyster sauce
¼ cup soy sauce
2 tablespoons sugar

Four 1½-pound lobsters (or 3 pounds salmon chunks or peeled shrimp)
¼ cup unsalted butter
12 broccoli florets
Lemon wedges for serving

Here, we give a classic Cantonese dish a new spin, and I think the results are phenomenal. The intensity of the preserved black beans brings out the natural sweet sea-saltiness of the lobster. (You can also make this dish with salmon or shrimp, which are easier on weeknights.) Serve with steamed white rice.

1. **To make the cilantro oil:** Fill a large bowl with water and ice and set aside. Bring a small pot of water to a boil and add the cilantro. As soon as the water returns to a boil, drain the leaves and transfer to the ice water. When cold, remove the cilantro from the water and squeeze all the water out of the leaves with your hands. Put the cilantro in a blender with the oil and salt. Purée until smooth, then strain through a fine-mesh sieve into a small bowl.

2. **To make the black bean sauce:** Heat the oil in a small pot over medium heat. Add the ginger and garlic and cook just until golden, then add the black beans, chile, oyster sauce, soy sauce, and sugar. Stir-fry until the sugar browns, about 3 minutes. Remove from the heat and set aside.

3. Fill a large bowl with water and ice and set aside. Bring a large pot of water to a rolling boil and salt it. Break off the lobster claws, remove the tails, and cut the heads lengthwise in half (your fishmonger can do this for you).

4. Add the claws to the boiling water and, after 2 min-

utes, the tails and heads. Cook for another 2 minutes, then drain and transfer to the prepared ice water bath. Halve the tails with the shell on (remove the vein from the tail meat if you like); extract the meat from the claws and bodies.

5. Heat the butter in a large skillet over medium-high heat. Add the tails, flesh side down, the broccoli, and the picked lobster meat and cook, stirring occasionally, until it begins to brown. Sprinkle half the reserved sauce on top, add 1 cup water, stir again, and cook until the meat is cooked through. Taste and add more sauce if you like.

6. Serve with the cilantro oil and lemon wedges on the side.

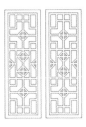

Lobster with Thai Herbs

Makes 4 servings

Four $1\frac{1}{2}$-pound lobsters
Salt
Cayenne pepper
1 tablespoon unsalted butter
1 teaspoon Green Curry Paste (page 200)
1 teaspoon red curry paste, store-bought is fine
1 teaspoon yellow curry paste, store-bought is fine
3 carrots, peeled and julienned
2 lemongrass stalks, smashed
6 kaffir lime leaves
$2\frac{2}{3}$ cups white port
2 apples, preferably Golden Delicious, peeled and julienned
$1\frac{1}{2}$ teaspoons ground turmeric
$\frac{1}{3}$ cup heavy cream
$\frac{1}{4}$ cup chopped fresh cilantro leaves

A Vong classic, and one of my all-time favorite dishes. It's full of flavors that explode in your mouth, all bound together, incredibly, by softly whipped cream. We usually serve this on a bed of lightly stir-fried bok choy, which I think is a nice touch. You can use a store-bought curry paste (or just one curry paste) in place of the homemade paste here, which is probably what I'd do if I were making this at home.

1. Preheat the oven to 450°F.

2. Fill a large bowl with ice and water and set aside. Bring a large pot of water to a rolling boil and salt it. Break off the lobster claws, remove the tails, and cut the heads lengthwise in half (your fishmonger can do this for you).

3. Add the claws to the boiling water and, after 2 minutes, the tails and heads. Cook for another 2 minutes, then drain and transfer to the prepared ice water bath. Halve the tails with the shell on (remove the vein from the tail meat if you like); extract the meat from the claws and bodies. Season the tails, claw meat, and body shells with salt and cayenne and place in the oven on a rimmed baking sheet. Cook for 5 minutes.

4. Heat the butter in a skillet over medium heat and cook the curry pastes together, stirring occasionally, until fragrant, about 3 minutes. Add the carrots, season with salt, and stir and cook slowly over medium-low heat.

5. Add the lemongrass, lime leaves, and 2 tablespoons water and cook until the water dissolves. Add the port, then boil the mixture to reduce by three-quarters, stirring occasionally, about 30 minutes.

6. Remove and discard the lemongrass and lime leaves. Add the apples and turmeric, simmer for 2 minutes, then remove from the heat and set aside.

7. Whisk the cream until it holds soft peaks. Stir into the sauce, season with salt, and reheat gently.

8. Put a lobster shell on each of four plates and put the meat in the shell; pour the sauce over, garnish with cilantro, and serve.

Various pots of simmering curry at the weekend food market, Aw Taw Kaw, in Bangkok

Squid Tempura in Smoked Chile Glaze

Makes 4 servings

CHILE GLAZE

2 dried ancho chiles
1 dried chipotle chile
⅓ cup sugar
4 garlic cloves, chopped
¼ cup fresh lime juice
¼ cup plus 2 tablespoons fresh lemon juice
¼ cup plus 2 tablespoons fresh orange juice
2 tablespoons nam pla (Thai fish sauce)

Corn or other oil for deep-frying
10 ounces small squid, the bodies cleaned and cut into ¾-inch rings, tentacles left whole
Tempura batter (page 124)
Salt
¼ cup fresh pea shoots, trimmed

This is like calamari in spirit, but infinitely better. The tempura batter is incredibly light and crisp and holds up well under the smoky sweet-and-sour glaze.

1. Put the chiles in a small skillet set over medium heat. Toast, turning the chiles occasionally, until dark brown and fragrant. Remove from the skillet, cool completely, and cut into ½-inch pieces.

2. Put the sugar in a small saucepan and add just enough water to wet it, about ¾ teaspoon. Shake the pan to distribute the sugar and water and caramelize over medium-high heat, shaking the pan occasionally. The sugar will gradually liquefy and darken. When it becomes deep amber, add the garlic and cook, stirring constantly, until golden, then add the chiles and cook, stirring constantly, until fragrant, about 1 minute. Add the citrus juices and stir until well combined.

3. Simmer until the mixture is very dark and syrupy. Remove from the heat and stir in the nam pla. Set aside.

4. Pour oil to a depth of 2 inches in a heavy, deep saucepan and heat to 400°F.

5. Dip the squid in the batter and transfer to the hot oil. Do not overcrowd the pan; work in batches if necessary. Cook until golden brown and really crisp, about 2 minutes. Drain on paper towels and season lightly with salt.

6. Toss the fried squid with the reserved chile glaze and garnish with pea shoots. Serve immediately.

Crab cooked and tied at the Aw Taw Kaw weekend market in Bangkok →

Soft-Shell Crabs

Makes 4 servings

TEMPURA BATTER

2¼ teaspoons sherry vinegar

1 tablespoon plus 1 teaspoon sesame oil

2¼ teaspoons salt

1¼ cups rice flour, plus more for dredging

¼ teaspoon baking soda

¼ teaspoon baking powder

PICKLES

2 fresh red Thai chiles

½ cup plus 2 tablespoons fresh lime juice

¼ cup plus 1 tablespoon sugar

2½ teaspoons salt

1 large cucumber, preferably European, seeded and cut into 3-inch-long thin slices

DIPPING SAUCE

¼ cup fresh lime juice

2 tablespoons chopped crystallized ginger

⅛ teaspoon salt, plus more to taste

¼ teaspoon extra virgin olive oil

1 cup grape seed, corn, or other neutral oil, plus more for deep-frying

¼ cup minced shallots

2 tablespoons peeled and minced fresh ginger

4 soft-shell crabs, cleaned (ask your fishmonger to do this, if you like)

½ cup rice flour

1 avocado, peeled, seeded, and thinly sliced

When soft-shell crabs are in season, they are great prepared this way. They are even better when served with the pickled cucumbers, crunchy shallot-ginger topping, and dipping sauce. Out of season, you can substitute your favorite crab cake.

1. **To make the tempura batter:** Put the vinegar, sesame oil, salt and ½ cup plus 2 tablespoons cold water in a bowl and mix well. Put the rice flour, baking soda, and baking powder in a separate bowl and whisk to combine. Add the dry ingredients to the wet ingredients and stir gently until smooth.

2. **To make the pickles:** Put the chiles in a small skillet and set over high heat. Cook, turning occasionally, until lightly charred. Remove from the heat, cool completely, stem, and mince.

3. Put the minced chiles, lime juice, sugar, and salt in a medium mixing bowl and stir until the sugar is dissolved. Add the cucumbers and toss well to coat. Set aside.

4. **To make the dipping sauce:** Put the lime juice, ginger, salt, and ¼ cup water in a blender. Purée until smooth, then strain through a fine-mesh sieve, pressing on the solids to extract as much liquid as possible. Transfer to a small saucepan and warm over medium

Gold Buddhas at →
the Shwedagon Paya
in Yangon (formerly
Rangoon)

heat. When warm to the touch, but not boiling, remove from the heat and stir in the olive oil. Set the sauce aside.

5. Heat ¾ cup of the grape seed oil in a small saucepan over medium-high heat. Add the shallots and cook, stirring constantly, until crisp and golden brown. Drain on paper towels, season lightly with salt, and set aside to cool.

6. Heat the remaining ¼ cup oil in a small saucepan over medium-high heat. Add the ginger and cook, stirring constantly, until crisp and browned. Drain on paper towels, season lightly with salt, and cool completely. Combine the shallots and ginger in a small mixing bowl and set aside at room temperature.

7. Meanwhile, pour oil to a depth of 3 inches in a heavy, deep saucepan and heat to 350°F.

8. Dredge the soft-shell crab in rice flour, then dip in tempura batter. Put in the hot oil, fry until crisp and golden, and drain on paper towels.

9. Arrange the avocado decoratively on a serving plate and season lightly with salt. Top with the shallot-ginger mixture. Drain the pickles, blot dry with paper towels, arrange in the center of the plate, and top with the crab. Spoon the sauce all around, and serve.

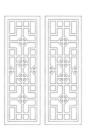

POULTRY

Chicken Paillard with Napa Salad

Makes 4 servings

4 cups fresh cilantro leaves
1 teaspoon freshly ground black pepper
One 8-inch block palm sugar, melted, or about ½ cup brown sugar
6 garlic cloves, peeled
½ cup nam pla (Thai fish sauce)
4 boneless, skinless chicken breasts, pounded until less than ½ inch thick
2 fresh red Thai chiles, seeded and finely minced
2 tablespoons granulated sugar
2 teaspoons whole black peppercorns, cracked
1 tablespoon rice vinegar
3 tablespoons fresh lime juice
3 tablespoons grape seed, corn, or other neutral oil
2 cups thinly sliced Napa cabbage
1 cup shredded carrot
1 cup shredded daikon radish
½ cup sliced red onion
½ cup sliced mango
¼ cup sliced fresh mint leaves, plus more for garnish
Salt

If you're looking for a refreshing yet substantial summer dish, this is it. Mango and mint add a playful sweetness to this light but assertive salad, which is nicely complemented by the grilled chicken. I love it.

You can buy palm sugar at any Asian market, but brown sugar is nearly as good.

1. Fill a large bowl with water and ice and set aside. Bring a small pot of water to a boil and add the cilantro. As soon as the water returns to a boil, drain the leaves, and transfer to the ice water. When cold, drain again, and transfer to a blender with the ground pepper, palm sugar, 4 garlic cloves, and half the nam pla. Purée until smooth. Spread a thin coat of this paste on the chicken breasts and marinate in the refrigerator for about 1 hour.

2. Meanwhile, make the salad. Mince the remaining garlic cloves, transfer to a mixing bowl, and whisk with the chiles, granulated sugar, peppercorns, vinegar, lime juice, oil, and remaining ¼ cup nam pla. In a large bowl, toss half the dressing with the cabbage, carrot, radish, onion, mango, and mint.

3. Start a charcoal or gas grill or broiler; the fire should be medium-hot and the grill rack should be about 4 inches from the heat source.

4. Grill the chicken breasts with the marinade until they are cooked through, 3 to 4 minutes a side. Cut the cooked breasts into 1-inch slices.

5. Mound the salad on a plate and top with another spoonful of dressing and the slices of chicken. Garnish with mint leaves, sprinkle lightly with salt, and serve.

Dill, long beans, and tamarind leaves from left to right, with Napa cabbage behind

Grilled Chicken with Kumquat-Lemongrass Dressing

Makes 4 servings

KUMQUAT-LEMONGRASS DRESSING

¼ cup fresh lime juice
2 tablespoons rice vinegar
2 tablespoons sugar
1 lemongrass stalk, trimmed, smashed, and chopped
4 kaffir lime leaves, chopped
3 ounces kumquats
1½ teaspoons grape seed, corn, or other neutral oil
1 shallot, minced
One 1-inch piece fresh ginger, minced
½ teaspoon sliced fresh red finger chile
½ teaspoon salt

2 teaspoons ground chili powder
2 teaspoons ground turmeric
¼ teaspoon salt, plus more to taste
1½ tablespoons sugar
4 boneless, skinless chicken breasts
2 candlenuts, shelled and chopped, or use Brazil or macadamia nuts
2 fresh red Thai chiles, seeded, and chopped
4 dried Thai chiles, soaked in hot water until softened and drained
2 garlic cloves, chopped
One ½-inch piece fresh ginger, chopped
One ½-inch piece fresh galangal, chopped
2 shallots, chopped
2 lemongrass stalks, trimmed, smashed, and chopped
1½ teaspoons tamarind pulp, soaked in ½ cup hot water and drained
2 teaspoons grape seed, corn, or other neutral oil
¾ cup coconut milk

An incredibly flavorful version of grilled chicken breast. First, you make a dry rub marinade; this is followed by a generous spice-mix coating, and it is all topped off by a bright, refreshing sauce.

1. **To make the dressing:** Put the lime juice, vinegar, and sugar in a small saucepan and bring to a boil, stirring occasionally. Remove from the heat, add the lemongrass and lime leaves and steep until the mixture is cool to the touch. Strain through a fine-mesh sieve and set aside.

2. Cut the kumquats crosswise into ¼-inch slices and pick out the seeds in each of the slices. Put the oil in a medium skillet and set over medium heat. Add the shallot and ginger and cook, stirring, until almost tender, about 30 seconds, then add the kumquat slices and reserved lime juice infusion. Bring the mixture to a steady simmer and cook for 30 seconds. Remove from the heat, add the chile and salt, and cool to room temperature. Use immediately or cover and refrigerate until ready to use.

(continued)

3. Stir together the chili powder, turmeric, salt, and 1 tablespoon of the sugar. Rub this mixture all over the chicken, cover, and refrigerate for at least 2 hours or as long as overnight.

4. Meanwhile, put the candlenuts, chiles, garlic, ginger, galangal, shallots, lemongrass, and tamarind in a blender and purée until smooth. Put the oil in a large saucepan and set over medium heat. Add the spice-mix paste and cook, stirring, until fragrant, 1 minute, then add the coconut milk, the remaining ½ tablespoon sugar, and ½ cup water. Cook, stirring constantly, for 20 minutes, then remove from the heat and cool completely.

5. Preheat the oven to 450°F. Start a charcoal or gas grill or broiler; the fire should be hot, and the grill rack should be about 4 inches from the heat source.

6. Season the chicken lightly with salt, then brush the spice-mix paste on the smooth side of the meat. Grill until nicely browned, turning once, then transfer to a baking dish large enough to hold the chicken in one layer. Place in the oven and roast until the meat is cooked through, 10 minutes. Cut the chicken breasts into 4 pieces each and arrange on serving plates. Spoon the dressing on top and serve.

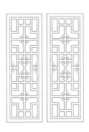

Roast Chicken with Chunky Miso Sauce and Grapefruit

Makes 4 servings

¼ cup plus 1 tablespoon extra virgin olive oil
One 3-pound chicken, cut into pieces
Salt and freshly ground white pepper
1 cup crème fraîche or sour cream
1 tablespoon chunky miso, or use any miso
1 tablespoon yuzu or lime juice
1 grapefruit, peeled and segmented between membranes, with juices reserved, and chopped into ½-inch cubes
1 fresh red Thai chile, seeded and minced
1 bunch frisée, leaves separated, washed, and dried
1 tablespoon fresh lemon juice

This is the quintessential Vong dish, half French and half Asian. But despite the fancy title and complex flavors, it's pretty easy to prepare and is luxuriously creamy when it's done. Substitute romaine or any other crunchy green for the frisée if you like; you can also make this dish with veal, pork, or any white meat.

1. Preheat the oven to 450°F.

2. Heat 2 tablespoons of the oil in a large ovenproof skillet over medium-high heat. Sprinkle the chicken pieces with salt and white pepper and add to the skillet, skin side down. Cook until they are very brown on one side, about 10 minutes, then turn the chicken and transfer to the oven and cook until cooked through, about 10 minutes more.

3. Meanwhile, put the crème fraîche and miso in a saucepan over low heat. Whisk the mixture together and warm gently; do not allow the mixture to boil. When bubbles begin forming around the edges, remove from the heat and whisk in the yuzu juice; set aside.

4. In a bowl, toss the grapefruit and its reserved juices with the chile and 2 tablespoons of the oil. In a separate bowl, toss the frisée with the lemon juice and remaining 1 tablespoon oil and season with salt.

5. Spoon the miso sauce into the bottom of four serving bowls. Center the chicken pieces on the sauce, then spoon the solids from the grapefruit mixture on top. Garnish with the frisée, drizzle on the remaining grapefruit juice, and serve.

Roast Chicken with Haricots Verts and Onion Compote

Makes 4 servings

SPICED JUS

1 cup Gewürztraminer or other slightly sweet, fruity wine
½ cup rice or other mild vinegar
⅓ cup soy sauce
¼ cup maple syrup
2 tablespoons honey
2 whole star anise
1 teaspoon black peppercorns
2 whole cloves
1 whole allspice berry, cracked
2 cinnamon sticks
2 teaspoons fennel seeds
1 teaspoon whole cumin seeds
12 fresh mint stems

CHIVE PURÉE

¼ cup snipped fresh chives
½ cup grape seed, corn, or other neutral oil

HARICOTS VERTS AND ONION COMPOTE

¼ cup extra virgin olive oil
1 large onion, sliced
8 garlic cloves, thinly sliced
Salt and freshly ground black pepper
¼ pound haricots verts, trimmed
½ fresh red finger chile, seeded and minced, or to taste

2 tablespoons clarified unsalted butter
One 3-pound chicken, cut into pieces

I call this sauce "spiced jus," because it isn't much more than that, just a bunch of flavors simmered together. (Yes, you have to gather a lot of ingredients, but they're all common enough.) But this simple combination becomes dazzling in its complexity. I also cook the garlic and onion slowly, until they are tender and sweet, and I love that combination with the crisp roast chicken.

1. Preheat the oven to 450°F.

2. **To make the spiced jus:** Combine the first 12 ingredients in a saucepan and bring to a boil. Cook for 10 minutes, then add the mint and remove from the heat. Cover and let steep for 10 minutes, then strain and set aside.

3. **To make the purée:** Fill a medium bowl with ice and water. Put the chives and grape seed oil in a blender and purée until completely smooth. Transfer to a small bowl and set the bowl over the ice water bath. Set aside.

4. **To make the compote:** Put the olive oil in a large skillet over medium-high heat. Add the onion and garlic, season with salt and pepper, and cook, stirring constantly, for about 2 minutes. Turn the heat to low and

cover. Cook the onion slowly, stirring occasionally, until it is very soft, about 20 minutes. Add the haricots verts and chile, cover again, and cook for another 5 minutes.

5. While the onion is cooking, heat the butter in a large ovenproof skillet over medium-high heat. Sprinkle the chicken pieces with salt and pepper and add to the skillet, skin side down. Cook until they are very brown on one side, about 10 minutes, then turn and transfer to the oven and cook until done, another 10 minutes or so.

6. Spoon the spiced jus into the bottom of four serving bowls, then top with the bean-onion compote and the chicken. Garnish with the chive purée and serve.

Roasted meat and Chinese sausage hanging outside at a street food stall in Yangon (formerly Rangoon) in Myanmar (formerly Burma)

POULTRY

Crunchy Baked Chicken with Glazed Baby Carrots

Makes 4 servings

CITRUS SOY SAUCE

2 teaspoons extra virgin olive oil
2 tablespoons minced shallots
2 teaspoons peeled and minced garlic
1½ cups Gewürztraminer or other fruity white wine
¾ cup fresh lemon juice
¼ cup plus 2 tablespoons soy sauce
1 cup plus 2 tablespoons unsalted butter
1½ teaspoons sesame oil

CRUNCHY BAKED CHICKEN

8 large egg yolks
1 teaspoon ground dried Thai chile
1 tablespoon soy sauce
1½ teaspoons sesame oil
1¾ cups Rice Krispies cereal
1 cup Total cereal
1 cup Special K cereal
¾ cup Corn Flakes cereal
2 tablespoons extra virgin olive oil, plus more for greasing
One 3-pound chicken, cut into pieces and boned
Salt and freshly ground white pepper

GLAZED BABY CARROTS

15 ounces baby carrots, cut into 1-inch-thick slices
¼ cup sugar
½ teaspoon salt
2 tablespoons fresh lime juice
2 tablespoons fresh orange juice
1 tablespoon unsalted butter
2 tablespoons chopped fresh tarragon

The supremely crunchy crust on this chicken comes not from deep-frying, but from a cereal coating. It's a nostalgic dish, reminiscent of Shake 'n Bake, but infinitely better. Baby carrots look fun on the side and the citrus glaze and fresh tarragon add a sophisticated twist.

Boat vendors on the Klong in Bangkok enjoying some shade

POULTRY

1. **To make the sauce:** Heat the olive oil in a large saucepan over medium-high heat. Add the shallots and garlic and cook, stirring, until golden brown, about 2 minutes. Add the wine, lemon juice, and soy sauce and cook, stirring occasionally, until the mixture has reduced to a syrupy consistency, about 20 minutes. Whisk in the butter until the mixture is emulsified and stir in the sesame oil. Keep the sauce warm until ready to serve.

2. **To make the chicken:** Mix the egg yolks, chile, soy sauce, and sesame oil in a large shallow dish and set aside. Put the cereals in a food processor and pulse just until coarsely ground. Transfer to another large shallow dish and set aside.

3. Preheat the oven to 450°F. Grease a large baking sheet with olive oil and set aside.

4. Heat a large skillet over medium-high heat until it is smoking, then add the olive oil. Sprinkle the chicken pieces with salt and white pepper and add to the skillet, skin side down. Cook until they are very brown and crispy on one side, about 10 minutes. Remove from the heat and put the chicken pieces, skin side up, on a rack to cool.

5. When the chicken has cooled, dip each piece, skin side down, first in the egg yolk mixture, then in the cereal mixture. Press the chicken firmly into the cereal to create a thick crust. Put the chicken pieces on the prepared baking sheet, crust side up, and transfer to the oven. Bake until the chicken is cooked through, about 10 minutes.

6. **To make the carrots:** While the chicken is baking, put the carrots in a large saucepan with the sugar, salt, and 1½ cups water. Cook over medium-high heat, stirring occasionally, until the mixture is almost dry and the carrots look glazed, about 5 minutes. Add the lime juice and orange juice and cook until the liquids are reduced by half, about 5 minutes. Stir in the butter until melted.

7. Serve the chicken with the reserved sauce on the side. Garnish the carrots with the tarragon and serve with the chicken.

Chicken Curry with Fat Noodles and Spring Vegetables

Makes 4 servings

CURRY MARINADE

5 lemongrass stalks, trimmed and cut into ½-inch pieces
5 shallots, cut into chunks
10 garlic cloves
2 tablespoons sugar
1 tablespoon yellow curry paste, store-bought is fine
¼ cup nam pla (Thai fish sauce)
1 tablespoon hot curry powder
1 tablespoon ground turmeric

One 3-pound chicken, cut into pieces
¼ cup extra virgin olive oil
1 onion, sliced
2 plum tomatoes, seeded and peeled
2 cups chicken stock, preferably homemade or canned low-sodium broth
5 cilantro stems
3 kaffir lime leaves
1 fresh red Thai chile
One 2-inch piece fresh galangal
1 lemongrass stalk, trimmed, smashed, and chopped
1½ cups coconut milk
Two 8-ounce blocks fresh wide rice noodles
3 tablespoons peanut oil
Salt
1 cup sliced carrots, optional
1 cup sliced mushrooms, optional
1 cup fresh or frozen peas, optional
1 cup peeled pearl onions, optional
Fresh lime juice

This deeply aromatic chicken curry is perfect with fat rice noodles, which I panfry on one side only, making them both soft and crisp. A fair amount of work, this dish, but worth it.

Baskets of fresh rice noodles at a local street market in Bangkok

1. Preheat the oven to 450°F.

2. **To make the marinade:** Put the ingredients in a blender with about 1/4 cup water and purée, stopping the machine to scrape down the sides as necessary. (Add a tiny bit more water, if necessary, to allow the machine to do its work.)

3. Rub a third of the marinade on the chicken pieces. Put half the olive oil in a large skillet over medium-high heat; when the oil is hot, add the chicken pieces and sear until brown on all sides, turning as necessary to brown evenly.

4. Heat the remaining 2 tablespoons olive oil in a large deep oven-proof casserole over medium heat and sweat the onion for about 5 minutes. Add 3 tablespoons of the marinade and cook, stirring, until fragrant, then mash in the tomatoes.

5. Add the seared chicken and chicken stock to the casserole and simmer for 5 minutes. Meanwhile, wrap the cilantro, lime leaves, chile, galangal, and lemongrass in cheesecloth and secure with kitchen string. Add to the pot, along with the coconut milk, and simmer for another 5 minutes. Cover, then place in the oven for about 1 hour, or until the chicken falls off the bone. When the chicken is done, remove the meat from the bones and return to the pan.

6. When the chicken is nearly cooked, slice the blocks of noodles lengthwise into 1-inch pieces. Do not separate the noodles. Heat the peanut oil in a large nonstick skillet over medium-high heat and add the noodle pieces, cut side down. Cook until the edges are crisp and the noodles are softened and just separated, about 3 minutes per side. Add a pinch of salt to the fried noodles and put in a deep plate.

7. If you're using the vegetables, lightly boil them in salted water and drain. Place the chicken meat on top of the noodles. Season the pan sauce with lime juice to taste, remove the cheesecloth bundle, and spoon the sauce over the chicken and noodles. Garnish with the vegetables and serve.

Chicken Wings with Ginger and Caramel Sauce

Makes 4 servings

CARAMEL

$\frac{1}{3}$ cup sugar

$\frac{1}{4}$ cup plus 2 tablespoons nam pla (Thai fish sauce)
2 garlic cloves, sliced
4 shallots, sliced
$2\frac{1}{2}$ pounds chicken wings
One 1-inch piece fresh ginger, julienned
2 teaspoons cracked black peppercorns, plus more for garnish
6 sprigs fresh cilantro

Although the base of this fairly standard Vietnamese dish is a caramel sauce, the garlic, shallots, and black pepper cut through the sweetness like a knife, providing terrific contrast. Since the last 45 minutes of the cooking time are unattended, this is a good dish for a night on which you want to entertain.

1. Preheat the oven to 450°F.

2. **To make the caramel:** Put the sugar in an oven-proof casserole and add just enough water to wet it, about 1 tablespoon. Shake the pan to distribute the sugar and water and caramelize over medium heat, shaking the pan occasionally. The sugar will gradually liquefy and darken; when it becomes golden brown, remove from the heat.

3. Carefully add the nam pla (it may spatter; hold the pan at arm's length), then return to the heat. Add the garlic and shallots and cook, stirring, until softened.

4. Add the chicken wings and coat with the sauce. Gently stir in the ginger and pepper and continue stirring until the chicken browns slightly, about 4 minutes. Cover and cook for 7 minutes, then transfer to the oven and cook for 45 minutes.

5. Remove the chicken wings, which should now be a rich caramel color, garnish with cilantro and cracked black pepper, and serve.

Red Curry Duck

Makes 4 servings

One 3-pound duck, cut into serving pieces, or 3 pounds duck legs
Salt and freshly ground black pepper
One 6-inch piece fresh ginger, finely chopped
4 shallots, sliced
1 carrot, chopped
2 lemongrass stalks, crushed
6 garlic cloves, crushed
1 tablespoon red curry paste, store-bought is fine
5 kaffir lime leaves, plus more for garnish
4 cups chicken stock, preferably homemade or canned low-sodium broth
1¾ cups coconut milk
1 fresh red Thai chile, seeded and puréed
1 tablespoon sambal belacan
1 fresh red finger chile, seeded and thinly sliced
¼ cup chopped fresh cilantro leaves
½ pineapple, peeled, cored, and puréed in a blender

Gamy duck is the perfect choice for this red curry sauce, where the spices bring out the richness of the duck without making it feel too heavy. This is a great dish to make ahead of time; skim off any fat after chilling, then reheat and serve.

1. Put the duck in a 12-inch skillet or casserole, preferably nonstick, and turn the heat to medium-high. Brown carefully on all sides, turning as necessary, and sprinkling with salt and pepper. Take the time to do this thoroughly, allowing up to 20 minutes total.

2. Remove the duck from the pan, leaving a couple of tablespoons of the rendered fat behind. Add the ginger, shallots, carrot, lemongrass, and garlic and cook, stirring, until golden, about 2 minutes, then add the curry paste, lime leaves, and half the chicken stock. Cook, stirring occasionally, until the mixture is boiling and fragrant, 2 minutes. Add the coconut milk and bring to a boil; nestle in the duck pieces, adding any accumulated juices. Adjust the heat so that the mixture simmers energetically but not violently, and cook, uncovered, for 15 minutes. Remove the breast pieces and stir in the chile purée. Add the remaining 2 cups chicken stock and continue cooking until the duck is tender, 20 to 40 minutes. Stir in the sambal belacan and season the curry sauce with salt and pepper to taste. Return the breast pieces to the pan and warm through.

3. Garnish the curry with the sliced red finger chile, lime leaves, cilantro, and pineapple purée.

Duck "Oriental"

Makes 4 servings

CURRY JUS RÔTI

½ pound chicken wings, cut into 3 or 4 pieces each
1½ teaspoons extra virgin olive oil
1 tablespoon diced onion
1 tablespoon diced carrot
1 tablespoon diced celery
1 garlic clove, chopped
1 teaspoon unsalted butter
¼ teaspoon red curry paste, store-bought is fine
¼ teaspoon Green Curry Paste, preferably homemade (page 200)
¼ teaspoon yellow curry paste, store-bought is fine
¼ cup dry white wine

SESAME-HONEY SAUCE

½ cup white sesame seeds
¼ cup honey
2 tablespoons unsalted butter

4 duck breasts, preferably on the bone
Salt and freshly ground black pepper
8 heads bok choy, trimmed
1 teaspoon baking soda
2 tablespoons unsalted butter
2 teaspoons fresh lime juice, plus more to taste
Duck Sticks (page 26), optional
Tamarind Ketchup (page 32)

When you combine all the components here, you have an incredible showstopper, a four-star dish that isn't too expensive or too difficult, but sure is luxurious. (If you're looking for a simpler version, just serve the duck breasts with the curry jus rôti and sesame-honey sauce; it's pretty great.) This is best served with Vegetable Fried Rice (page 228).

1. **To make the jus rôti:** Preheat the oven to 500°F and place a rack in the lowest possible position (if you can roast on the floor of the oven, so much the better).

2. Combine the chicken and olive oil in a roasting pan just large enough to hold the chicken in one layer. Roast for about 45 minutes, stirring and scraping occasionally, until the meat is nicely browned. Add the vegetables and garlic and stir and scrape once or twice, then return to the oven for about 20 minutes more, stirring once or twice.

3. Stir again, scraping the bottom of the pan well, and carefully add 1½ cups water. Return to the oven and simmer for 30 minutes. Remove from the oven, cool slightly, and strain. Keep the oven on.

4. Meanwhile, melt the butter in a large stockpot over medium heat. Add the curry pastes and cook, stirring occasionally, until fragrant, about 3 minutes. Add the wine, mix well, and cook until the mixture is reduced by half. Stir in the strained stock and reduce until thickened slightly. Set aside.

(continued)

Strings of →
jasmine flowers

5. **To make the sauce:** Put the sesame seeds and honey in a small saucepan over low heat. Cook, stirring frequently, until caramelized and golden brown, about 15 minutes. Remove from the heat, stir in the butter, cool, and set aside.

6. Season the duck breasts with salt and pepper, put in a roasting pan, transfer to the oven, and roast until medium-rare, 10 minutes. Remove from the oven, cool, and debone, keeping the meat in one or two pieces each.

7. Meanwhile, bring a medium pot of water to a boil. Add the bok choy and baking soda and cook until the bok choy is bright green and just tender, about 3 minutes. Drain immediately and set aside.

8. Melt the butter in a large skillet over medium-high heat. Add the duck breasts, skin side down, and cook just until crisp. Remove from the heat, cool slightly, then cut each into ½-inch slices.

9. Bring the curry jus rôti to a boil in a saucepan, then stir in the sesame-honey sauce. Remove from the heat and season to taste with lime juice. Spoon this sauce onto one side of each serving plate and arrange the duck slices on top. Put the Duck Sticks, if using, and the bok choy on the other side and the Tamarind Ketchup in the center. Serve immediately, preferably with fried rice.

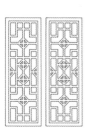

Peking Duck

Makes 4 servings

PEKING DUCK

3 tablespoons honey
3 tablespoons dark soy sauce
2 tablespoons apple cider vinegar
One 6-pound duck

PEKING DUCK CREPES

2¾ cups all-purpose flour
2 tablespoons sesame oil

¼ cup plus 2 tablespoons hoisin
1 tablespoon sugar
4 scallions, trimmed, cut into 2-inch lengths, and thinly sliced
1 cucumber, peeled, seeded, and cut into 2 x 1-inch batons
Shrimp chips, optional

Peking duck is definitely a special-occasion dish. The crackling sweet skin and savory gamy meat taste heavenly when wrapped in homemade chewy crepes. The hardest part of cooking Peking duck is finding room in your refrigerator for the marinating process. The skin needs to dry out completely to acquire its distinctive crunch. (Ideally, the duck should cook hanging by a meat hook in your oven too.) Once the duck is properly marinated, the rest is quite straightforward.

1. **To make the duck:** Put the honey, soy sauce, and vinegar in a medium saucepan with 4½ cups water and bring the mixture to a boil, stirring occasionally. Remove from the heat and cool completely.

2. Use a meat hook or kitchen twine to hold the duck up by its neck. Hold the duck over a large mixing bowl and spoon half the honey mixture over the duck. Make sure the duck is completely coated. Discard the sauce in the bowl and refrigerate the remaining sauce.

3. Hang the duck in your refrigerator over a large mixing bowl and refrigerate overnight. Set up a small fan in your refrigerator to blow the duck dry while it chills. (A small battery-operated fan works well.) Spoon the remaining honey sauce over the duck every 2 hours for the first 6 hours of its chilling time. The skin of the duck should feel as dry and as stiff as parchment paper after it has chilled overnight.

4. Preheat the oven to 475°F.

5. Put the duck on a rack in a roasting pan, breast side up. Pour ⅔ cup water in the pan to prevent splattering. Cook for 15 minutes, then turn the heat down to 350°F and continue cooking for 1 hour and 10 minutes. If the water dries out, add another ½ cup. Remove the duck from the oven and let it rest in the pan for 10 minutes.

6. **Make the crepes** while the duck is cooking. Put the flour in a large mixing bowl and add 1 cup very hot water in a slow, steady stream while mixing with chopsticks or a wooden spoon. If the mixture is still dry after all the water has been added, add more water, 1 tablespoon at a time, just until the dough holds together. Transfer to a lightly floured surface and knead for 8 minutes. Put the dough back in the bowl, cover with plastic wrap, and let rest for 30 minutes.

7. Uncover the dough and knead again for 5 minutes. Roll the dough into an 18-inch-long log and cut the log evenly into 18 pieces. Shape each piece of dough into a ball.

8. Fill a shallow dish with the sesame oil. Dip one side of one ball into the sesame oil and press the ball, oiled side down, onto another ball of dough. Roll the two flattened balls together into one 6-inch circle. Repeat with the remaining balls of dough.

9. Heat a large nonstick skillet over medium heat. Add a round of dough and cook until the dough is dry and flecked with brown spots. Flip and cook the other side until dry. Repeat with the remaining dough. When the cooked crepes are cool, peel each round apart into 2 crepes.

10. Use a cleaver or sharp carving knife to cut the duck into bite-size pieces, removing all the bones. Arrange the duck on a serving platter.

11. Stir together the hoisin, sugar, and 1 tablespoon water. Instruct your guests to spread some hoisin sauce onto a crepe and to fill the crepe with the duck, scallions, and cucumber. Serve with the shrimp chips on the side, if you like.

Squab "à l'Orange" with Crystallized Tamarind

Makes 4 servings

SAUCE

½ cup fresh orange juice
2 tablespoons soy sauce
¼ cup plus 2 tablespoons rice vinegar
1 tablespoon Shaoxing wine
1 whole star anise
2 tablespoons roughly chopped fresh ginger
¼ cup sugar
1 tablespoon black tea leaves, preferably oolong
Salt

4 semi-boneless squabs (see headnote)
1 tablespoon unsalted butter, plus more as needed
1 teaspoon ground star anise
Salt and freshly ground black pepper
Twelve ¼-inch pieces crystallized tamarind candy
1 Asian pear, peeled, cored, and cut into thin wedges (or use a Granny Smith apple)
1 teaspoon coarse salt

This new version of a French classic is much easier than the original, and so much more fragrant; the tea leaves really transform the sauce, and I find that squab is more satisfying here than duck (which also works well). The crystallized tamarind is a nice touch, but you can leave it out if you have trouble finding it (which you should be able to do in most Asian markets).

To "semi-bone" the squabs, just take a sharp boning knife and cut straight down along either side of the breast; you'll end up with a boneless breast attached to the bone-in leg and wing.

1. Preheat the broiler.

2. **To make the sauce:** Put the first 6 ingredients in a blender and purée. Transfer the mixture to a saucepan and stir in the sugar and tea over medium heat. Bring to a boil, stirring occasionally, then remove from the heat, cover, and steep for 5 minutes. Cool the mixture completely, then strain through a fine-mesh sieve and season to taste with salt. Set aside.

3. Rub the squab with the butter, then season it with the anise, salt, and pepper. Put it on a buttered baking sheet, skin side up.

4. Broil until medium-rare, 5 minutes. Spoon the sauce onto the serving plates and put the broiled squab on top. Garnish with the tamarind candy, Asian pear, and salt, and serve.

Squab with Egg Noodle Pancake

Makes 4 servings

3½ tablespoons unsalted butter
1 cup pearl onions, peeled
Salt
8 long slices fresh ginger, julienned
2 tablespoons honey
2 tablespoons jus rôti, store-bought is fine, or use chicken stock, preferably homemade or canned low-sodium broth
1 tablespoon fresh lime juice
1 cup trimmed fresh sugar snap peas
¼ cup chopped fresh chive buds or chives
4 semi-boneless squabs (see headnote)
Freshly ground black pepper
1 teaspoon cumin seeds, toasted and ground (see page 27)
¼ teaspoon ground ginger
¼ teaspoon medium curry powder
¼ teaspoon ground cinnamon
Egg Noodle Pancake (page 240)

Here I like to add the spice mixture to the birds immediately after cooking and not before because I find it changes the nature of this dish, giving the crisp squab a fresh, fragrant coating of aromatics that is not overpowering. Served with quickly made Egg Noodle Pancakes, which everyone loves, this dish is both impressive and quick.

To "semi-bone" the squabs, just take a sharp boning knife and cut straight down along either side of the breast; you'll end up with a boneless breast attached to the bone-in leg and wing.

1. Melt 2 tablespoons of the butter in a large skillet over medium heat. Add the pearl onions, season with salt, and cook, stirring occasionally, until nicely browned, at least 10 minutes. Add the ginger and honey and continue cooking until caramelized, then stir in the jus rôti. Season with the lime juice, remove from the heat, and set aside.

2. Fill a large bowl with water and ice and set aside. Bring a small pot of water to a boil and add the sugar snap peas and chive buds. Cook just until bright green and tender, drain, and transfer to the ice water. When cold, drain again and set aside.

3. Preheat the broiler and set the rack 4 to 6 inches from the heat source.

4. Use 1 tablespoon of the butter to grease the bottom of a roasting pan. Season both sides of the birds with salt and pepper and place on the roasting pan, skin side up. Combine the spices and set aside.

5. Broil the birds until the skin is brown and crisp and the bird rare, about 5 minutes. Let them rest for a minute or two, then sprinkle them on both sides with a pinch of the spice mixture. Mix their juices in with the cooked onions.

6. Melt the remaining ½ tablespoon butter in a medium skillet over medium heat. Add the sugar snap peas, season with salt, and add 1 tablespoon water. Cook, stirring occasionally, until the sugar snap peas are heated through.

7. Put an Egg Noodle Pancake in the center of each of four serving plates. Put the squab on the cakes, top with the onions, and spoon the onion juices all around. Garnish with the chive buds and sugar snap peas and serve.

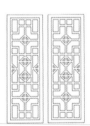

MEAT

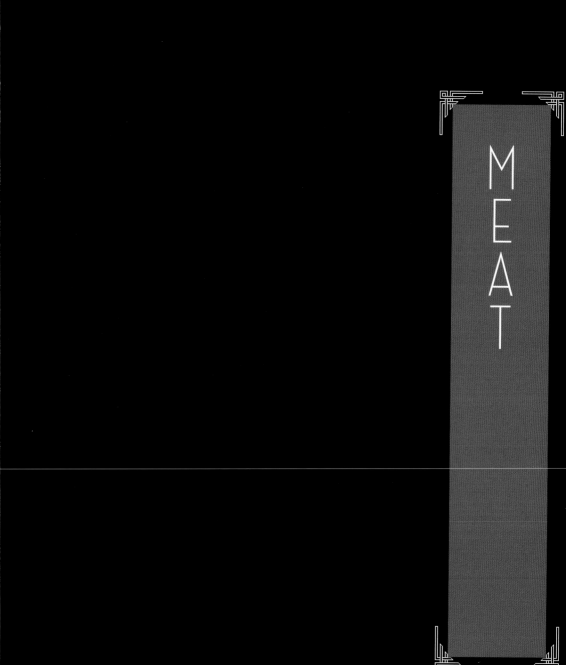

Charred Sirloin with Soy, Garlic, and Coriander

Makes 4 servings

½ cup light soy sauce
¼ cup regular soy sauce
½ tablespoon dark soy sauce
1 fresh green Thai chile, halved lengthwise
1 fresh red Thai chile, halved lengthwise
3 dried Thai chiles, seeded and crushed
1½ tablespoons coriander seeds, toasted (see page 62) and crushed
¼ cup bourbon
¼ cup crushed fresh cilantro leaves
¼ cup crushed fresh Thai basil leaves
¼ cup crushed fresh mint leaves
Four 8-ounce sirloin or ribeye steaks, each about 1-inch thick, at room temperature
2 teaspoons garlic salt
¼ cup unsalted butter
8 cups fresh spinach leaves
Salt
1 tablespoon white sesame seeds, toasted (see page 15)

As if grilled sirloin weren't good enough already, I infuse it with soy and finish it with a fresh dressing built around coriander. Wilted spinach is the perfect accompaniment. Here's what I do to make garlic salt, and you can do it too: Buy deep-fried garlic (Thai markets sell it) and mix it with salt—the stuff is great!

1. Put the first 8 ingredients into a medium saucepan and set over high heat. Bring to a boil, then immediately remove from the heat and add the cilantro, basil, and mint. Stir well, then set aside to cool, uncovered, to room temperature. When cool, purée in a blender and strain through a fine-mesh sieve, extracting all the liquid; set aside. (You can do this a day or two in advance if you like.)

2. Start a charcoal or gas grill or broiler; the fire should be hot, and the grill rack should be about 5 inches from the heat source.

3. Brush the steaks generously with the soy infusion, reserving any leftover sauce, season with garlic salt, and set on the grill. Cook the first side for 3 minutes, then cook the other side for another 5 minutes for medium-rare. Remove from the grill and let rest.

4. Meanwhile, melt the butter in a large skillet over medium-high heat. When the butter smells nutty, add the spinach and season with salt. Cook, stirring occa-

sionally, just until almost wilted. Then stir in the toasted sesame seeds and divide the spinach evenly among the serving plates.

5. Cut the steaks crosswise into 1-inch slices and brush with the reserved sauce. Put the steak slices on top of the spinach and serve.

Altar of offering in the streets of Bangkok

MEAT

Beef Brisket with Onions and Chile

Makes 4 servings

3 tablespoons extra virgin olive oil
½ fresh red finger chile, seeded and thinly sliced
2 onions, diced
2½ pounds beef brisket
Salt and freshly ground black pepper
2 carrots, diced
1 celery stalk, diced
5 cups chicken stock, preferably homemade or canned low-sodium broth, plus more as needed
1 pound fresh egg noodles
Soy sauce

I think of this as an Alsatian-Jewish-Chinese dish, so it's representative of both my roots and the things I love. You've got oven-braised beef brisket, transformed by a caramelized onion crust; the chile adds a great kick.

1. Preheat the oven to 325°F.

2. Heat the oil in a skillet over medium-low heat. Add the chile and half the diced onions and cook, stirring occasionally, until brown. Remove from the heat and cool.

3. Meanwhile, trim excess fat off the brisket, leaving a thin, even layer of fat on top. Season the meat generously with salt and pepper and put it in a roasting pan. Scatter the carrots, celery, and remaining onions around the brisket.

4. Press the caramelized onions onto the top of the brisket to form a crust. Pour in enough stock so that everything but the crust is covered. Cover the pan with foil and transfer to the oven.

5. Cook the meat, basting every half hour, until it is very tender, 2 to 3 hours. Remove the pan from the oven and allow the brisket to cool in its juices before carving.

6. Meanwhile, bring a large pot of water to a boil. Salt it generously and add the egg noodles. Cook, stirring occasionally, until al dente, about 4 minutes. Drain.

7. Divide the noodles and pan juices among the serving bowls and top with slices of the beef. Season to taste with soy sauce and serve.

Sirloin Steaks with Garlic Soy Butter and Pickled Bell Peppers

Makes 4 servings

This is an extreme dish, a take on Chinese stir-fried beef with peppers, in which bold flavors combine to enhance the sirloin centerpiece. You can make the pickled bell peppers ahead of time; just bring them back to room temperature before serving.

PICKLED BELL PEPPERS

4 bell peppers, preferably an assortment of red, orange, and yellow, halved lengthwise and seeded
1 teaspoon cayenne pepper, plus more as needed
2 tablespoons extra virgin olive oil
¼ cup champagne or white wine vinegar
2 tablespoons rice vinegar
2 tablespoons elderflower syrup or honey
2 tablespoons Shaoxing wine
2 tablespoons sugar
1 teaspoon nam pla (Thai fish sauce)
½ teaspoon ground cloves

2 tablespoons extra virgin olive oil
1 garlic clove, thinly sliced
1 cup soy sauce
¾ cup plus 2 tablespoons unsalted butter, cut into small pieces
2 teaspoons freshly ground black pepper
Four 8-ounce sirloin steaks, each about 1 inch thick, at room temperature

1. Preheat the oven to 300°F.

2. **To make the peppers:** Put the peppers, cut side down, on a foil-lined baking sheet. Sprinkle them with the cayenne, drizzle with the oil, cover with foil, and put into the oven. Cook until very tender, about 1 hour. Remove the peppers from the oven, peel, mince, and transfer to a mixing bowl.

3. Meanwhile, put the vinegars, syrup, wine, sugar, nam pla, and cloves in a saucepan. Bring to a boil, then remove from the heat and cool. Strain the sauce over the peppers in the bowl, mix well, and set aside.

4. Heat the oil in a medium skillet over low heat. Add the garlic and cook until very soft, about 5 minutes. Transfer the garlic and soy sauce to a blender and blend until smooth. Return the garlic-soy mixture to the skillet, add ¾ cup of the butter, and set over low heat. Whisk the mixture until the butter is melted, but do not boil. Season with the pepper.

5. Put the remaining 2 tablespoons butter in a large skillet and increase the heat to medium-high. When the butter melts, add the steaks and increase the heat to

high. Sear for 3 minutes, then turn. Sear on the second side for 3 minutes; lower the heat and cook until they reach your desired level of doneness, about 8 minutes total for medium-rare.

6. Spoon the garlic-soy butter sauce on the bottom of the serving plates, put a steak in the center of each plate, and top with the pickled peppers. Serve immediately.

A fruit and vegetable vendor in the heart of Bangkok

Sautéed Lamb Chops with Garlic, Lemon, and Chile

Makes 4 servings

CRUMB CRUST
½ cup extra virgin olive oil
¾ cup Japanese panko bread crumbs
Salt and freshly ground black pepper
¼ cup minced garlic
¼ cup minced fresh lemon zest
2 tablespoons minced fresh cilantro leaves

SWEET-AND-SOUR GELÉE
¼ cup red wine vinegar
2 tablespoons Shaoxing wine
1 tablespoon rice vinegar
1 tablespoon sweet white wine
2 tablespoons honey
2 tablespoons sugar
¼ red bell pepper, cored and seeded
1 dried Thai chile
1 whole clove
½ teaspoon agar-agar

2 tablespoons unsalted butter
2 tablespoons extra virgin olive oil
8 lamb rib or loin chops
Salt and freshly ground pepper

This is a fun and completely different take on lamb chops—the crumb crust, flavored with lemon zest, garlic, and cilantro, is served aside the lamb chops instead of being cooked to a crisp on top. A sweet-and-sour gelée adds another dimension of texture and flavor to the dish. To eat, dip the lamb in the bread crumbs and jelly.

1. Preheat the oven to 450°F.

2. **To make the crust:** Heat half the oil in a large skillet over medium heat. Add the panko crumbs and cook, stirring occasionally, until golden. Season with salt and pepper, then drain on paper towels. Heat the remaining ¼ cup oil in another large skillet over medium-high heat. Add the garlic and cook, stirring occasionally, until golden and sticky, 5 to 10 minutes. Drain and season with salt. Combine the panko crumbs and garlic in a mixing bowl and stir in the lemon zest and cilantro. Set aside.

3. **To make the gelée:** Put the first 9 ingredients in a medium saucepan and set over medium heat. Bring to a boil and simmer for 30 seconds. Remove from the heat and transfer to a blender. Blend until smooth, strain into a saucepan, and skim any foam off the top. Put over medium-low heat and whisk in the agar-agar. Bring to a boil and cook for 1 minute. Remove from the heat and pour onto a rimmed baking sheet or plate set over ice. Set aside.

4. Put the butter and oil in a large skillet over high heat. Season the lamb chops with salt and pepper and add to the skillet once the butter melts. Brown one side, then turn the chops and transfer to the oven. Cook until medium-rare, about 5 minutes more.

5. Mound the panko mixture on each of the serving plates. Top with the meat and spoon the sweet-and-sour gelée on top. Serve immediately.

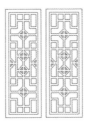

Lamb Shank Braised with Green Curry and Vegetables

Makes 4 servings

GREEN CURRY PASTE

2 lemongrass stalks, trimmed and chopped
1 teaspoon cumin seeds, toasted (see page 27)
1 cup fresh cilantro stems
1 tablespoon chopped fresh galangal
2 garlic cloves, chopped
2 fresh green finger chiles, seeded and minced
2 fresh green Thai chiles, seeded and minced
1 teaspoon belacan, or dried shrimp
2 shallots, chopped
2 lime leaves, chopped
1/4 cup nam pla (Thai fish sauce)
2 tablespoons sugar

4 lamb shanks
3 tablespoons extra virgin olive oil
Salt and freshly ground black pepper
1 lemongrass stalk, trimmed, smashed, and cut into 2-inch pieces
One 1-inch piece fresh galangal, sliced
2 fresh green Thai chiles
2 kaffir lime leaves
1 1/4 cups fresh cilantro leaves, plus sprigs for garnish
1 onion, sliced
2 cups chicken stock, preferably homemade or canned low-sodium broth
1 1/2 cups coconut milk
12 baby carrots, peeled
12 baby turnips, peeled
4 scallions, trimmed and julienned
1/2 cup fresh peas
1/2 cup fresh fava beans
2 Thai eggplants, trimmed and cut into chunks
1 tablespoon unsalted butter

Lamb is one of my favorite meats for curry and shanks, especially, simply melt into the spices. This Thai-style curry is so good, though, that you can make it vegetarian and omit the lamb; and you can use any vegetables you like, not just the ones I chose. Note that this dish requires overnight marination.

1. **To make the curry paste:** Put the ingredients in a blender. Blend until the consistency of a fine paste, scraping down the sides of the bowl as necessary.

2. Rub all but 1/4 cup of the curry paste onto the lamb shanks. Cover both the lamb shanks and the curry paste and refrigerate overnight.

3. Heat half the oil in a large skillet over high heat. Season the lamb with salt and pepper and add to the pan. Sear until nicely browned, then turn and sear the other side. Remove from the heat and set aside.

4. Put the lemongrass, galangal, chiles, lime leaves, and ¼ cup of the cilantro leaves in a piece of cheesecloth. Wrap and secure the sachet with kitchen string.

5. Heat the remaining 1½ tablespoons oil in a large deep pot or Dutch oven, which can later be covered, over medium heat. Add the onion and cook until softened, about 5 minutes. Add the reserved curry paste and cook, stirring occasionally, until fragrant, about 3 minutes. Add the lamb shanks, stock, 1 cup of the coconut milk, and the sachet. Bring to a boil and then lower the heat and simmer, partially covered, until the meat is falling off the bone, at least 1 hour and probably longer.

6. Remove the meat to another platter, cover, and refrigerate until serving time. Remove the sachet and chill the sauce, covered, in the refrigerator. When it has chilled, remove the fat with a spoon.

7. Meanwhile, fill a large bowl with water and ice and set aside. Bring a small pot of water to a boil and add the remaining cilantro leaves (reserving the sprigs for garnish). As soon as the water returns to a boil, drain the leaves and transfer to the ice water, reserving the cooking liquid. When cold, drain again, and put the leaves in a blender with 2 tablespoons of the reserved liquid. Purée until smooth and set aside.

8. Fill a large bowl with water and ice and set aside. Bring a large pot of water to a boil. Add the carrots, turnips, scallions, peas, and beans and cook just until tender, about 3 minutes. Immediately transfer to the ice water, drain, and set aside.

9. Bring the skimmed sauce back to a steady simmer in a large saucepan. Add the meat and eggplant and cook until the meat is reheated and the eggplant tender, about 15 minutes. Stir in the cilantro purée and remaining ½ cup coconut milk.

10. Melt the butter in a skillet over medium heat. Add the carrots, turnips, scallions, peas, and beans, season to taste with salt, and sauté to reheat.

11. Put the lamb in the center of the serving plates. Spoon the eggplant and green curry sauce and the sautéed vegetables around the lamb, garnish with cilantro sprigs, and serve.

Steamed Lamb Shanks

Makes 4 servings

1 red bell pepper, cored, seeded, and minced
2 teaspoons ground cumin
8 kaffir lime leaves
4 lemongrass stalks, trimmed, smashed, and minced
5 fresh red Thai chiles, seeded and minced
8 garlic cloves, minced
12 whole cloves
¼ cup rice vinegar
4 fresh cilantro stems
4 lamb shanks

This is an interesting braise, combining Thai spices with a simple steaming technique that preserves every ounce of the lamb juices and all the flavors of the seasonings. Serve with steamed white rice and vegetables.

1. Prepare a steamer.

2. Combine all the ingredients with ¼ cup water in a large, heavy-duty Ziploc bag. Seal and shake gently to coat the lamb with the marinade. Transfer the bag to the steamer, standing the lamb shanks up on their fat parts, and steam until the lamb is very tender, 2½ to 3 hours, refilling the steamer with water as necessary. Remove the lamb shanks from the bag and serve.

Pork Chops with Chile Glaze

Makes 4 servings

CHILE GLAZE

1 dried ancho chile
1 dried chipotle chile
3 tablespoons sugar
2 garlic cloves, minced
1 tablespoon plus 2 teaspoons fresh lime juice
2½ tablespoons fresh lemon juice
2½ tablespoons fresh orange juice
1 tablespoon nam pla (Thai fish sauce)

4 center-cut bone-in loin pork chops, about 1 inch thick, at room temperature
Salt and freshly ground black pepper

I love a well-grilled pork chop—crisp on the outside, with all the meaty juices captured inside. When done properly, a grilled pork chop is fantastic. With this simple chile glaze, it's even better!

1. **To make the chile glaze:** Put the chiles in a small skillet set over medium heat. Toast, turning the chiles occasionally, until dark brown and fragrant. Remove from the skillet, cool completely, and cut into ½-inch pieces.

2. Put the sugar in a small saucepan and add just enough water to wet it, about ½ teaspoon. Shake the pan to distribute the sugar and water and then caramelize over medium-high heat, shaking the pan occasionally. The sugar will gradually liquefy and darken; when it becomes dark brown, add the garlic. Cook, stirring, for 30 seconds. Add the chiles and mix well, then stir in the citrus juices. Cook, stirring constantly, until the mixture becomes syrupy. Remove from the heat and stir in the nam pla. Cool to room temperature and strain.

3. Start a charcoal or gas grill or broiler; the fire should be hot, and the grill rack should be about 4 inches from the heat source.

4. Season the chops with salt and pepper and sear over the hottest part of the grill for 2 minutes per side, taking care not to let them burn. Then move them to a cooler part of the grill and cook, turning once or twice, until done, about 15 minutes more.

5. Put the pork chops on serving plates and brush liberally with the chile glaze. Serve immediately.

Baby Back Ribs with Barbecue Sauce

Makes 4 servings

RIBS

1 tablespoon salt
2 cups sliced fresh ginger
1 fresh red Thai chile
1 cup soy sauce
2 racks baby back ribs

BARBECUE SAUCE

1 cup hoisin
2 tablespoons five-spice powder
1 garlic clove, minced
3 fresh red Thai chiles, seeded and minced
1 tablespoon fresh orange zest, finely minced
⅓ cup soy sauce
2 tablespoons champagne or white wine vinegar
¼ cup honey

1 orange, sliced crosswise, for garnish

Everyone loves barbecued ribs and the addition of orange zest and Asian spices gives these tender ribs complex and intriguing overtones.

1. **To prepare the ribs:** Stir together the salt, ginger, chile, and soy sauce in a large stockpot. Add the ribs and 4 quarts water and bring to a boil over high heat. Turn the heat to low and simmer until the meat is just about to fall off the bone, about 2 hours. Transfer the ribs to a roasting pan.

2. Meanwhile, **make the barbecue sauce:** Stir together the hoisin, five-spice powder, garlic, chiles, orange zest, soy sauce, and half the vinegar in a saucepan. Cook over high heat, stirring occasionally, for 15 minutes. Then lower the heat and stir in the honey and remaining 1 tablespoon vinegar until well blended.

3. Preheat the broiler.

4. Remove the barbecue sauce from the heat and brush on top of the ribs. Put the ribs under the broiler and cook until crisp on top, about 5 minutes. Transfer the ribs to a serving plate, garnish with orange slices, and serve.

Pork Vindaloo

Makes 4 servings

2 garlic cloves, chopped
One 1-inch piece fresh ginger, chopped
2 fresh red finger chiles, stemmed and seeded
½ cup red wine vinegar
1 tablespoon whole cumin seeds, finely ground
1 tablespoon paprika
½ teaspoon freshly ground black pepper
2 pounds pork butt, cut into 1½-inch cubes
1 tablespoon grape seed, corn, or other neutral oil, plus more for deep-frying
1 green cardamom pod
1 whole clove
1 cinnamon stick
2 onions, preferably Spanish, diced
1 teaspoon salt, plus more to taste
1 tablespoon sugar, plus more to taste
½ cup fresh Thai basil leaves
½ cup thinly sliced garlic
1 small jicama, peeled and julienned
2 tablespoons sliced fresh red Thai chiles

One of the most popular Indian curries, vindaloo pairs vinegar with fragrant spices like cinnamon, clove, and cardamom. The resulting flavors are wonderfully complex and warm. This dish is great for making ahead, since the flavors intensify with time. Simply reheat when ready to serve.

1. Put the first 7 ingredients in a blender and blend until the mixture becomes a wet paste. Put the pork in a shallow baking dish and coat the cubes with the spice mixture. Cover and refrigerate for at least 1 hour.

2. When ready to cook, heat the oil in a large skillet or casserole, which can later be covered, over medium heat. Add the cardamom, clove, and cinnamon and cook, stirring, until fragrant, 30 seconds. Add the onions and cook, stirring occasionally, until the onions are softened and translucent, but not browned, about 5 minutes.

3. Add the pork with its marinade, stir, and bring to a boil. Adjust the heat so the mixture simmers gently, then cover and cook until the pork is tender, about 1½ hours, seasoning with salt and sugar after 45 minutes. Stir from time to time; if the mixture dries out, add a little water. (If you choose to prepare the dish in advance, stop the cooking at this point. Let the curry sit at room temperature for up to a couple of hours, or cover and refrigerate for up to a day. If you like, skim excess fat before reheating and proceeding, adding a little water if necessary.)

(continued)

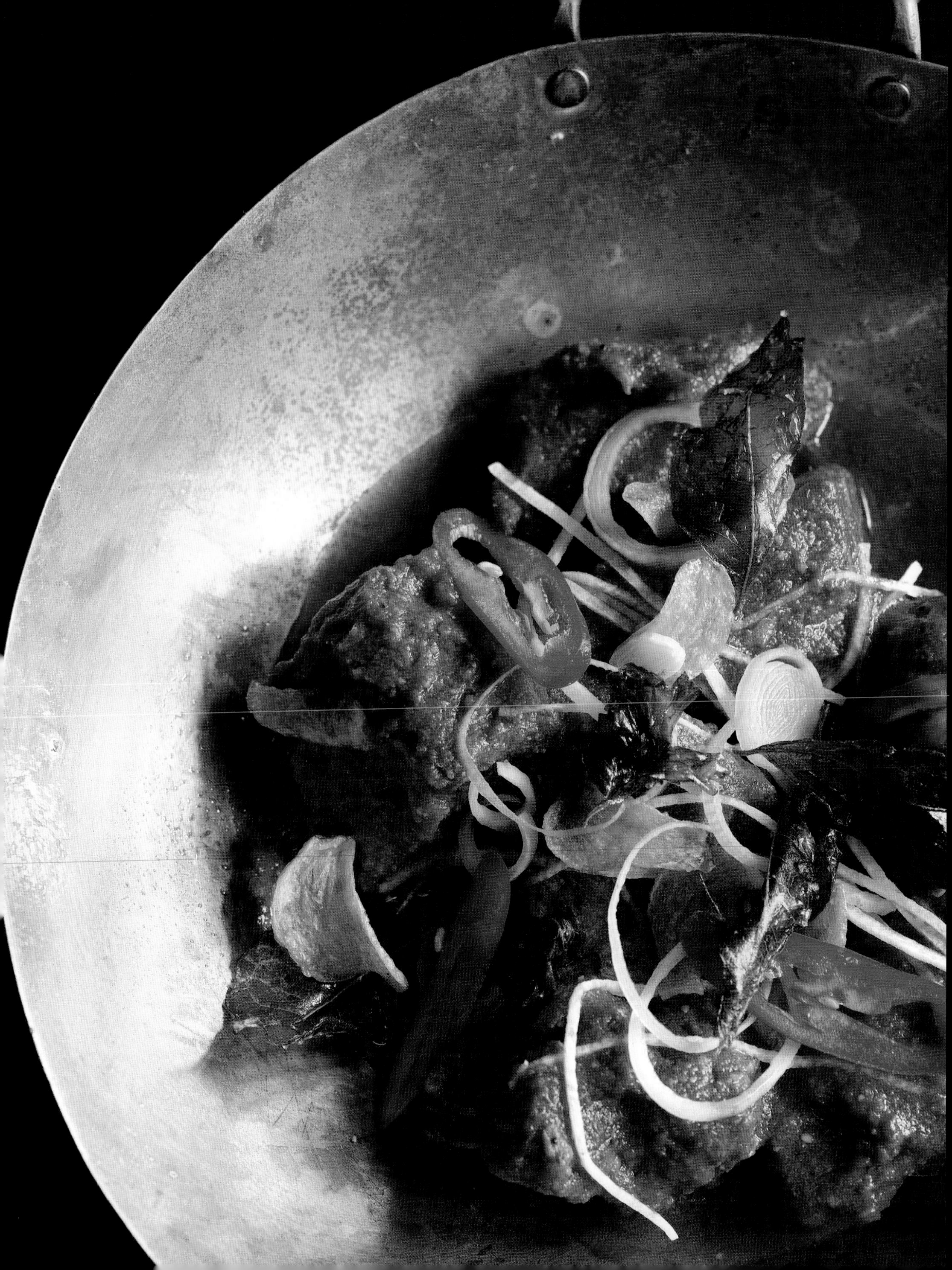

4. Pour oil to a depth of 1 inch in a heavy, deep saucepan and heat to 350°F. Carefully add the basil and cook, turning occasionally, until crisp. Remove with a slotted spoon and drain on paper towels. Add the sliced garlic and cook, turning occasionally, until golden brown and crisp. Remove with a slotted spoon and drain on paper towels. Season to taste with salt.

5. Taste and adjust the seasoning, garnish with the jicama, basil, garlic, and slivered chiles, and serve.

The art of →
crispy pork skin

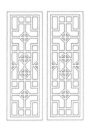

หมแดดเดียว

VEGETABLES

Spicy Ginger Tofu

Makes 4 servings

3 tablespoons minced fresh ginger
1½ tablespoons soy sauce
1 teaspoon chopped fresh green Thai chiles
1 teaspoon ground turmeric
2 teaspoons sugar
1 teaspoon salt, plus more to taste
One 12-ounce block firm tofu, patted dry and cut into 1-inch cubes
¼ cup grape seed, corn, or other neutral oil
1 onion, sliced
2 shallots, minced
1 garlic clove, minced
2 tablespoons chopped peanuts, plus more for garnish
¼ cup fresh Thai basil leaves, plus more for garnish

This dish takes some patience, since you need to brown the tofu first, but the time is well worth it: The tofu develops a nice brown crust around its silky interior.

1. Whisk together the ginger, soy sauce, chiles, turmeric, sugar, and salt in a shallow dish until well combined. Add the tofu pieces, turning to coat. Cover and refrigerate for at least 1 hour and up to 24 hours.

2. Heat half the oil in a nonstick skillet over medium heat and add the onion, shallots, and garlic. Sauté, stirring occasionally, until fragrant and softened, about 3 minutes. Season with salt, turn the heat to low, and add 3 tablespoons water to keep the vegetables moist.

3. Meanwhile, heat the remaining 2 tablespoons oil in another nonstick skillet and add the tofu. Do not crowd, making sure the pieces are kept separate. After the tofu is browned on one side, about 3 minutes, turn the pieces carefully and brown another side, about 3 minutes. Repeat until all sides are browned.

4. Transfer the browned tofu to the onion sauté and top with the chopped peanuts and basil. Season with salt, garnish with more peanuts and basil, and serve.

Steamed Mushrooms with Ginger and Sticky Rice

Makes 4 servings

- ⅔ cup sticky (sometimes also called glutinous) rice
- 2 cups mixed fresh mushrooms, preferably equal parts enoki, shiitake, honshimeji, oyster, and maitake, trimmed and sliced as necessary
- ½ cup good sake, preferably Pride of the Village Sake
- ¼ cup sugar
- 2 tablespoons extra virgin olive oil
- ¼ cup minced fresh ginger
- Salt
- ¼ cup rice vinegar, plus more as needed
- 8 fresh mint leaves

The method of "steaming" the mushrooms here is actually a style of poaching that keeps in all the flavors. When paired with the syrupy ginger dressing, the mushrooms are heavenly, a spectacular side dish or the perfect centerpiece for a vegetarian meal.

1. Rinse the rice, then soak it in water to cover for at least 1 hour (24 hours is also fine). Prepare a steamer. Drain the rice, then wrap in cheesecloth and put in the steamer above boiling water. Steam until tender, about 30 minutes.

2. Put the mushrooms in a small pot with about ½ cup water over medium heat and cover. After a couple of minutes, uncover the pot and turn the heat to high. Cook, stirring occasionally, until the water is mostly reduced. Remove from the heat.

3. Put the sake and sugar in another small pot and stir until the sugar is dissolved. Bring to boil, then remove from the heat. Heat the oil in a small skillet and add the ginger. Season with salt and cook until softened and fragrant, about 2 minutes. Add the vinegar and deglaze, stirring frequently, until the mixture is syrupy. Stir in the sake-sugar mixture, remove from the heat, then season to taste with more vinegar.

4. Put the rice in the bottom of four serving bowls, top with the mushrooms and dressing, garnish with mint, and serve.

Water Chestnuts, Sugar Snap Peas, and Shiitakes

Makes 4 servings

- 3 tablespoons grape seed, corn, or other neutral oil
- 6 fresh small shiitake mushrooms, trimmed
- 4 wood ear mushrooms, soaked in water for ½ hour, then drained and chopped.
- 1 tablespoon peeled and minced fresh ginger
- ½ cup peeled and sliced fresh water chestnuts
- 1 cup sugar snap peas, strings removed and ends trimmed
- 2 tablespoons soy sauce
- Salt

Crunchy, salty, and sweet, this quick stir-fry takes advantage of fresh vegetables by treating them simply. A hint of ginger and a splash of soy sauce are all you need.

1. Heat 1 tablespoon of the oil in a wok or large skillet over medium-high heat. Add the mushrooms, ginger, and 1 tablespoon water and stir-fry until browned and softened, about 2 minutes. Then add another tablespoon oil, the water chestnuts, and 1 tablespoon water and stir-fry for another minute. Add the remaining tablespoon oil, the sugar snap peas, and 1 tablespoon water and stir-fry for another 2 minutes.

2. Season with the soy sauce and salt to taste and serve.

Stir-Fried Corn and Broccoli

Makes 4 servings

1 large broccoli stalk
2 tablespoons grape seed, corn, or other neutral oil
1 cup fresh corn kernels or slices of baby corn
1 lemongrass stalk, trimmed and minced
1 fresh red Thai chile, seeded and minced
1 garlic clove, minced
Soy sauce
Salt, optional

In this little stir-fry, I keep the vegetables crisp and add fragrant lemongrass, chile, and garlic, with just a little bit of soy sauce. This steaming-stir-fry technique really brings all the flavors to life.

1. Cut the broccoli florets off the stalk and cut any large florets into smaller pieces. Peel the stem and cut into ⅛-inch-thick slices at an angle.

2. Heat the oil in a wok or large skillet over high heat. When the oil is hot, add the broccoli and corn and stir-fry for about 1 minute. Add 3 tablespoons water and continue to stir-fry until the broccoli is bright green and just tender.

3. Turn the heat to medium and stir in the lemongrass, chile, and garlic and cook, stirring occasionally, until fragrant and tender, about 2 minutes. Season to taste with soy sauce and, if needed, salt. Serve immediately.

Steamed Spicy Eggplant

Makes 4 servings

1 pound Japanese eggplants, trimmed and peeled
1 teaspoon peanut oil
3 garlic cloves, minced
1 scallion, trimmed and thinly sliced
1 tablespoon chili paste
1¼ teaspoons sugar
3 tablespoons soy sauce
1 tablespoon Shaoxing wine
1 tablespoon sesame oil
2½ teaspoons rice vinegar, preferably Japanese

Steaming eggplant is a popular cooking technique in China and Japan. And for good reason. The eggplant becomes tender and juicy—soft enough to melt in your mouth, but still firm enough to hold its shape. Tossed with a spicy and savory marinade, the eggplant absorbs all the aromatic flavors.

1. Prepare a steamer.

2. Cut the eggplants lengthwise into quarters and then cut each piece crosswise in half. Put the eggplants in the steamer, cover, and cook until tender, about 10 minutes.

3. Meanwhile, heat the oil in a small skillet over medium-high heat. Add the garlic and cook, stirring, until golden brown, about 4 minutes. Transfer to a mixing bowl with the remaining ingredients and stir well.

4. Add the eggplant to the marinade and toss gently until well mixed. Serve warm.

Green Curry Vegetables

Makes 4 servings

GREEN CURRY SAUCE

2 teaspoons coriander seeds
1 teaspoon cumin seeds
¾ teaspoon freshly ground black pepper
5 fresh green Thai chiles, roughly chopped
4 shallots, roughly chopped
12 garlic cloves, roughly chopped
1 bunch fresh cilantro, including roots, washed thoroughly and roughly chopped
One 2-inch piece fresh galangal, roughly chopped

GREEN CURRY VEGETABLES

2 cups chicken stock, preferably homemade or low-sodium canned broth
2 cups coconut milk
2 cups chopped fresh cilantro leaves
Salt
20 sugar snap peas, strings removed and ends trimmed
4 Thai eggplants, stemmed and cut lengthwise into eighths
8 fresh water chestnuts, peeled and quartered
4 fresh red finger chiles, cut into ½-inch pieces
8 okra, trimmed and halved lengthwise
8 baby corn, husks removed, trimmed, and halved lengthwise
12 asparagus, trimmed and cut into 1-inch pieces at an angle
One 8-inch piece bamboo shoot, cut into thin wedges
1 head broccoli, broken into small florets
4 kaffir lime leaves, halved lengthwise and middle vein removed
¼ cup green peppercorns, canned are fine
¼ cup nam pla (Thai fish sauce)

All the flavor in this dish comes from the cilantro roots. The green curry sauce is just amazing with heat from the chiles and freshness from the aromatic herbs. The list of vegetables here is just a guideline. Use whatever vegetables are fresh at the market, except for leafy or root vegetables. Steamed white rice is a must for this dish.

1. **To make the sauce:** Put the coriander seeds, cumin seeds, and black pepper in a mortar and grind to a medium-fine consistency with a pestle. Alternatively, use a spice grinder and grind to a medium-fine consistency.

2. Transfer the spices to a blender with the remaining ingredients and ½ cup water. Blend and add another ¼ cup water in a slow, steady stream with the machine running. Blend until smooth, scraping down the sides of the bowl as necessary.

(continued)

3. **To make the vegetables:** Bring the chicken stock and coconut milk to a boil in a large saucepan over medium-high heat. Turn the heat to low and simmer until reduced by half, about 20 minutes.

4. Add the curry sauce to the mixture and stir well to combine. Remove from the heat and transfer to a blender. Blend for 2 minutes, then add the chopped cilantro leaves and blend until smooth. Set aside.

5. Fill a large bowl with water and ice and set aside. Bring a medium pot of water to a boil and salt it generously. Add the sugar snap peas and eggplant. Cook until the peas are bright green, about 2 minutes, then immediately transfer to the ice water bath. When cold, drain and set aside.

6. Put the curry sauce into a medium saucepan and set over medium heat. Add the remaining vegetables, lime leaves, and green peppercorns. When the sauce comes to a boil, add the reserved snap peas and eggplant and the nam pla. Cook for another 4 minutes. Serve immediately.

A basket of betel leaves →
in a vegetable market in Bagan
(formerly Pagan), Myanmar
(formerly Burma)

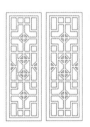

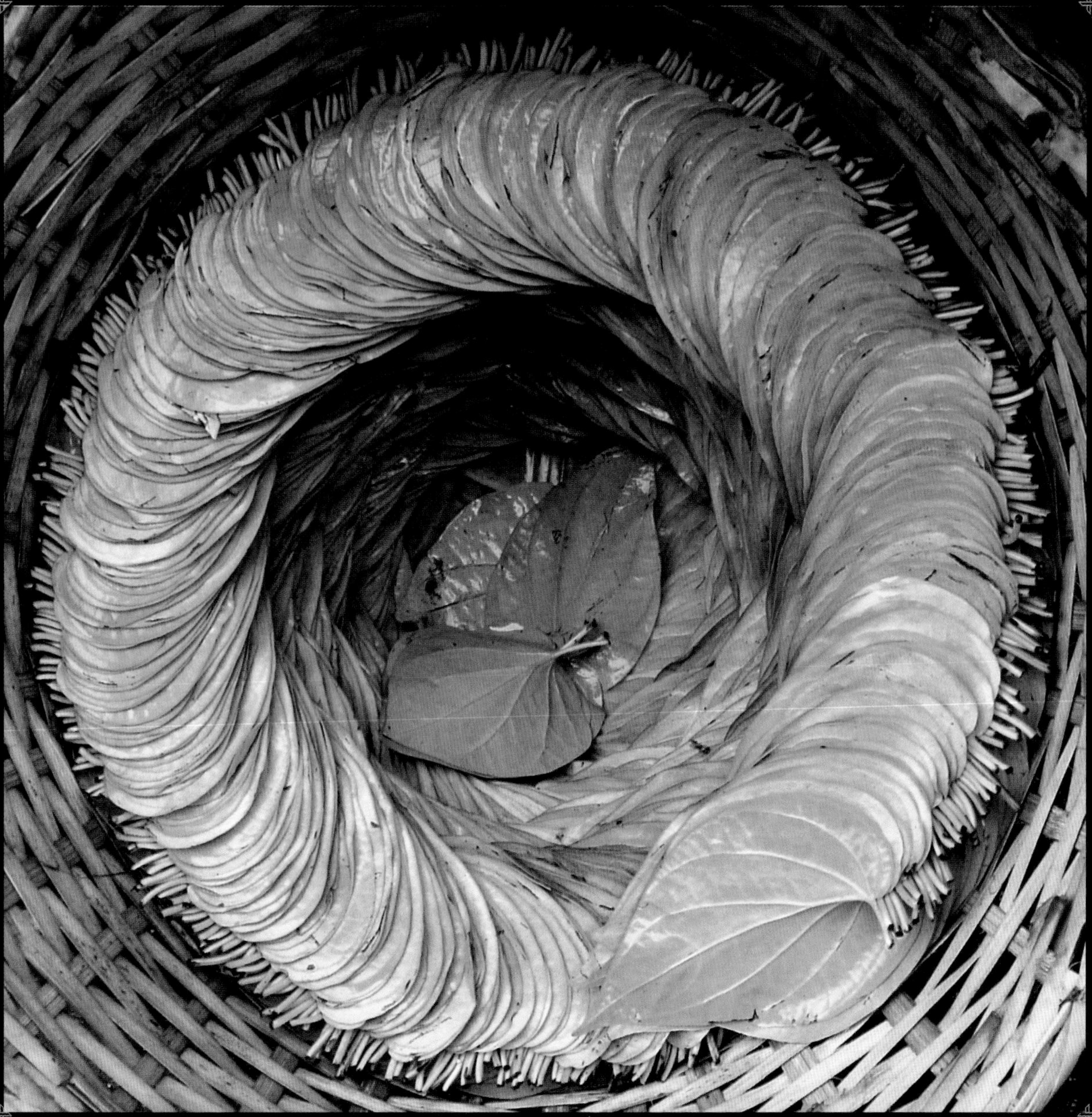

RICE & NOODLES

Coconut Sticky Rice

Makes 4 servings

1 cup sweet rice (also called glutinous rice), soaked overnight in cold water
½ cup coconut milk
1½ teaspoons nam pla (Thai fish sauce)
⅓ teaspoon sugar
4 banana leaves

This is the best accompaniment to any saucy Asian-flavored dish. The rice grains are tender, but still chewy, and have a rich, subtle sweetness. Steaming the rice in banana leaves imparts an incomparable aroma to the dish.

Bundles of rice in banana leaves on the streets of Bangkok

1. Prepare a steamer. Drain the rice and wrap loosely in cheesecloth. Place in the steamer and cook until tender, sticky, and elastic, about 10 minutes. Unwrap and let cool for a minute.

2. Transfer the rice to a large mixing bowl and stir in the coconut milk, nam pla, and sugar. Taste and adjust the seasonings if you like.

3. Cut the banana leaves so that you have four 8 x 10-inch rectangles, with the grain of the leaves running the long way. Place one long end closest to your body and spoon a quarter of the rice mixture onto the middle of the leaf. Fold one long end over, then the other, and finally the two shorter ends. Seal with a toothpick or string. Repeat with the remaining leaves. (At this point, you may refrigerate the packages for up to 2 days.)

4. When you're ready to serve, steam the packages over boiling water until hot, about 10 minutes, or microwave for a couple of minutes to reheat.

Pineapple Fried Rice

Makes 4 servings

3 tablespoons grape seed, corn, or other neutral oil
¾ cup cubed fresh pineapple
¾ cup diced onion
3 cups day-old cooked rice
1½ cups trimmed bean sprouts
1½ cups sliced Napa cabbage
½ cup fresh red Thai chile seeded and minced, or to taste
1 teaspoon soy sauce, or to taste
1 teaspoon sesame oil, or to taste
1 teaspoon nam pla (Thai fish sauce), or to taste
1 scallion, trimmed and thinly sliced

Pineapple fried rice has become a staple in most Thai restaurants, but is usually too sweet and bland at the same time. I make it with crisp vegetables and fresh pineapple. Caramelize the pineapple and onion well and serve this right away—the difference is amazing.

Be sure to use leftover rice for this and any other fried rice dish you might make.

1. Heat the oil in a wok or large skillet over medium-high heat. Add the pineapple and onion and cook until caramelized, 5 to 10 minutes. Stir in the rice and cook until nicely colored, then stir in the bean sprouts and cabbage.

2. When the vegetables start to soften, stir in the chile, soy sauce, sesame oil, and nam pla. Taste and adjust the seasoning, then transfer to your serving bowls, top with the scallion, and serve.

Ginger Fried Rice

Makes 4 servings

½ cup rendered chicken fat or neutral oil
2 tablespoons minced garlic
2 tablespoons minced fresh ginger
Salt
2 cups thinly sliced leeks, white and pale green parts only
4 cups day-old cooked rice, preferably jasmine, at room temperature
2 teaspoons sesame oil
4 teaspoons soy sauce
1 tablespoon grape seed, corn, or other neutral oil
4 large eggs

This take on fried rice is so deeply satisfying it has become one of my new favorite dishes—really. Quick and easy, but elegant enough to serve at a dinner party.

1. Melt half the fat in a large skillet over medium heat. Add the minced garlic and ginger and season lightly with salt. Cook, stirring occasionally, until crisp and browned. Drain on paper towels and set aside.

2. Meanwhile, melt the remaining fat in a large deep skillet over medium-low heat, then add the leeks. Cook, stirring occasionally, until softened, about 10 minutes. They should be very tender, but not browned. Season to taste with salt.

3. Add the rice and cook, stirring well, until heated through. Season to taste with salt, then remove from the heat. Put a quarter of the rice into a small bowl and gently press down into the bowl. Invert the bowl onto a serving plate. The rice will unmold in a small dome. Drizzle ½ teaspoon of the sesame oil and 1 teaspoon of the soy sauce around the mound of rice. Repeat with the remaining rice.

4. Put the grape seed oil in a nonstick skillet and fry the eggs, sunny-side up, until the edges are set, but the yolk is still runny. Put the eggs on top of the mounds of rice. Top each mound of rice and egg with some of the garlic-ginger crisps and serve immediately.

Vegetable Fried Rice

Makes 4 servings

- 1/4 cup plus 2 tablespoons grape seed, corn, or other neutral oil
- 2 large eggs, lightly beaten
- 4 baby corn, trimmed and sliced
- 1 1/4 teaspoons salt, plus more to taste
- 1 1/4 teaspoons sugar, plus more to taste
- 4 choy sum stalks, trimmed and cut into 1 1/2-inch lengths
- 1 carrot, sliced
- 4 snow peas, trimmed and sliced
- 2 Chinese long beans, trimmed and cut into 1 1/2-inch lengths
- 2 Napa cabbage leaves, trimmed and sliced
- 1/4 cup green peas, preferably fresh
- 1/2 onion, sliced
- 4 asparagus stalks, trimmed and cut into 1 1/2-inch lengths
- 1/4 cup trimmed bean sprouts
- 4 cups day-old cooked rice

There is nothing flashy about this dish—just a load of fresh vegetables, stir-fried until crisp and tender, and tossed with rice. The result is intensely satisfying and comforting.

1. Heat 2 teaspoons of the oil in a wok or large skillet over medium-high heat. Add the eggs and cook, stirring, just until set. Transfer to a plate and set aside. Wipe out the wok and heat 1 teaspoon oil in the wok over high heat. Add the baby corn, season with 1/8 teaspoon of the salt and 1/8 teaspoon of the sugar, and cook, stirring, just until tender-crisp and brightly colored. Transfer to a large plate and set aside. Repeat with the remaining vegetables, cooking and seasoning each separately and setting aside on the same large plate.

2. Heat the remaining 2 tablespoons oil in the wok over medium-high heat. Add the rice, eggs, and vegetables and cook, stirring, until the rice is warmed through. Season to taste with salt and sugar, transfer to serving bowls, and serve immediately.

Singapore Noodles

Makes 4 servings

$\frac{1}{2}$ pound dried rice vermicelli, soaked in hot water until softened and drained
$\frac{1}{4}$ cup grape seed, corn, or other neutral oil, plus more as needed
2 ounces shrimp, peeled, deveined, and cut into $\frac{1}{2}$-inch dice
2 ounces boneless, skinless chicken breasts or thighs, cut into $\frac{1}{2}$-inch dice
2 ounces scallops, cut into $\frac{1}{2}$-inch dice
$\frac{1}{2}$ cup thinly sliced onion
$\frac{1}{4}$ cup thinly sliced red bell pepper
$\frac{1}{4}$ cup thinly sliced green bell pepper
Salt
1 tablespoon curry powder
1 large egg, beaten
$\frac{1}{4}$ cup trimmed bean sprouts
2 ounces crabmeat, picked over for shells and cartilage
1 tablespoon sesame seeds, toasted (see page 15)

This is street food at its best, thin noodles and vegetables, generously seasoned with curry powder and given substance with seafood and chicken. You can, of course, vary the types of protein and vegetables you use, or omit the protein altogether and make it vegetarian.

1. Bring a medium pot of water to a boil. Add the vermicelli and cook just until softened, about 1 minute, then drain immediately and set aside.

2. Heat half the oil in a medium skillet over medium-high heat. Add the shrimp and chicken and brown nicely, then add the scallops and cook, stirring occasionally, for another minute. Remove from the heat.

3. Heat the remaining 2 tablespoons oil in a large nonstick skillet over medium-high heat. Add the onion and cook until browned, then stir in the peppers. When the peppers are brightly colored and beginning to soften, add the noodles, sprinkle with salt, and toss with half the curry powder. Add more oil if necessary.

4. Push the noodle mixture to one side and crack the egg onto the other side. Let the egg sit until it is firm, about 1 minute, then toss it with the noodles, breaking it into smaller pieces. Toss in the bean sprouts, crab, remaining $1\frac{1}{2}$ teaspoons curry powder, and the shrimp mixture. Taste and adjust the curry powder and salt, garnish with sesame seeds, and serve.

Lime Noodles with Vegetables, Basil, and Sesame

Makes 4 servings

1¼ cups plus 2 tablespoons grape seed, corn, or other neutral oil
10 garlic cloves, thinly sliced
¾ cup fresh lime juice
½ cup sugar
2 cups fresh basil leaves, preferably Thai
1½ cups fresh mint leaves
¾ cup white sesame seeds, toasted (see page 15), plus more for garnish
1 tablespoon salt, plus more as needed
About ½ pound assorted vegetables: carrots, parsnips, broccoli (stems are fine), bell peppers, etc., peeled and julienned
1 pound ¼-inch-wide dried rice noodles, soaked in hot water until softened and drained
½ cup unsalted butter

A huge hit for us: spicy, sour, sweet, and herbaceous. This is among the greatest noodle dishes ever.

1. Put 3 tablespoons of the oil in a medium skillet over medium-low heat. Add the garlic and cook, stirring occasionally, until the garlic turns golden, about 10 minutes; set aside.

2. Meanwhile, combine the lime juice and sugar in a small saucepan and bring to a boil. Set aside.

3. Fill a large bowl with water and ice and set aside. Bring a small pot of water to a boil and add the basil and mint leaves. As soon as the water returns to a boil, drain the leaves and transfer to the ice water. When cold, drain again and squeeze dry. Purée in a blender with the sesame seeds, garlic, salt, and 1 cup of the oil. (This herb paste will keep, refrigerated, for 2 days.)

4. Heat the remaining 3 tablespoons oil in a skillet over high heat. Add the vegetables and some salt and cook, tossing, just until brightly colored. Keep warm.

5. Bring a large pot of water to a boil and salt it. Cook the noodles until tender, 30 seconds. Drain and transfer to a large skillet set over high heat with the butter and lime syrup; add salt to taste and cook, tossing, until well mixed and creamy. Put the noodles in a warmed serving bowl; drizzle liberally with the basil-mint paste, top with the vegetables, garnish with the sesame seeds, and serve.

Calamansi with the top →
cut off at Newton Circus
food stalls in Singapore

Pad Thai with Crab and Shrimp

Makes 4 servings

2 cups Sweet-and-Sour Sauce (page 133)
¼ cup nam pla (Thai fish sauce)
¼ cup fresh lime juice
1 tablespoon plus 1 teaspoon sugar
2 tablespoons grape seed, corn, or other neutral oil
4 garlic cloves, chopped
2 shallots, chopped
6 medium shrimp, peeled, deveined, and halved
4 ounces crabmeat, picked over for shells and cartilage
2 large eggs, lightly beaten
1 pound ¼-inch-wide dried rice noodles, soaked in hot water until softened
⅔ cup trimmed bean sprouts
2 scallions, trimmed and roughly chopped
¼ cup chopped fresh cilantro leaves, plus more for garnish
¼ cup chopped fresh basil leaves, preferably Thai plus more for garnish
⅓ cup peanuts, chopped
4 lime wedges for serving

Here, we've taken the iconic dish of American Thai restaurants and made it tastier and more beautiful, with fresh crabmeat and fresh herbs. Since this is a quick stir-fry, it's great as a one-dish meal. Your friends will rave about how your version is better than any they've eaten in a restaurant.

1. In a small bowl, stir together the Sweet-and-Sour Sauce, nam pla, lime juice, and sugar until the sugar is dissolved. Set aside.

2. Heat the oil in a wok or large skillet over medium-high heat. Add the garlic and shallots and cook until softened, about 1 minute, then add the shrimp. Cook just until pink, then stir in the crabmeat and eggs. Add the noodles and cook for 1 minute, then stir in the sauce.

3. Once everything is well coated, stir in the bean sprouts and scallions and cook until slightly softened. Stir in the cilantro, basil, and peanuts. Remove from the heat, garnish with fresh herbs and lime wedges, and serve.

Chile-Garlic Egg Noodles

Makes 4 servings

1 cup extra virgin olive oil
1 cup sliced shallots
1 cup sliced garlic
Salt
2 roasted red finger chiles, diced
2 roasted red bell peppers, diced
2½ teaspoons nam pla (Thai fish sauce)
½ cup soy sauce
½ cup honey
¼ cup sherry vinegar
2 tablespoons rice vinegar
1 pound fresh egg noodles
¼ cup chopped fresh mint leaves
¼ cup chopped fresh Thai basil leaves
½ cup chopped scallions

For years, I have seen dishes like this offered throughout Asia as one-dish lunches; it's great on its own or as an appetizer. The heat from the chiles is toned down by the honey, huge amounts of sweet shallots and garlic, and herbs. The combination of full, robust flavors makes this dish deeply satisfying.

1. Heat the oil in a heavy saucepan over low heat. Add the shallots and garlic and season lightly with salt. Cook, stirring occasionally, until the mixture bubbles, then continue to cook until the shallots are very soft, about 20 minutes. Drain the mixture through a fine-mesh sieve and transfer to a large mixing bowl. Add the chiles, peppers, and nam pla. Stir well; taste and adjust the seasoning.

2. Combine the soy sauce, honey, and vinegars in a saucepan over medium heat. Bring to a boil, stirring occasionally, then remove from the heat and cool.

3. Bring a pot of water to a boil. Add the noodles and cook until al dente, about 3 minutes, then drain and rinse quickly.

4. Put the noodles and soy-honey mixture in a large mixing bowl and toss until the noodles are well coated. To serve, put a bundle of noodles at the bottom of each serving plate. Spoon on the chile-garlic sauce, garnish with mint, basil, and scallions, and serve.

Shanghai Noodles with Golden Garlic and Soft Tofu

Makes 4 servings

1 small bunch (½ ounce) fresh Thai basil stems
1 small bunch (½ ounce) fresh mint stems
1½ cups chicken stock, preferably homemade or canned low-sodium broth
3 teaspoons salt, plus more to taste
3 tablespoons extra virgin olive oil, plus more for garnish
1 cup thinly sliced garlic
¼ cup thinly sliced fresh serrano chiles
1½ pounds fresh Shanghai noodles
1 cup fresh pea shoots
1 cup sliced fresh Thai basil leaves
One 8-ounce block soft tofu, quartered and chilled
Fleur de sel

Shanghai noodles, made with a flour-based dough, are thick and hearty. The combination of fresh herbs and cold tofu makes this dish refreshingly light. This is a great summer lunch and perfect as a vegetarian entrée.

1. Bring 1½ cups water to a boil in a large saucepan. Add the basil and mint stems, cover, and remove from the heat. Let sit for 5 minutes, then strain through a fine-mesh sieve. Return the strained liquid to the saucepan and discard the solids. Stir in the chicken stock and salt and set aside.

2. Heat the oil in a large saucepan over medium-high heat. Add the garlic and cook, stirring, until golden, about 4 minutes. Add the chiles and reserved herb stock, and turn the heat to low.

3. Bring a large pot of water to a boil. Add the noodles and cook just until tender, but still chewy, about 3 minutes. Drain, rinse under cold water just to separate the noodles, drain again, and add to the garlic mixture.

4. Stir in the pea shoots and sliced basil and remove from the heat. Divide the noodles among four serving bowls and spoon the sauce from the pan over the noodles. Top with a block of tofu, drizzle lightly with olive oil, and sprinkle with fleur de sel. Serve immediately.

Spicy Egg Noodles with Vegetables

Makes 4 servings

VEGETABLE SAUCE

¼ cup soy sauce
⅛ teaspoon salt
2 teaspoons cornstarch mixed with 1 tablespoon water
1 tablespoon grape seed, corn, or other neutral oil
4 garlic cloves, minced
½ lemongrass stalk, trimmed and minced
¼ teaspoon minced fresh green Thai chile

SPICY EGG NOODLES

Salt
1¼ pounds fresh egg noodles, preferably ⅛ inch thick
2 broccoli stems, trimmed, peeled, and julienned
8 thin asparagus stalks, trimmed, halved lengthwise, and cut into 2-inch lengths
3 tablespoons grape seed, corn, or other neutral oil
½ cup thinly sliced garlic
1 small bunch garlic chives, trimmed and cut into ½-inch lengths at an angle
2 teaspoons crushed red pepper flakes
¼ red bell pepper, stemmed, seeded, and julienned
¼ yellow bell pepper, stemmed, seeded, and julienned
¼ orange bell pepper, stemmed, seeded, and julienned
2 carrots, julienned
2 tablespoons Guilin chili sauce
2 tablespoons hoisin
½ cup white sesame seeds, toasted (see page 15)

The crisp vegetables add not only vibrant color to this dish but also a distinct freshness. The heartiness of the noodles, paired with a flavorful sauce, makes this an ideal vegetarian entrée.

1. **To make the vegetable sauce:** In a small bowl, stir together the soy sauce, salt, cornstarch mixture, and 1 cup water and set aside.

2. Heat the oil in a large saucepan over medium-high heat. Add the garlic, lemongrass, and chile and cook, stirring, until deep golden brown and fragrant, about 1 minute. Add the soy sauce mixture and bring to a boil. Remove from the heat and set aside.

3. **To make the noodles:** Bring a large pot of water to a boil; salt lightly and add the noodles. Cook just until tender, but not yet soft. Drain, rinse under cold water, and drain again. Set aside.

4. Fill a large bowl with water and ice and set aside. Bring a medium saucepan of water to a boil, salt lightly, and add the broccoli and asparagus. Cook just until tender and bright green, about 2 minutes. Drain and transfer to the ice water. When cold, drain again.

5. Heat 2 tablespoons of the oil in a small saucepan and add the garlic. Cook, stirring occasionally, until golden brown and crisp. Remove with a slotted spoon and drain on paper towels. Set aside.

6. Heat the remaining tablespoon oil in a wok or large skillet over high heat. Add the garlic chives and red pepper flakes and cook, stirring, until fragrant, about 30 seconds. Add the peppers and carrots, season lightly with salt, and cook, stirring, just until bright and tender, about 2 minutes. Add the broccoli, asparagus, noodles, vegetable sauce, chili sauce, and hoisin and cook, stirring, until everything is well mixed and warmed through. If the sauce seems too thick, add a tablespoon of water. Taste and adjust the seasoning.

7. Transfer to a serving plate and garnish with the fried garlic and sesame seeds. Serve immediately.

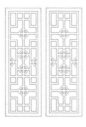

Scallion Pancakes

Makes 9 pancakes

- 1 tablespoon rice vinegar
- 1 tablespoon soy sauce
- 4 scallions, trimmed and minced, green and white parts separated
- 2 cups all-purpose flour
- 1½ teaspoons salt, plus more as needed
- 1 tablespoon grape seed, corn, or other neutral oil, plus more for frying
- 3 tablespoons sesame oil, plus more as needed

These are incredibly labor-intensive—more work than making puff pastry—but worth it, I think. Crisp, flaky, chewy, aromatic with scallions, and rich with sesame oil—the best way to serve these is to eat them one by one as you fry them.

Empty baskets at the end of the day

1. In a small bowl, whisk together the vinegar, soy sauce, half the minced white scallions, and 2 tablespoons water. Set the dipping sauce aside.

2. Combine the flour and salt in the bowl of a standing mixer with the dough hook. With the mixer running on medium-low, add the oil and 3/4 cup boiling water, then add more water as needed to make a soft, pliable dough. Divide the dough into 3 pieces and knead well on a floured board. Cover with a kitchen towel and let rest for 20 minutes.

3. Roll each piece of dough into a 6-inch-long cylinder and cut into three 2-inch pieces. Roll each piece into a circle, 6 inches in diameter. Brush each circle with sesame oil and sprinkle with the remaining scallions. Roll up each circle as you would a jelly roll and seal the edges. Slightly flatten the dough, then coil like a snail and seal the end. Flatten the dough with the palm of your hand. Repeat this process: roll, flatten, coil, and flatten again.

4. Let the pancakes rest, covered, for 20 minutes, then flatten with your hand and roll out into a thin, flat circle. Stack the pancakes between floured sheets of parchment paper.

5. Pour oil to a depth of 1/4 inch in a large skillet and place over medium-high heat. Add a pancake and fry until crisp, then turn and fry the other side until crisp. Drain on paper towels and repeat with the remaining pancakes. Cut each pancake into quarters and serve with the reserved dipping sauce.

Egg Noodle Pancake

Makes 4 servings

Salt

¾ pound thin fresh egg noodles (lo mein)

¼ cup minced chives

2 tablespoons chili garlic sauce

3 tablespoons grape seed, corn, or other neutral oil, plus more as needed

This pancake serves as the base for squab (see page 188), but goes well with any poultry dish and is the perfect bottom layer for many stir-fries. Kids especially will enjoy eating it alone.

1. Bring a large pot of water to a boil and salt it. Add the noodles and cook for 3 minutes. Drain, rinse under cold water, and drain again.

2. In a large bowl, toss the noodles with the chives, chili garlic sauce, 1 tablespoon of the oil, and salt; taste and adjust the seasoning as necessary. (I make this pancake fairly fiery, but you need not.)

3. Film the bottom of a heavy 8-inch skillet, preferably nonstick, with the remaining 2 tablespoons oil and turn the heat to medium-high. When the oil shimmers, add the noodle mix. Spread it out evenly and press it down a little with your hands or the back of a spatula.

4. Cook for 2 minutes, then turn the heat down a bit and continue to cook until the cake is holding together and is nicely browned on the bottom, about 10 minutes more. Turn, adding a little more oil if necessary. (The easiest way to do this: Slide the cake out onto a plate, cover with another plate, invert the plates, and slide the cake back into the pan.)

5. Cook on the other side until brown, then serve hot or at room temperature.

**Sweet crepes filled with banana →
and drizzled with condensed milk**

DESSERTS

Coconut and Tapioca Parfait with Tropical Fruits

Makes 6 servings

PALM SUGAR-ROASTED PINEAPPLE

1 pineapple, peeled, cored, and diced
1 cup palm sugar
1 vanilla bean, halved lengthwise and seeds scraped
¼ teaspoon salt
½ teaspoon fresh lime zest

LIME FROZEN YOGURT

2 cups whole milk
2 cups granulated sugar
¼ teaspoon salt
2 cups plain whole-milk yogurt
2 limes
¼ cup Meyer's rum

2½ cups coconut milk
¾ cup palm sugar
1 vanilla bean, halved lengthwise and seeds scraped
Salt
2 cups large pearl tapioca, preferably ¼-inch-diameter pearls
1 cup whole milk
1 cup diced cantaloupe or papaya
1 mango, peeled and diced
4 kiwis, peeled and diced
⅓ cup chopped fresh mint leaves

A treat often found on the streets of Southeast Asia, Taiwan, and Hong Kong, this dessert-with-a-straw is given a wonderful boost by the addition of vanilla and mint. You can omit the palm sugar-roasted pineapple if you don't have the time, but it is truly wonderful. Finish with any fruit, from fresh cherries to chopped peaches; the coconut tapioca goes with just about anything.

1. **To make the pineapple:** Put the diced pineapple, palm sugar, vanilla (both seeds and pod), and salt in a large skillet and set over high heat.

2. Cook, stirring occasionally, until the sugar melts. Turn the heat down to low and simmer, stirring every 10 minutes, until the mixture is dry, about 40 minutes. The mixture should simmer continuously, but not burn. When done, the mixture will be deep golden brown.

3. Remove from the heat and cool in the skillet. Add the lime zest and continue to cool to room temperature. Remove and discard the vanilla pod. Transfer the mixture to a bowl, cover, and refrigerate for at least 2 hours.

4. **To make the frozen yogurt:** Put the milk, granulated sugar, and salt in a large saucepan and set over medium heat. Stir constantly until the sugar melts. Remove from the heat and whisk in the yogurt.

5. Zest the limes directly into the mixture, then juice the limes into the mixture, straining out any seeds. Whisk in the rum until everything is well combined. Transfer to a

mixing bowl and chill in the refrigerator (or over a bowl of ice, which is faster). If time allows, cover and refrigerate overnight. Transfer the mixture to an ice cream machine and freeze according to the manufacturer's instructions.

6. Bring the coconut milk, palm sugar, vanilla (both seeds and pod), and a pinch of salt to a boil in a large saucepan. Turn the heat to low and simmer, stirring occasionally, until the sugar melts, about 5 minutes. Transfer to a medium mixing bowl and set aside.

7. Bring a large pot of water to a boil and add a pinch of salt. Add the tapioca and cook, stirring, until the water returns to a rapid boil. Continue cooking and stirring until the tapioca is almost clear, about 10 minutes. The tapioca should be tender, but still chewy. Drain, rinse under cold water, drain again, and immediately transfer to the coconut soup. Stir in the milk.

8. Fill a large bowl with ice and water and set the tapioca mixture over it to cool. When cool, stir in the roasted pineapple, cantaloupe or papaya, mango, kiwi, and mint. Mix well, remove the vanilla pod, and transfer the mixture to tall serving cups. Top with a scoop of the lime frozen yogurt and serve immediately with a fat straw and spoon.

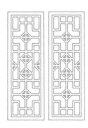

Coconut Panna Cotta with Exotic Fruit Salad

Makes 6 servings

SIMPLE SUGAR SYRUP

1½ cups sugar

COCONUT PANNA COTTA

1¼ cups whole milk

¾ cup unsweetened grated coconut

¼ cup plus 2 tablespoons sugar

2¼ gelatin sheets, soaked in cold water until softened and drained, or 2 teaspoons powdered gelatin softened in 1½ tablespoons cold water

¼ teaspoon vanilla extract

1½ cups heavy cream

SORBET AND SALAD

1 cup passion fruit purée

¼ pineapple, peeled, cored, and diced

2 mangoes, peeled, pitted, and diced

1 vanilla bean, halved lengthwise and seeds scraped

2 kiwis, peeled and sliced

½ pint strawberries, stemmed and sliced

2 tablespoons passion fruit seeds

2 tablespoons sliced fresh mint leaves

Substituing coconut milk for the usual cream transforms traditional panna cotta into a thrilling new sweet. The nutty overtones from the coconut milk are perfect with the colorful array of tropical fruit. Use any fruit you like, as long as it is fresh and sweet.

1. **To make the syrup:** Put the sugar in a medium saucepan with 1½ cups water. Bring the mixture to a boil, stirring to dissolve the sugar, and boil until clear and slightly thickened, about 7 minutes. Remove from the heat and cool completely.

2. **To make the panna cotta:** Bring the milk, coconut, and ¼ cup of the sugar to a boil in a medium saucepan, stirring occasionally, about 5 minutes. Remove from the heat and steep until the mixture is room temperature.

3. Fill a large bowl with water and ice and set aside. Bring the coconut milk mixture back to a boil and stir in the gelatin until it melts. Whisk in the vanilla and the remaining 2 tablespoons sugar and strain through a fine-mesh sieve into a medium mixing bowl. Set the bowl over the ice water bath. Set aside until cool.

4. Meanwhile, whisk the cream in a large bowl to medium-soft peaks. Whisk the coconut milk mixture into the cream until well incorporated. Divide the mixture among 6 ceramic ramekins and refrigerate until set, about 2 hours.

5. **To make the sorbet:** Stir 1 cup of the sugar syrup with the passion fruit purée and 1 cup water until well

blended. Transfer the mixture to an ice cream machine and freeze according to the manufacturer's instructions.

6. **To make the salad:** Put the remaining sugar syrup in a bowl with the pineapple, mango, and vanilla seeds. Toss gently until everything is well combined.

7. When ready to serve, run a thin-bladed knife around the edge of each ramekin and unmold the panna cottas onto serving plates. Put a scoop of the passion fruit sorbet next to the panna cotta and spoon the pineapple mixture all around. Top with the kiwi, strawberries, passion fruit seeds, and mint. Serve immediately.

Here I am with a very unusual-looking pineapple at the Aw Taw Kaw weekend market in Bangkok

Passion Fruit Soufflé

Makes 6 servings

1 tablespoon unsalted butter
1 cup sugar, plus more for sprinkling
½ cup pastry cream powder
1½ cups passion fruit purée
1 cup whole milk
7 large egg whites

Passion fruit is a great flavor for soufflés, making this sweet-tart dessert light and rich. Though you must bake these immediately before serving, you can make the batter and fill the ramekins ahead of time and refrigerate, uncovered, for up to 8 hours. This makes it an ideal dessert for my restaurants and for your home.

1. Preheat the oven to 350°F. Generously butter and sugar six 3-ounce ramekins, including the tops of the rims.

2. Put the pastry cream powder in a saucepan. Add ¼ cup of the passion fruit purée and whisk until the mixture is pasty. Add the milk and whisk until the powder has dissolved. Finally, add the remaining 1¼ cups passion fruit purée and whisk until well combined.

3. Set the saucepan over low heat and cook, whisking continuously. As soon as the mixture thickens and forms ribbons, remove it from the heat. The mixture should be completely smooth without any lumps. (If there are lumps, strain the mixture.) Transfer to a large mixing bowl and let cool until just warm, then cover with plastic wrap, pressing the plastic directly on the surface.

4. Put ¼ cup plus 1 tablespoon water in a medium saucepan and add 1 cup sugar. With a clean pastry brush, use the water to wash down the sides of the saucepan, making sure there are no residual sugar granules. Set the saucepan over low heat and cook, undisturbed, until the sugar reaches the hard-ball stage, about 118°F.

5. Meanwhile, put the egg whites in the bowl of an electric mixer. Whisk at medium speed until soft peaks form. When the cooked sugar syrup reaches 118°F, turn the mixer speed to high, and add the syrup to the egg whites in a slow, steady stream along the side of the mixer bowl. After all the cooked sugar has been added, turn the speed to low and continue whisking until the mixture cools slightly. You can test the temperature by feeling the bowl; it should be warm.

6. Remove the plastic wrap from the pastry cream and whisk in a quarter of the egg white mixture. When well combined, add the remaining egg whites and fold in gently. When everything is well combined, fill the ramekins to above the rim and make a peak in the center. Put the ramekins on a baking sheet, transfer to the oven, and bake for 7 minutes. The soufflés should rise about 2 inches above the rim and have a nice caramelized top. Serve immediately.

Roaming the aisles at the Aw Taw Kaw weekend market in Bangkok

Passion Fruit Pavlova

Makes 6 servings

PASSION FRUIT SORBET
¾ cup granulated sugar
3 cups passion fruit purée

MERINGUE
8 large egg whites
1 cup granulated sugar
2 cups confectioners' sugar

½ cup heavy cream
½ cup passion fruit seeds

Pavlova, Australia's national dessert, is essentially a meringue cup filled with ice cream and whipped cream. Passion fruit is often the flavor of choice and I've chosen to stick with that tasty tradition here.

1. **To make the sorbet:** Put the granulated sugar in a medium saucepan with 1 cup water. Bring the mixture to a boil, stirring occasionally. Remove from the heat and stir in the passion fruit purée. Transfer to a mixing bowl and cool in the refrigerator (or over a bowl of ice, which is faster) until completely chilled. Transfer the mixture to an ice cream machine and freeze according to the manufacturer's instructions.

2. **To make the meringue:** Preheat the oven to 200°F.

3. Put the egg whites in the bowl of an electric mixer. Whisk at medium speed until soft peaks form. With the machine running, add the granulated sugar in a slow, steady stream. When the whites are stiff, gently fold in the confectioners' sugar.

4. Spoon the mixture evenly, to a thickness of ¼ inch, into half-circle silicone molds, 3½ inches in diameter and 1⅝ inches deep. (If you do not have silicone demi-sphere molds, you can use 4-ounce ceramic ramekins.) You want the meringue to resemble small cups or bowls when baked.

(continued)

5. Bake until completely dry, about 2 hours. Remove from the oven, unmold carefully, and cool completely in a dry place on a rack.

6. While the meringue is cooling, put the cream in the bowl of an electric mixer. Whisk at medium speed until medium-soft peaks form.

7. Put a small mound of cream in the center of each serving dish. Gently press a meringue cup onto the cream and put a scoop of the passion fruit sorbet into each cup. Top with another cup, garnish with the passion fruit seeds, and serve immediately.

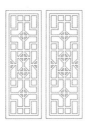

Thai Jewels and Fruits on Crushed Coconut Ice

Makes 6 servings

Phenomenal in taste and appearance, this complex dessert contains bizarre ingredients and techniques, though at its heart is an assortment of different fruits. (There's some shopping to do, but you can find these unusual ingredients in most well-stocked Thai or Chinese markets.) Water chestnuts—considered a fruit in Thailand—are the real attraction here. Mango, passion fruit, kiwi, Asian pear, or pomegranate seeds can be substituted for any of the fruits below. In any case, the goal is different shapes, textures, and colors that match well.

MALI SAUCE

¾ cup palm sugar
1 vanilla bean, halved lengthwise and seeds scraped
Salt
1 tablespoon mali syrup

COCONUT SAUCE

3½ cups coconut milk
2 vanilla beans, halved lengthwise and seeds scraped
1 cup granulated sugar
1 teaspoon salt
1 cup whole milk

9 ounces fresh water chestnuts, peeled and cut into ¼-inch dice (about 2 cups)
½ cup red sala syrup, preferably Hale's Blue Boy brand, available in Thai markets
1½ teaspoons green pandan paste, preferably Koepoe-Koepoe brand
Salt
3 cups tapioca starch
Two 10½-ounce bottles coconut juice, preferably Bangkok Market brand
1 cup palm seeds, rinsed and quartered
1 cup thinly sliced jackfruit
1 cup diced red papaya

1. **To make the mali sauce:** Put the palm sugar, vanilla (both seeds and pod), and a pinch of salt in a medium saucepan with 1 cup water. Set over medium heat and cook, stirring occasionally, until the sugar is melted. The mixture does not need to come to a boil.

2. Remove from the heat, stir in the mali syrup, and cool to room temperature. Set aside.

3. **To make the coconut sauce:** Put the coconut milk, vanilla (both seeds and pod), granulated sugar, and salt in a medium saucepan over medium heat. Cook, stirring occasionally, until the sugar is completely dissolved.

4. Remove from the heat and stir in the milk and ⅓ cup of the mali sauce. Set aside to cool to room temperature. Remove the vanilla pods.

(continued)

5. Meanwhile, divide the water chestnuts between 2 mixing bowls. Add the red sala syrup to one bowl and the green pandan paste to the other. Mix well to coat and color the water chestnuts. Let sit for at least 10 minutes, or cover and refrigerate for as long as overnight.

6. Drain the water chestnuts into 2 separate colanders and reserve the soaking liquid, keeping the colors separate. Add ⅓ cup mali sauce to each bowl of reserved liquid and mix well. Set aside.

7. Fill 2 large bowls with water and ice and set aside. Bring a large pot of water to a boil and add a pinch of salt. Meanwhile, toss the red water chestnuts with half the tapioca starch in a colander. Shake vigorously not only to coat well but also to remove any excess starch, which can cause clumping. Add the red water chestnuts to the boiling water and cook, stirring occasionally, until they float to the surface, about 10 minutes. Drain, transfer to an ice water bath, and cool completely. Drain again and transfer to the red mali sauce. Repeat with the green water chestnuts, putting them in the green mali sauce at the end. Set aside.

8. Remove the pieces of coconut from the coconut juice and slice. Set aside. Transfer the coconut juice to a sturdy, large Ziploc bag and freeze. When completely frozen, pound the frozen juice until it becomes finely crushed ice.

9. Drain the red and green water chestnuts and combine in a large mixing bowl. Add the coconut meat, palm seeds, jackfruit, and red papaya and toss well. Divide the coconut ice among the serving bowls. Top with the fruit, then pour the coconut sauce and reserved mali sauce, to taste, over to cover the ice and fruit. Serve immediately with a spoon.

Thai Sundae

Makes 6 servings

RICE PUDDING ICE CREAM

1⅓ cups whole milk
⅓ cup sugar
1 tablespoon jasmine rice, washed well and drained
2 large egg yolks
⅓ cup heavy cream
½ vanilla bean, halved lengthwise and seeds scraped

RICE CRISPIES

Nonstick cooking spray, as needed
2 tablespoons sugar
¾ cup Rice Krispies cereal

CHOCOLATE CREAM

2 large egg yolks
1 tablespoon plus 1 teaspoon sugar
¼ cup whole milk
¼ cup heavy cream
2¼ ounces bittersweet chocolate, chopped

ESPRESSO GRANITÉ

¼ cup strong brewed espresso
1½ tablespoons Simple Sugar Syrup (page 246)

¾ cup freshly whipped cream

This sophisticated sundae looks beautiful in martini glasses and the combination of different flavors makes it exotic and fun to eat. If you are making the ice cream yourself, it is best to build the sundae immediately after the ice cream comes out of the ice cream machine. Otherwise, substitute high-quality vanilla ice cream and soften it slightly.

1. **To make the ice cream:** Bring ¾ cup of the milk and 1 teaspoon of the sugar to a boil over medium heat in a medium saucepan. Add the rice, turn the heat to low, and simmer the mixture until the rice is tender, about 5 minutes. The mixture should still be a little wet. Transfer to a large mixing bowl, cool completely, and chill in the refrigerator (or over a bowl of ice, which is faster).

2. Whisk together the egg yolks and remaining sugar in a large mixing bowl until pale yellow and thick. Set aside.

3. Bring the cream, vanilla (both seeds and pod), and remaining milk to a boil in a large saucepan. Remove from the heat and set aside for 15 minutes. Return to the heat. When bubbles begin to form around the edges of the pan, pour a third of the hot cream onto the egg yolk mixture, whisking constantly, until well incorporated. Return that mixture to the saucepan, whisking constantly. Set the mixture over low heat and cook, stirring, until thick enough to coat the back of a spoon, about 15 minutes. Strain the custard through a fine-mesh sieve into a large mixing bowl and chill in the refrigerator (or over a bowl of ice, which is faster).

4. Put the rice pudding in the back or bottom of an ice cream machine, then add the custard. Freeze according to the manufacturer's instructions.

5. **To make the crispies:** Spray a baking sheet with the cooking spray and set aside.

6. Put the sugar in a small saucepan and set over medium heat. Cook, undisturbed, until it becomes light golden brown. Remove from the heat and immediately, and carefully, stir in the cereal. When the cereal is well coated, transfer it to the prepared baking sheet and spread in a thin even layer.

7. When the mixture starts to cool, separate the cereal into individual granules. Cool completely until crisp.

8. **To make the chocolate cream:** Whisk together the egg yolks and sugar in a large mixing bowl and set aside. Warm the milk and cream in a large saucepan over high heat until bubbles form around the edges of the pan. Pour half of the milk mixture onto the yolk mixture, whisking constantly, until well incorporated. Return that mixture to the saucepan, set over low heat, and cook, whisking constantly, until thickened slightly, about 3 minutes.

9. Add the chocolate to the saucepan and whisk until melted and nicely combined. Remove the saucepan from the heat and continue to whisk until smooth. Cool slightly, then put 3 tablespoons of the chocolate cream into each of six martini glasses. The cream should come one-third of the way up the sides. Transfer the glasses to the refrigerator until the cream is cool and firm.

10. **To make the granité:** Put the espresso, syrup, and ¼ cup water into a 13 x 9-inch shallow baking dish. Mix well and transfer to the freezer. Freeze, whisking the mixture thoroughly every 5 minutes, until frozen and nicely aerated into ice shavings.

11. When the chocolate cream has cooled, scoop 3 heaping tablespoons of rice pudding ice cream on top of the chocolate and smooth to form an even surface. Top the ice cream with 2 heaping tablespoons of the espresso granité, then spoon 2 large dollops of whipped cream atop that and smooth across the top of the glass. Garnish with 1 heaping tablespoon of the rice crispies and serve.

Warm Rice Pudding and Passion Fruit Sherbet

Makes 6 servings

PASSION FRUIT SHERBET
2 cups passion fruit purée
¼ cup fresh orange juice
3 ripe bananas, peeled and roughly chopped
1⅓ cups sugar
1 teaspoon salt

RICE PUDDING
1 cup whole milk
1 cup skim milk
1 cup thick coconut milk
1 cinnamon stick
1 vanilla bean, halved lengthwise and seeds scraped
1 teaspoon salt
1¼ cups jasmine rice, washed well and drained
1 cup sugar
¼ cup raisins, soaked in warm water and drained
1¼ cups heavy cream
1 teaspoon fresh lime zest

1 tablespoon passion fruit seeds

This is a classic combination of Thai flavors—bitter, sour, salty, and sweet—in a dessert. (The lime zest provides a subtle bitter overtone.)

You can make the rice pudding ahead of time and refrigerate it until ready to serve. Bring the pudding to room temperature and then torch the sugar and add the passion fruit sherbet and seeds immediately before serving.

1. **To make the sherbet:** Put the ingredients and 1¾ cups water into a large saucepan and set over medium-low heat. Bring to a steady simmer and cook, stirring occasionally, for 5 minutes.

2. Remove from the heat and transfer to a blender. Blend until smooth, then transfer to a mixing bowl and chill in the refrigerator (or over a bowl of ice, which is faster), stirring occasionally, until cold. Transfer the chilled mixture to an ice cream machine and freeze according to the manufacturer's instructions.

3. **To make the rice pudding:** Bring the milks, coconut milk, cinnamon, vanilla (both seeds and pod), and salt to a boil in a large saucepan. Add the rice to the boiling coconut milk mixture and stir well. Scrape the bottom of the saucepan to make sure none of the rice sticks. Turn the heat to low and simmer, uncovered, stirring occasionally, until the mixture is dry and all the liquid has been absorbed into the rice, about 30 minutes. Do not let the mixture brown at all.

(continued)

4. Remove from the heat and immediately stir in $\frac{2}{3}$ cup of the sugar until it melts. Stir in the raisins and set aside to cool.

5. Meanwhile, whisk the cream to soft peaks. When the rice pudding has completely cooled, fold in the whipped cream and lime zest. Do not fold in the cream until the pudding has cooled, or the cream will collapse. The rice pudding should now be loose, with the rice kernels separated. Remove the vanilla pod and cinnamon stick.

6. Divide the rice pudding among six serving bowls and tap the bowls against a counter so that the pudding is even across the top. Sprinkle about 1 tablespoon sugar over each bowl and torch the sugar until it caramelizes to a deep golden brown. Spoon the passion fruit seeds over the rice pudding and serve the passion fruit sherbet on the side.

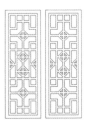

Seasonal Fruit Plate with Lime-Spiced Salt

Makes 6 servings

½ cup raw sugar, such as Muscovado
½ fresh red finger chile or 2 fresh red Thai chiles, seeded and minced
1 teaspoon fresh lime zest
1 tablespoon fleur de sel
¼ cup granulated sugar
½ pineapple, peeled, cored, and sliced
1 papaya, peeled, seeded, and sliced
2 kiwis, peeled and quartered
1 mango, peeled, seeded, and sliced
2 apples, peeled, cored, and sliced

Fruit plates are a popular dessert throughout Asia. Here, the standard is spiced up with a salty-spicy-sweet dip. You can really use any fruits here—choose whatever is in season. The ones listed here are simply suggestions.

1. Mix the raw sugar, chile, and lime zest in a mixing bowl. Stir in the fleur de sel and granulated sugar. This mixture will keep in an airtight container for up to 2 days, but will lose its aroma over time.

2. Serve the mixture in individual dipping dishes accompanied by the fruit. Instruct your guests to dip the fruit in the mixture and enjoy.

Chocolate and Vietnamese Coffee Tart with Condensed Milk Ice Cream

Makes two 10-inch tarts, about 12 servings

CONDENSED MILK ICE CREAM

2 cups whole milk
½ teaspoon salt
6 large egg yolks
¾ cup sweetened condensed milk

VIETNAMESE COFFEE SAUCE

½ cup sweetened condensed milk
1½ tablespoons brewed espresso or 2 teaspoons Trabelit coffee extract
¼ teaspoon salt

TART DOUGH

½ cup unsalted butter, at room temperature, plus more for greasing the pan
1¾ cups all-purpose flour, plus more for dusting
¼ cup almond flour
¼ cup cocoa powder
1 cup confectioners' sugar
¼ teaspoon salt
1 large egg
Nonstick vegetable oil spray

CHOCOLATE-COFFEE GANACHE

12 ounces semisweet or bittersweet chocolate, chopped
1¾ cups heavy cream
½ cup evaporated milk
⅓ cup Vietnamese or Café du Monde ground coffee
½ teaspoon salt
2 large eggs
¼ cup Trimoline or sweetened condensed milk

Beautifully dark and rich, this tart has a silky coffee ganache filling. The light, flaky crust is the perfect complement—not too sweet, but still chocolaty. If you don't have time to make the sauce and ice cream, you can serve this with fresh whipped cream or good vanilla ice cream.

1. **To make the ice cream:** Warm the whole milk and salt in a medium saucepan over medium heat just until bubbles begin to form around the edges. Whisk the yolks until broken and add a third of the warm milk in a slow, steady stream, whisking constantly. Return that mixture to the saucepan and cook over low heat, stirring constantly, until the mixture is thick enough to coat the back of a spoon.

2. Remove from the heat and stir in the sweetened condensed milk. Strain through a fine-mesh sieve into a bowl and cool in the refrigerator (or over a bowl of ice, which is faster). Transfer to an ice cream machine and freeze according to the manufacturer's instructions.

3. **To make the sauce:** Stir the ingredients together until well incorporated. Chill in the refrigerator until thickened.

4. **To make the dough:** Put the butter, flour, almond flour, cocoa powder, confectioners' sugar, and salt in a food processor and pulse until the mixture resembles cornmeal. With the machine running, add the egg and process just until the mixture comes together.

5. Transfer the dough to a large sheet of plastic wrap and pat into two 1-inch-thick circles. Cover tightly with 2 sheets of plastic wrap and chill in the refrigerator until firm, at least 4 hours and preferably overnight.

6. Unwrap the dough and transfer to a lightly floured work surface. Roll out one disk of the dough, turning it occasionally, until it is ⅛ inch thick. Use non-stick vegetable oil spray to grease a 10-inch round tart pan and transfer the dough to the pan. Trim the edges, brush off any excess flour from the dough, and cover with plastic wrap. Transfer to the freezer and freeze for at least 30 minutes, or as long as overnight. Repeat with the other piece of dough.

7. Preheat the oven to 325°F and position a rack in the bottom of the oven.

8. Poke holes all over the frozen dough using a fork. Line the dough with parchment paper and fill with pie weights, or use rice or dried beans. Bake for 15 minutes, remove the weights and parchment, and bake until the dough is dry to the touch, about 5 more minutes. Cool completely on a rack. Keep the oven on and turn the heat down to 275°F.

9. **Meanwhile, make the ganache:** Put the chocolate in a large mixing bowl and set aside. Bring the cream, evaporated milk, coffee, and salt to a simmer over low heat in a small saucepan. Strain through a fine-mesh sieve over the chocolate and whisk the mixture immediately.

10. Once the chocolate has melted and become smooth and shiny, whisk in the eggs, one at a time, until smooth. Whisk in the sweetened condensed milk until well incorporated and smooth. Set aside.

11. Pour the ganache into the cooled tart shells, smooth out the top, and bake for 10 minutes, then turn the pans and bake for 10 more minutes. The middle should still jiggle slightly, but not be wet. Remove from the oven and cool completely.

12. To serve: Cut the tarts into wedges. Spoon some coffee sauce on each serving plate, set the tarts beside it, and put a scoop of the ice cream on the other side. Serve immediately.

Ovaltine Kulfi with Caramelized Banana and Spiced Milk Chocolate Sauce

Makes 12 servings

SPICED CARAMEL POPCORN

¼ cup unsalted butter
½ teaspoon salt
½ teaspoon baking soda
1 cup plus 2 tablespoons sugar
1 tablespoon glucose or corn syrup
1 tablespoon fresh lemon juice
5½ cups unbuttered, unsalted popcorn
¼ cup mukwa, Indian-spiced candied fennel seeds

OVALTINE KULFI

4 cups heavy cream
1 vanilla bean, halved lengthwise and seeds scraped
1 teaspoon salt
1 cup Ovaltine powder
14 ounces milk chocolate, chopped

5 baby bananas
3 tablespoons plus 1 teaspoon sugar

SPICED MILK CHOCOLATE SAUCE

¾ cup evaporated milk
¼ cup sweetened condensed milk
½ cinnamon stick
½ vanilla bean, halved lengthwise and seeds scraped
¼ teaspoon salt
¼ gelatin sheet, soaked in cold water until softened and drained, or ½ teaspoon powdered gelatin, softened in 1 teaspoon cold water
5 ounces milk chocolate, chopped

CARAMEL SAUCE

¾ cup heavy cream
½ vanilla bean, halved lengthwise and seeds scraped
¼ teaspoon salt
½ cup sugar
1½ teaspoons fresh lemon juice
1½ teaspoons unsalted butter

Sort of like a high-class Nestlé Crunch ice cream bar, this treat is fun to eat, yet sophisticated. Kulfi, a frozen popsicle-type treat from South Asia, is given a new world twist here with the addition of Ovaltine. The subtle malt and chocolate flavors make this rich and satisfying.

(continued)

1. **To make the popcorn:** Preheat the oven to 275°F. Line a rimmed baking sheet with a Silpat.

2. Put the butter, salt, and baking soda in a small bowl and mix well; set aside. Put the sugar and glucose in a large skillet and wet with the lemon juice and 2 tablespoons water. Set over high heat and stir until well combined. Cook, undisturbed, until the mixture begins to color, about 3 minutes. Continue to cook, stirring occasionally, until it becomes deep golden brown. Remove from the heat and carefully stir in the butter mixture. Add the popcorn and stir well to coat.

3. Transfer the popcorn to the prepared baking sheet and spread in a single even layer. Bake until dry, about 10 minutes. Remove from the oven and stir carefully. Bake for another 10 minutes, then remove from the oven and stir again. Cool completely so that the caramel dries and hardens.

4. Toss the popcorn with the mukwa. Set aside in an airtight container.

5. **To make the kulfi:** Bring the cream, vanilla (both seeds and pod), and salt to a steady simmer over medium heat in a large saucepan. Cook, stirring occasionally, until the cream has thickened and reduced by about half, about 45 minutes. Vigorously whisk in the Ovaltine powder until the mixture is smooth, then remove from the heat and add the chocolate. Stir until the chocolate melts. The mixture should be totally smooth and have a fudgelike consistency.

6. Strain the mixture through a fine-mesh sieve and immediately transfer to a rimmed half-sheet pan. Cover with plastic wrap and transfer to the freezer. Freeze until almost set, about 45 minutes, then cut into 4 X 1-inch rectangles. Continue to freeze until the mixture is completely hard.

7. Peel and halve the baby bananas lengthwise. Put the halves between sheets of plastic wrap and flatten to 1/4 inch thick. Transfer to the freezer and freeze until hardened.

8. **To make the chocolate sauce:** Bring the evaporated milk, sweetened condensed milk, cinnamon, vanilla (both seeds and pod), and salt to a steady simmer over medium-low heat in a large saucepan. Cook, whisking constantly, for 2 minutes.

9. Remove from the heat, add the softened gelatin, and stir until it melts. Add the chocolate and stir until it melts. Strain through a fine-mesh sieve into a bowl, cover with plastic wrap, and chill in the refrigerator.

10. **To make the caramel sauce:** Warm the cream, vanilla (both seeds and pod), and salt over low heat in a large saucepan. Meanwhile, put the sugar in a small saucepan and wet with the lemon juice. Set over medium heat and cook, undisturbed, until it becomes dark golden brown, about 7 minutes.

11. Lower the heat under the caramel and very carefully ladle in a spoonful of the warm cream. Whisk to combine, then ladle in another spoonful. Continue, whisking constantly, until all the cream has been incorporated. Do not splatter; the caramel is very hot. Whisk in the butter, then remove from the heat and set aside to cool. When cool, remove the vanilla pod.

12. When ready to serve, remove the bananas from the freezer, unwrap, and place on a cookie sheet. Sprinkle each banana with 1 teaspoon sugar and torch or place under the broiler until caramelized. Transfer the Ovaltine kulfi to the serving plates, top with the 6 banana slices, garnish with the popcorn, and spoon the caramel sauce and chocolate sauce on the side. Serve immediately.

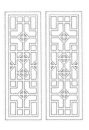

Caramelized Banana Cake with Crunchy Praline and Caramel Ice Cream

Makes 12 servings

CARAMEL ICE CREAM

1 cup heavy cream
1 cup whole milk
¼ vanilla bean, halved lengthwise and seeds scraped
⅔ cup sugar
4 large egg yolks
½ teaspoon sea salt

BANANA CHIPS

2 ripe bananas, puréed until smooth
1 tablespoon plus 1 teaspoon sugar

PRALINE CRUNCH

½ cup praline paste, preferably Valrhona
2 tablespoons roughly chopped bittersweet chocolate
1 cup chopped feuilletine pieces
2 tablespoons hazelnuts

CHOCOLATE SAUCE

¼ cup corn syrup
2 tablespoons glucose or corn syrup
2 tablespoons grape seed, canola, or other neutral oil
¾ cup heavy cream
8 ounces bittersweet chocolate, roughly chopped
¼ cup whole milk

BANANA CAKE

1 cup plus 2 tablespoons all-purpose flour
⅓ cup hazelnut flour
½ teaspoon baking powder
½ teaspoon baking soda
½ teaspoon salt
¾ cup unsalted butter, plus more for greasing the pan
1⅓ cups sugar, plus more for garnish
2 large eggs
½ cup plus 2 tablespoons sour cream
1 banana, puréed until smooth, plus 2 bananas, sliced, for garnish

Here, the humble banana is transformed into a rich cake and crisp chips. With a crunchy chocolate praline and complex caramel ice cream, this dessert is heavenly. The cake is also good on its own if you want a quick weeknight dessert.

1. **To make the ice cream:** Bring the cream, milk, and vanilla (both seeds and pod) to a light boil in a medium saucepan and remove from the heat. Stir together the sugar and 2 tablespoons water in a small saucepan and set over medium heat. Cook, shaking the pan occasionally, until the mixture becomes deep amber. Remove from the heat.

2. Whisk the eggs in a medium mixing bowl just until broken and add the warm cream mixture in a slow, steady stream while whisking constantly; repeat with the

caramel. Add the salt, then strain through a fine-mesh sieve into a bowl and cool in the refrigerator (or over a bowl of ice, which is faster). Transfer to an ice cream machine and freeze according to the manufacturer's instructions.

3. **To make the banana chips:** Preheat the oven to 200°F. Line a rimmed baking sheet with a Silpat.

4. Spread the puréed banana on the Silpat in a thin, even layer. Sprinkle with the sugar and bake until dried and hard, about 1 hour. Cool completely in the pan.

5. **To make the praline:** Line a rimmed baking sheet with a Silpat. Put the praline paste and chocolate in a double boiler or heatproof mixing bowl set over a saucepan of simmering water. Warm, stirring occasionally, until melted. Add the feuilletine and hazelnuts and stir well. Spread the mixture on the Silpat in a thin, even layer. Chill, uncovered, in the refrigerator until set. Roughly chop and keep refrigerated until ready to serve.

6. **To make the chocolate sauce:** Bring the corn syrup, glucose, oil, and ¼ cup of the cream to a boil in a medium saucepan set over medium-high heat. Remove from the heat and add the chocolate. Let sit for 1 minute, then stir until the chocolate is completely melted. Add the milk and remaining ½ cup cream and stir until smooth. Set aside at room temperature until ready to serve.

7. **To make the cake:** Preheat the oven to 325°F. Lightly butter a rimmed quarter-sheet pan or a 13 x 9-inch cake pan. Line with parchment paper and butter the parchment.

8. Sift the flours, baking powder, baking soda, and salt together; set aside. Cream the butter and sugar together in an electric mixer fitted with the paddle attachment at high speed for 12 minutes. Add the eggs, one at a time, then turn the speed to medium-low and slowly add the sifted dry ingredients. Add the sour cream and mix just until everything is combined.

9. Gently fold in the puréed banana and spread the batter in the prepared pan. Bake until the cake is dark brown and a tester inserted in the center comes out clean, about 30 minutes. Cool for 5 minutes in the pan, then invert onto a cooling rack, peel off the parchment paper, and cool completely.

10. When the cake has cooled, use a 3-inch round biscuit cutter to cut the cake into 12 circles. Put a round of cake in the center of a serving plate and top with a single layer of banana slices. Sprinkle the

banana slices with sugar and torch to caramelize the sugar to a golden brown color. Repeat with the remaining cake rounds.

11. Mound 2 tablespoons of the praline crunch next to the cake. Top the praline with a scoop of the caramel ice cream and garnish the ice cream with the banana chips. Spoon the chocolate sauce all around. Serve immediately.

Banana bud at a local street market

Vietnamese Coffee Ice Cream

Makes about 1 quart

¾ cup whole milk
1 vanilla bean, halved lengthwise and seeds scraped
¼ teaspoon salt
3¼ cups heavy cream
1¼ cups sugar
¼ cup Vietnamese or Café du Monde ground coffee
7 large egg yolks

I love drinking Vietnamese coffee, but I enjoy it even more in this frozen form. If you can't find Vietnamese or Café du Monde ground coffee, you can also make this with good ground French Roast.

1. Bring the milk, vanilla (both seeds and pod), salt, and half the cream to a simmer over medium heat in a large saucepan. Remove from the heat and set aside.

2. Put the sugar in a small saucepan and add just enough water to wet it, about 1 tablespoon. Shake the pan to distribute the sugar and water and caramelize over medium-high heat, shaking the pan occasionally. The sugar will gradually liquefy and darken; when it becomes golden brown, after about 5 minutes, remove from the heat and carefully add the warmed milk mixture (it may spatter; hold the pan at arm's length), then return to the heat. Cook, stirring, until the mixture returns to a steady simmer. Remove from the heat and whisk in the coffee.

3. Whisk the yolks in a large mixing bowl just until broken and add ½ cup of the hot coffee cream in a slow, steady stream while whisking constantly. Return that mixture to the saucepan and cook over low heat, stirring constantly, until thick enough to coat the back of a spoon, about 10 minutes.

4. Strain through a fine-mesh sieve into a medium-size bowl, stir in the remaining cream, and cool in the refrigerator (or over a bowl of ice, which is faster). Transfer to an ice cream machine and freeze according to the manufacturer's instructions.

Young Ginger Ice Cream

Makes about 1 quart

2⅔ cups heavy cream
1⅓ cups whole milk
One 7-inch piece fresh young ginger, peeled and chopped
1⅓ cups palm sugar
¼ teaspoon salt
7 large egg yolks

Young ginger, which doesn't pack as much heat as mature ginger, adds a floral and herbaceous spice to this ice cream. The rich palm sugar rounds out the flavors.

1. Bring the cream, milk, ginger, palm sugar, and salt to a simmer, stirring occasionally, over medium heat in a large saucepan. Remove from the heat.

2. Whisk the yolks in a large mixing bowl just until broken and add ½ cup of the hot cream in a slow, steady stream while whisking constantly. Return that mixture to the saucepan and cook over low heat, stirring constantly, until thick enough to coat the back of a spoon.

3. Strain through a fine-mesh sieve into a medium-size bowl and cool in the refrigerator (or over a bowl of ice, which is faster). Transfer to an ice cream machine and freeze according to the manufacturer's instructions.

Green Tea Ice Cream

Makes about 1 quart

2⅔ cups heavy cream
1⅓ cups whole milk
1⅓ cups sugar
¼ teaspoon salt
7 large egg yolks
¼ cup matcha (green tea powder)

Homemade green tea ice cream is far more aromatic than the store-bought kind. Choose a high-quality green tea powder. The ice cream will only be as good as the tea you put into it.

1. Bring the cream, milk, sugar, and salt to a simmer, stirring occasionally, over medium heat in a large saucepan. Remove from the heat.

2. Whisk the yolks in a large mixing bowl just until broken and add ½ cup of the hot cream in a slow, steady stream while whisking constantly. Return that mixture to the saucepan and cook over low heat, stirring constantly, until thick enough to coat the back of a spoon, about 10 minutes.

3. Strain through a fine-mesh sieve into a medium-size bowl and whisk in the matcha until completely dissolved and well incorporated. Cool in the refrigerator (or over a bowl of ice, which is faster). Transfer to an ice cream machine and freeze according to the manufacturer's instructions.

Coconut Sorbet

Makes about 1 quart

2 cups plus 2 tablespoons coconut milk
½ cup whole milk
½ cup heavy cream
1 teaspoon sugar
¼ cup plus 2 tablespoons Simple Sugar Syrup (page 246)
¼ cup plus 2 tablespoons Malibu rum

The fresh nutty flavors of coconut really come out when frozen into a sorbet. This is an ideal accompaniment to chocolate desserts.

1. Bring the coconut milk, milk, cream, and sugar to a simmer, stirring occasionally, over medium heat in a large saucepan. Remove from the heat and transfer to a medium mixing bowl.

2. Cool in the refrigerator (or over the bowl of ice water, which is faster) until cold. Stir in the syrup and rum. Transfer to an ice cream machine and freeze according to the manufacturer's instructions.

Clockwise from top left: →
passion fruit sherbet, green tea ice cream, coconut sorbet, Vietnamese coffee ice cream, strawberry, vanilla, and red wine sorbet

Strawberry, Vanilla, and Red Wine Sorbet

Makes about 1 quart

2 pounds strawberries, stemmed and quartered
1 cup dry red wine
1½ cups sugar, plus more to taste
4 vanilla beans, halved lengthwise and seeds scraped
3 tablespoons fresh lemon juice

Light and sophisticated, this is an elegant ending to any meal.

1. Put the strawberries, wine, sugar, and vanilla (both seeds and pods) and lemon juice in a large bowl and set aside for 45 minutes.

2. Remove the vanilla pods, transfer the mixture to a blender, and purée until smooth. Taste and adjust the sugar, if desired. Transfer to an ice cream machine and freeze according to the manufacturer's instructions.

A traditional street → dessert of coconut milk and rice flour called *kanom krok*

NAVY MARINE
KIKILALA

Sources

Your best bet for finding a lot of the Asian ingredients used in this book is your local Asian market. Well-stocked supermarkets and specialty, gourmet, and natural food markets may also carry many of the ingredients.

Mail- and Internet-Order Sources

Amazon.com
www.amazon.com
This is actually a great one-stop shop for specialty dry ingredients. The "Gourmet Food" store category carries items from many different sources, but you can order from all of them through your single Amazon account while purchasing other items as well.

Ethnic Grocer
www.ethnicgrocer.com
Specializes in ingredients from around the world. A good one-stop shop for exotic ingredients.

Foods of India
121 Lexington Avenue
New York, NY 10016
(212) 683-4419
This wonderful place for Indian spices and ingredients, like tandoori spice mix (see page 135), ships to all fifty states. You can order by phone too.

Kalustyan's
123 Lexington Avenue
New York, NY 10016
(212) 685-3451
www.kalustyans.com
A good source for South Asian spices and herbs, as well as nuts and specialty items.

Melissa's World Variety Produce, Inc.
P.O. Box 21127
Los Angeles, CA 90021
(800) 588-0151
www.melissas.com
Ships fresh, exotic, and hard-to-find organic produce.

Penzeys Spices
P.O. Box 933
Muskego, WI 53150
(414) 679-7207
www.penzeys.com
High-quality spices, whole and ground, from around the world.

Temple of Thai
www.templeofthai.com
A great one-stop shop for Southeast Asian ingredients.

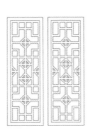

Index

A

Almond flour, 4
Ammonia powder, 4, 133
Anise
coconut-anise vinaigrette, mixed lettuces with, 86–87
Appetizers, 14–69
braised pork belly with shallot, 69
charred chile-rubbed beef skewers with Thai basil dipping sauce, 66–67
chicken buns, 30–31
chicken samosas with cilantro-yogurt dip, 27–29
chili prawns with sweet sesame walnuts, 40–41
cold sesame noodles 66, 15–16
crab fritters with three dipping sauces, 32–33
duck sticks, 26
dumplings: black pepper crab, 34–36; shrimp and pork, 37–38
grilled oyster mushroom and avocado carpaccio, 68
hamachi with chile-citrus sorbet and mango, 55
mussels steamed with lemongrass, Thai basil, dried chile, and coconut juice, 46
raw beef with five condiments, 61
rolls: chicken and shrimp egg rolls, 21–22; crispy vegetable rolls, 19–20; lobster summer rolls, 17–18; mushroom spring rolls with galangal emulsion, 24–25
satay: chicken, 62; pork, 65
shrimp: cakes, with cucumber-peanut relish, 39; and chicken egg rolls, 21–22; seared, with gingered butternut squash, 43–45; toasts, with water chestnuts, 42
soy-cured salmon, Asian pear, and cilantro crème fraîche, 56
Thai fried chicken wings with hot-and-sour sauce and salted mango, 59–60
tuna: ribbons, with ginger marinade, 51–52; rice cracker-crusted, with spicy citrus sauce, 49; seared, with Sichuan pepper and soy-mustard sauce, 48; shaved tuna, chile tapioca, Asian pear, and lime, 53–54
Apples, slow-baked halibut with onions, coconut, and, 119
Artichoke, curried, spiced cod with, 108–109
Asian pear
shaved tuna, chile tapioca, Asian pear, and lime, 53–54
soy-cured salmon, Asian pear, and cilantro crème fraîche, 56
Asian-style pickles, 19–20
Asparagus
green curry vegetables, 219–220
salad, with Chinese mustard, 94
Avocado
grilled oyster mushroom and avocado carpaccio, 68
and radish salad, with onion tempura, 95–96

B

Bamboo shoots, 4
Banana
caramelized banana cake with crunchy praline and caramel ice cream, 268–270
Ovaltine kulfi with caramelized banana and spiced milk chocolate sauce, 264–267
"Barbecued" red snapper, Thai style, 128
Barbecue sauce, baby back ribs with, 205
Basil, Thai. *See* Thai basil
Bean curd sheets. *See* Tofu skin(s)
Beans. *See* Chinese long beans; Green beans
Bean sprouts
shrimp and bean sprout salad, 104
Beef
brisket, with onions and chile, 195
charred chile-rubbed beef skewers with Thai basil dipping sauce, 66–67
charred sirloin with soy, garlic, and coriander, 193–194
raw, with five condiments, 61
sirloin steaks with garlic soy butter and pickled bell peppers, 196–197
Bell peppers, pickled, sirloin steaks with garlic soy butter and, 196–197
Bird peppers, 9. *See also* Chile(s)
Black bean(s)
ginger–garlic–black bean crumbs, skate wings with, 124–127
sauce, lobster with broccoli and, 154–155
Black pepper crab dumplings, 34–36
Black pepper shrimp with "sun-dried" pineapple, 151
Black sea bass
crispy, with sweet-and-sour sauce and green tea, 133–134
with fragrant coconut juice, 130–132
Black sesame vinaigrette, 147
Bok choy, salmon glazed with lime leaf with cinnamon and, 138–139
Boston lettuce salad with lemon-licorice dressing, 88
Broccoli, Chinese, 5
Broccoli
green curry vegetables, 219–220

lobster with black bean sauce and, 154–155
stir-fried corn and, 216
Broth
fragrant lemongrass, shrimp dumplings with, 81–82
ginger, steamed salmon in, 140
lime-coconut, 53–54
mushroom-ginger, with sea scallops, 72
Browned butter vinaigrette, 122
Buns, chicken, 30–31
Butternut squash
gingered, seared shrimp with, 43–45
roasted, shrimp with, 147
sautéed, grilled swordfish with, 129

C

Cabbage
"fish" with wok-fried Napa cabbage, 141–142
Napa cabbage salad, chicken paillard with, 166–167
shredded cabbage salad, 90
shredded vegetable salad, 91
Café du Monde coffee, 4
Cake, caramelized banana, with crunchy praline and caramel ice cream, 268–270
Cakes, shrimp, with cucumber-peanut relish, 39
Caramel
caramelized banana cake with crunchy praline and caramel ice cream, 268–270
Ovaltine kulfi with caramelized banana and spiced milk chocolate sauce, 264–267
sauce, chicken wings with ginger and, 178
Carpaccio, grilled oyster mushroom and avocado, 68
Carrots
crunchy baked chicken with glazed baby carrots, 174–175
Chicken, 166–178
buns, 30–31
crunchy baked, with glazed baby carrots, 174–175
curry, with fat noodles and spring vegetables, 176–177
grilled, with kumquat-lemongrass dressing, 169–170
paillard, with Napa salad, 166–167
roast: with chunky miso sauce and grapefruit, 171; with haricots verts and onion compote, 172–173
samosas, with cilantro-yogurt dip, 27–29
satay, 62
and shrimp egg rolls, 21–22
Singapore noodles, 229
in soups: chicken and coconut milk, 77; chicken noodle with Chinese vegetables, 78–79; hot-and-sour soup, 74
Thai fried chicken wings with hot-and-sour sauce and salted mango, 59–60
wings, with ginger and caramel sauce, 178
Chicken stock, Chinese, 78–79
Chile(s), 8, 9
beef brisket with onions and, 195
charred chile-rubbed beef skewers with Thai basil dipping sauce, 66–67
chile-citrus sorbet, hamachi with mango and, 55
chile-garlic egg noodles, 233
chile mayonnaise, 17–18
glaze, pork chops with, 203
lime-chile salt, 95–96
lime-spiced salt, seasonal fruit plate with, 261
red finger chiles, 8
sautéed lamb chops with garlic, lemon, and, 198–199
shaved tuna, chile tapioca, Asian pear, and lime, 53–54
smoked chile glaze, squid tempura in, 158
soy and chile mignonette sauce, 32–33
Thai chiles, 9
Chili pastes, 4, 5
Chili prawns with sweet sesame walnuts, 40–41
Chili sauce, 4
Malaysian, cod with, 113–114
Chinese broccoli, 5
Chinese chicken stock, 78–79
Chinese long beans, 5
mango salad, cherry tomato, long bean, and tamarind, 93
in shrimp cakes with cucumber-peanut relish, 39
Chinese mustard, asparagus salad with, 94
Chinese vegetables, chicken noodle soup with, 78–79
Chocolate
chocolate and Vietnamese coffee tart with condensed milk ice cream, 262–263
cream, Thai sundae with, 256–257
Ovaltine kulfi with caramelized banana and spiced milk chocolate sauce, 264–267
sauce, for caramelized banana cake with crunchy praline and caramel ice cream, 268–270
Chutney, tomato, monkfish with tandoori spices and, 135
Cilantro
cilantro crème fraîche, soy-cured salmon with Asian pear and, 56
cilantro-yogurt dip, chicken samosas with, 27–29
oil, 154
Cinnamon, salmon glazed with lime leaf with bok choy and, 138–139
Citrus. *See also specific types*
chile-citrus sorbet, hamachi with mango and, 55
citrus soy sauce, 174–175
sauce, spicy, rice cracker–crusted tuna with, 49
vinaigrette, 95–96
Coconut, coconut juice, 5
black sea bass with fragrant coconut juice, 130–132
coconut and tapioca parfait with tropical fruits, 244–245
coconut-anise vinaigrette, mixed lettuces with, 86–87
coconut milk and chicken soup, 77
coconut panna cotta with exotic fruit salad, 246–247
coconut-poached halibut and eggplant, 120–121
coconut sauce, 253
coconut sorbet, 274

coconut sticky rice, 224
coconut tuiles, 86
crushed coconut ice, Thai jewels and fruits on, 253–254
lime-coconut broth, 53–54
mussels steamed with lemongrass, Thai basil, dried chile, and coconut juice, 46
shaved tuna, chile tapioca, Asian pear, and lime, 53–54
slow-baked halibut with apples, onions, and coconut, 119
Cod
with Malaysian chili sauce, 113–114
spiced, with curried artichoke, 108–109
steamed, with caramelized onion, ginger, and scallions, 110
Coffee, 4
chocolate and Vietnamese coffee tart with condensed milk ice cream, 262–263
espresso granité, Thai sundae with, 256–257
Vietnamese coffee ice cream, 271
Compote, haricots verts and onion, roast chicken with, 172–173
Condensed milk ice cream, chocolate and Vietnamese coffee tart with, 262–263
Confit, shallot, braised pork belly with, 69
Coriander, charred sirloin with soy, garlic, and, 193–194
Corn. *See also* Popcorn
and crab soup, 76
green curry vegetables, 219–220
stir-fried broccoli and, 216
Crab(s)
black pepper crab dumplings, 34–36
corn and crab soup, 76
fritters, with three dipping sauces, 32–33
pad Thai with shrimp and, 232
Singapore noodles, 229
soft-shell crabs, 161–162
Crème fraîche, cilantro, soy-cured salmon with Asian pear and, 56
Crepes, for Peking duck, 184–185
Crispy vegetable rolls, 19–20
Cucumber(s)
cucumber-peanut relish, shrimp cakes with, 39
marinated with orange peel, 89
pickles, 161
Curry
about curry pastes, 5
chicken, with fat noodles and spring vegetables, 176–177
curried artichoke, spiced cod with, 108–109
curry jus rôti, 181
green, lamb shank braised with vegetables and, 200–201
green curry lentils, salmon in tofu skin with, 136–137
green curry vegetables, 219–220
lobster with Thai herbs, 156–157
red curry duck, 179

D

Desserts, 244–276
caramelized banana cake with crunchy praline and caramel ice cream, 268–270
chocolate and Vietnamese coffee tart with condensed milk ice cream, 262–263
coconut and tapioca parfait with tropical fruits, 244–245
coconut panna cotta with exotic fruit salad, 246–247
coconut sorbet, 274
green tea ice cream, 273
Ovaltine kulfi with caramelized banana and spiced milk chocolate sauce, 264–267
passion fruit Pavlova, 251–252
passion fruit soufflé, 248–249
seasonal fruit plate with lime-spiced salt, 261
strawberry, vanilla, and red wine sorbet, 276
Thai jewels and fruits on crushed coconut ice, 253–254
Thai sundae, 256–257
Vietnamese coffee ice cream, 271
warm rice pudding and passion fruit sherbet, 259–260
young ginger ice cream, 272
Dip, cilantro-yogurt, chicken samosas with, 27–29
Dipping sauce(s)
cilantro crème fraîche, soy-cured salmon and Asian pear with, 56
crab fritters with three dipping sauces, 32–33
Thai basil, charred chile-rubbed beef skewers with, 66–67
Dressing. *See also* Vinaigrette
kumquat-lemongrass, grilled chicken with, 169–170
lemon-licorice, Boston lettuce salad with, 88
spicy sour dressing, 97
Dried shrimp, 5
Duck
duck "Oriental," 181–182
duck sticks, 26
Peking duck, 184–185
red curry duck, 179
Duck mustard, 21
Dumplings
black pepper crab, 34–36
shrimp, with fragrant lemongrass broth, 81–82
shrimp and pork, 37–38

E

Egg drop soup
hot-and-sour soup, 74
tomato, 73
Egg noodles. *See* Noodles
Eggplant
coconut-poached halibut and, 120–121
green curry vegetables, 219–220
steamed spicy eggplant, 217
Egg rolls, chicken and shrimp, 21–22
Eggs, ginger fried rice with, 227
Elderflower syrup, 5
Emulsion
galangal, mushroom spring rolls with, 24–25
mint, 130
Espresso granité, Thai sundae with, 256–257

F

Fish, 108–143
black sea bass: crispy, with sweet-and-sour sauce and green tea,

133–134; with fragrant coconut juice, 130–132
cod: with Malaysian chili sauce, 113–114; spiced, with curried artichoke, 108–109; steamed, with caramelized onion, ginger, and scallions, 110
"fish" with wok-fried Napa cabbage, 141–142
halibut: Cha Ca La Vong, 117–118; coconut-poached halibut and eggplant, 120–121; slow-baked, with apples, onions, and coconut, 119
hamachi with chile-citrus sorbet and mango, 55
monkfish with tandoori spices and tomato chutney, 135
red snapper, "barbecued" Thai style, 128
salmon: glazed with lime leaf, bok choy, and cinnamon, 138–139; soy-cured salmon, Asian pear, and cilantro crème fraîche, 56; steamed, in ginger broth, 140; in tofu skin with green curry lentils, 136–137
skate: steamed, with tarragon and toasted sesame seeds, 122–123; wings, with ginger–garlic–black bean crumbs, 124–127
sole, poached, with watercress and noodles, 115–116
swordfish, grilled, with sautéed butternut squash, 129
tuna: ribbons, with ginger marinade, 51–52; rice cracker–crusted, with spicy citrus sauce, 49; seared, with Sichuan pepper and soy-mustard sauce, 48; shaved tuna, chile tapioca, Asian pear, and lime, 53–54
Fish fumet, 115
Fish sauce, 7
Fried rice
ginger, 227
pineapple, 225
vegetable, 228
Fritters, crab, with three dipping sauces, 32–33
Frozen yogurt, lime, 244–245
Fruit. *See also specific fruits*
exotic fruit salad, coconut panna cotta with, 246–247
seasonal fruit plate with lime-spiced salt, 261
Thai jewels and fruits on crushed coconut ice, 253–254
tropical fruits, coconut and tapioca parfait with, 244–245
Fumet, fish, 115

G

Gai lan, 5
Galangal, 6
emulsion, mushroom spring rolls with, 24–25
Ganache, chocolate-coffee, 262–263
Garlic
charred sirloin with soy, coriander, and, 193–194
chile-garlic egg noodles, 233
garlic-ginger-basil sauce, steamed lobster with, 152
ginger–garlic–black bean crumbs, skate wings with, 124–127
golden, Shanghai noodles with soft tofu and, 235
sautéed lamb chops with lemon, chile, and, 198–199
Gelée
sweet-and-sour, 198
vinegar, lobster summer rolls with, 17–18
Ginger
broth, steamed salmon in, 140
chicken wings with caramel sauce and, 178
garlic-ginger-basil sauce, steamed lobster with, 152
gingered butternut squash, seared shrimp with, 43–45
ginger fried rice, 227
ginger–garlic–black bean crumbs, skate wings with, 124–127
marinade, ribbons of tuna with, 51–52
mushroom-ginger broth with sea scallops, 72
spicy ginger tofu, 212
steamed cod with caramelized onion, scallions, and, 110
steamed mushrooms with sticky rice and, 213
syrup, 43
young ginger ice cream, 272
Glutinous rice. *See* Sticky rice
Glutinous rice flour, 6
Golden needles. *See* Lily buds
Granité, espresso, 256–257
Grapefruit
citrus vinaigrette, 95–96
roast chicken with chunky miso sauce and, 171
Green beans. *See also* Chinese long beans
haricots verts and onion compote, roast chicken with, 172–173
Green curry
green curry lentils, salmon in tofu skin with, 136–137
green curry vegetables, 219–220
lamb shank braised with vegetables and, 200–201
Green papaya(s), 6
green papaya rémoulade, 32–33
Green tea, 7
black sea bass with sweet-and-sour sauce and, 133–134
ice cream, 273

H

Halibut
Cha Ca La Vong, 117–118
coconut-poached eggplant and, 120–121
slow-baked, with apples, onions, and coconut, 119
Hamachi with chile-citrus sorbet and mango, 55
Haricots verts and onion compote, roast chicken with, 172–173
Hartshorn. *See* Ammonia powder
Hazelnut oil, 6
Herbs, Thai, lobster with, 156–157
Honey
sesame-honey sauce, 181–182
Hot-and-sour sauce, Thai fried chicken wings with salted mango and, 59–60
Hot-and-sour soup, 74
Hot bean pastes, 4

Hue Dew (Hua Diao) wine. *See* Shaoxing wine

I

Ice, crushed coconut, Thai jewels and fruits on, 253–254
Ice cream
caramel, caramelized banana cake with crunchy praline and, 268–270
condensed milk, chocolate and Vietnamese coffee tart with, 262–263
green tea, 273
rice pudding, Thai sundae with, 256–257
Vietnamese coffee, 271
young ginger, 272
Ingredients
pantry items, 4–10
sources, 280–281

J

Jasmine syrup. *See* Mali syrup
Jus
jus rôti, 181
spiced jus, 172

K

Ketchup, tamarind, 32–33
Kulfi, Ovaltine, with caramelized banana and spiced milk chocolate sauce, 264–267
Kumquat-lemongrass dressing, grilled chicken with, 169–170

L

Lamb
charred lamb salad, 103
chops, sautéed, with garlic, lemon, and chile, 198–199
shanks: braised with green curry and vegetables, 200–201; steamed, 202
Laver, 7
Lemon
lemon-licorice dressing, Boston lettuce salad with, 88
sautéed lamb chops with garlic, chile, and, 198–199
Lemongrass
broth, fragrant, shrimp dumplings with, 81–82
kumquat-lemongrass dressing, grilled chicken with, 169–170
mussels steamed with Thai basil, dried chile, coconut juice, and, 46
Lemon verbena oil, 119
Lentils, green curry, salmon in tofu skin with, 136–137
Licorice powder, 6
lemon-licorice dressing, Boston lettuce salad with, 88
Lily buds, 6
Lime
lime-chile salt, 95–96
lime-coconut broth, 53–54
lime frozen yogurt, 244–245
lime-spiced salt, seasonal fruit plate with, 261
noodles, with vegetables, basil, and sesame, 230
shaved tuna, chile tapioca, Asian pear, and lime, 53–54
Lime leaf, 6
salmon glazed with, with bok choy and cinnamon, 138–139
Lobster(s)
with black bean sauce and broccoli, 154–155
lobster summer rolls, 17–18
steamed, with garlic-ginger-basil sauce, 152
with Thai herbs, 156–157
Long beans. *See* Chinese long beans
Lotus root, 6–7

M

Mail-order sources, 280–281
Malaysian chili sauce, cod with, 113–114
Mali syrup, 7
mali sauce, 253
Mango
hamachi with chile-citrus sorbet and, 55
mango salad, cherry tomato, long bean, and tamarind, 93
salted, Thai fried chicken wings with hot-and-sour sauce and, 59–60
Matcha, 7. *See also* Green tea
Mayonnaise
chili, 17–18
green papaya rémoulade, 32–33
sauce, stir-fried shrimp with, 148
Meat. *See* Beef; Lamb; Pork
Mignonette sauce, soy and chile, 32–33
Mint emulsion, 130
Miso sauce, chunky, roast chicken with grapefruit and, 171
Monkfish with tandoori spices and tomato chutney, 135
Mushroom(s)
grilled oyster mushroom and avocado carpaccio, 68
mushroom-ginger broth with sea scallops, 72
salad of wild mushrooms and greens, 100
spring rolls, with galangal emulsion, 24–25
steamed, with ginger and sticky rice, 213
water chestnuts, sugar snap peas, and shiitakes, 214
Mussels steamed with lemongrass, Thai basil, dried chile, and coconut juice, 46
Mustard
Chinese, asparagus salad with, 94
duck mustard, 21
mustard sauce, 95–96
papaya, grilled shrimp with, 146
soy-mustard sauce, seared tuna with Sichuan pepper and, 48

N

Nam pla, 7. *See also* Fish sauce
Nam prik, 19–20
pineapple, 37–38
Napa cabbage. *See* Cabbage
Noodles, 229–237
beef brisket with onions and chile, 195
chicken noodle soup with Chinese vegetables, 78–79
chile-garlic egg noodles, 233
cold sesame noodles 66, 15–16
egg noodle pancake, 240; squab with, 188–189
fat, chicken curry with spring vegetables and, 176–177
lime, with vegetables, basil, and sesame, 230

pad Thai with crab and shrimp, 232
poached sole with watercress and, 115–116
Shanghai, with golden garlic and soft tofu, 235
Singapore noodles, 229
spicy egg noodles with vegetables, 236–237
Nori, 7
Nuoc cham, 117
Nuoc mam, 7. *See also* Fish sauce

O

Oil
cilantro, 154
cinnamon, 138
lemon verbena, 119
Thai basil, 66
Onion(s)
beef brisket with chile and, 195
caramelized, steamed cod with ginger, scallions, and, 110
and haricots vert compote, roast chicken with, 172–173
slow-baked halibut with apples, coconut, and, 119
tempura, avocado and radish salad with, 95–96
Orange
cucumber marinated with orange peel, 89
squab "à l'orange" with crystallized tamarind, 187
Ovaltine kulfi with caramelized banana and spiced milk chocolate sauce, 264–267
Oyster mushrooms
grilled oyster mushroom and avocado carpaccio, 68

P

Pad Thai with crab and shrimp, 232
Palm sugar, 7
Pancake(s)
egg noodle, 240; squab with, 188–189
scallion, 238–239
Panna cotta, coconut, with exotic fruit salad, 246–247
Pantry items, 4–10
sources, 280–281
Papaya, 6
green papaya rémoulade, 32–33
papaya mustard, grilled shrimp with, 146
Parfait, coconut and tapioca, with tropical fruits, 244–245
Passion fruit purée, 7
passion fruit Pavlova, 251–252
passion fruit sherbet, warm rice pudding and, 259–260
passion fruit sorbet, coconut panna cotta and exotic fruit salad with, 246–247
passion fruit soufflé, 248–249
Pavlova, passion fruit, 251–252
Peanut(s)
cold sesame noodles 66, 15–16
cucumber-peanut relish, shrimp cakes with, 39
sauce: chicken satay with, 62; halibut Cha Ca La Vong with, 117–118
Peas
green curry vegetables, 219–220
water chestnuts, sugar snap peas, and shiitakes, 214
Peking duck, 184–185
Pepper. *See* Black pepper; Sichuan pepper
Peppers. *See* Bell peppers; Chile(s)
Pickles
Asian-style, 19–20
cucumber, 161
pickled bell peppers, sirloin steaks with garlic soy butter and, 196–197
Pineapple
coconut and tapioca parfait with tropical fruits, 244–245
nam prik, shrimp and pork dumplings with, 37–38
pineapple fried rice, 225
"sun-dried," black pepper shrimp with, 151
Ponzu, 7
Popcorn
spiced caramel popcorn, 264–266
Pork
baby back ribs with barbecue sauce, 205
belly, braised, with shallot, 69
chops, with chile glaze, 203
satay, 65
and shrimp dumplings, 37–38
vindaloo, 206–208
Potatoes
crunchy potato salad, 101
Poultry. *See* Chicken; Duck; Squab
Praline, crunchy, caramelized banana cake with caramel ice cream and, 268–270
Prawns. *See also* Shrimp
chili prawns with sweet sesame walnuts, 40–41
Pudding, rice
rice pudding ice cream, Thai sundae with, 256–257
warm, with passion fruit sherbet, 259–260
Pumpkin seeds, seared shrimp and gingered butternut squash with, 43–45

R

Radish and avocado salad with onion tempura, 95–96
Red curry duck, 179
Red finger chiles, 8. *See also* Chile(s)
Red snapper, "barbecued" Thai style, 128
Red wine
strawberry, vanilla, and red wine sorbet, 276
Relish, cucumber-peanut, shrimp cakes with, 39
Rémoulade, green papaya, 32–33
Ribs
baby back ribs with barbecue sauce, 205
Rice, 9, 224–228
coconut sticky rice, 224
ginger fried rice, 227
pineapple fried rice, 225
rice pudding ice cream, Thai sundae with, 256–257
steamed mushrooms with ginger and sticky rice, 213
sushi rice, 122
warm rice pudding and passion fruit sherbet, 259–260
Rice cracker–crusted tuna with spicy citrus sauce, 49
Rice flour, 6

Rice paper, 8
Rice vinegar, 8
Rolls
chicken and shrimp egg rolls, 21–22
crispy vegetable rolls, 19–20
lobster summer rolls, 17–18
mushroom spring rolls with galangal emulsion, 24–25

S

Salad(s), 86–104
asparagus, with Chinese mustard, 94
avocado and radish, with onion tempura, 95–96
Boston lettuce, with lemon-licorice dressing, 88
charred lamb salad, 103
crunchy fried squid salad, 97–98
crunchy potato salad, 101
cucumber marinated with orange peel, 89
exotic fruit, coconut panna cotta with, 246–247
mango salad, cherry tomato, long bean, and tamarind, 93
mixed lettuces with coconut-anise vinaigrette, 86–87
Napa cabbage, chicken paillard with, 166–167
shredded cabbage salad, 90
shredded vegetable salad, 91
shrimp and bean sprout, 104
of wild mushrooms and greens, 100
Salmon
glazed with lime leaf, bok choy, and cinnamon, 138–139
soy-cured salmon, Asian pear, and cilantro crème fraîche, 56
steamed, in ginger broth, 140
in tofu skin with green curry lentils, 136–137
Salt
lime-chile salt, 95–96
lime-spiced, seasonal fruit plate with, 261
Samosas, chicken, with cilantro-yogurt dip, 27–29
Satay
chicken, 62
pork, 65
Sauce(s)
barbecue, baby back ribs with, 205
caramel: chicken wings with ginger and, 178; Ovaltine kulfi with caramelized banana, spiced milk chocolate sauce, and, 264–267
chocolate: for caramelized banana cake with crunchy praline and caramel ice cream, 268–270; spiced milk chocolate, Ovaltine kulfi with caramelized banana and, 264–267
citrus soy sauce, 174–175
coconut sauce, 253
garlic-ginger-basil, steamed lobster with, 152
green curry, 219
green papaya rémoulade, 32–33
hot-and-sour, Thai fried chicken wings with salted mango and, 59–60
Malaysian chili sauce, cod with, 113–114
mali sauce, 253
mayonnaise, stir-fried shrimp with, 148
miso, chunky, roast chicken with grapefruit and, 171
mustard sauce, 95–96
nuoc cham, 117
peanut, chicken satay with, 62
peanut, halibut Cha Ca La Vong with, 117–118
pineapple nam prik, shrimp and pork dumplings with, 37–38
sesame-honey, 181–182
soy and chile mignonette, 32–33
soy-mustard, seared tuna with Sichuan pepper and, 48
spiced jus, 172
spicy citrus, rice cracker–crusted tuna with, 49
sweet-and-sour, black sea bass with green tea and, 133–134
Thai basil dipping sauce, charred chile-rubbed beef skewers with, 66–67
tomato: "barbecued" red snapper with, 128; shrimp with, 148
Vietnamese coffee, 262
Scallions
scallion pancakes, 238–239
steamed cod with caramelized onion, ginger, and, 110
Scallops
mushroom-ginger broth with sea scallops, 72
Singapore noodles, 229
Schutz, Pierre, 2–3
Seafood. *See* Fish; Shellfish; *specific types*
Sea scallops. *See* Scallops
Sesame
black sesame vinaigrette, 147
cold sesame noodles 66, 15–16
lime noodles with vegetables, basil, and, 230
sesame-honey sauce, 181–182
sweet sesame walnuts, chili prawns with, 40–41
toasted sesame seeds, steamed skate with tarragon and, 122–123
Shallot, braised pork belly with, 69
Shanghai noodles with golden garlic and soft tofu, 235
Shaoxing wine, 8
Shellfish, 146–162. *See also* Crab(s); Lobster(s); Shrimp; Squid
Sherbet. *See also* Sorbet
passion fruit, warm rice pudding and, 259–260
Shiitakes, water chestnuts, and sugar snap peas, 214
Shrimp
and bean sprout salad, 104
black pepper shrimp with "sun-dried" pineapple, 151
cakes, with cucumber-peanut relish, 39
chicken and shrimp egg rolls, 21–22
chili prawns with sweet sesame walnuts, 40–41
dumplings, with fragrant lemongass broth, 81–82
grilled, with papaya mustard, 146
pad Thai with crab and, 232
and pork dumplings, 37–38
with roasted butternut squash, 147
seared, with gingered butternut squash, 43–45
Singapore noodles, 229
stir-fried, with two flavors, 148
toasts, with water chestnuts, 42

Shrimp, dried, 5
Shrimp paste, 8
Sichuan pepper, seared tuna with soy-mustard sauce and, 48
Singapore noodles, 229
66 restaurant, 3
Skate
steamed, with tarragon and toasted sesame seeds, 122–123
wings, with ginger–garlic–black bean crumbs, 124–127
Soft-shell crabs, 161–162
Sole, poached, with watercress and noodles, 115–116
Sorbet. *See also* Sherbet
chile-citrus, hamachi with mango and, 55
coconut, 274
passion fruit: coconut panna cotta and exotic fruit salad with, 246–247; passion fruit Pavlova, 251–252
strawberry, vanilla, and red wine, 276
Soufflé, passion fruit, 248–249
Soup(s), 72–82
chicken and coconut milk (tom yum gai), 77
chicken noodle, with Chinese vegetables, 78–79
corn and crab, 76
hot-and-sour, 74
mushroom-ginger broth with sea scallops, 72
shrimp dumplings with fragrant lemongass broth, 81–82
tomato egg drop soup, 73
Soy
charred sirloin with garlic, coriander, and, 193–194
and chile mignonette sauce, 32–33
chili pastes with, 4
citrus soy sauce, 174–175
garlic soy butter, sirloin steaks with pickled bell peppers and, 196–197
soy-cured salmon, Asian pear, and cilantro crème fraîche, 56
soy-mustard sauce, seared tuna with Sichuan pepper and, 48
Spiced caramel popcorn, 264–266
Spiced jus, 172
Spiced milk chocolate sauce, Ovaltine kulfi with caramelized banana and, 264–267
Spice Market, 3
Spring rolls, mushroom, with galangal emulsion, 24–25
Squab
with egg noodle pancake, 188–189
"à l'orange," with crystallized tamarind, 187
Squash, butternut
gingered, seared shrimp with, 43–45
roasted, shrimp with, 147
sautéed, grilled swordfish with, 129
Squid
crunchy fried squid salad, 97–98
tempura, in smoked chile glaze, 158
Star anise, 8–9
Sticky rice, 9
coconut sticky rice, 224
steamed mushrooms with ginger and, 213
Stock
chicken, Chinese, 78–79
fish fumet, 115
Strawberry, vanilla, and red wine sorbet, 276
Sugar snap peas
green curry vegetables, 219–220
water chestnuts, sugar snap peas, and shiitakes, 214
Sumac, 9
Summer rolls, lobster, 17–18
Sundae, Thai, 256–257
Sushi rice, 122
Sweet-and-sour gelée, 198
Sweet-and-sour sauce, black sea bass with green tea and, 133–134
Sweet rice. *See* Sticky rice
Sweet rice flour, 6
Sweet sesame walnuts, chili prawns with, 40–41
Swordfish, grilled, with sautéed butternut squash, 129
Syrup, ginger, 43

T

Tamarind
crystallized, squab "à l'orange" with, 187
mango salad, cherry tomato, long bean, and tamarind, 93
tamarind ketchup, 32–33
Tamarind candy, 5
Tamarind paste, 9
Tandoori spices, monkfish with tomato chutney and, 135
Tapioca
and coconut parfait with tropical fruits, 244–245
shaved tuna, chile tapioca, Asian pear, and lime, 53–54
Taro, 9
Tarragon, steamed skate with toasted sesame seeds and, 122–123
Tart, chocolate and Vietnamese coffee, with condensed milk ice cream, 262–263
Tea. *See* Green tea
Tempura
batter, 124, 161
onion, avocado and radish salad with, 95–96
skate wings with ginger–garlic–black bean crumbs, 124–127
soft-shell crabs, 161–162
squid, in smoked chile glaze, 158
Thai basil, 9
dipping sauce, charred chile-rubbed beef skewers with, 66–67
garlic-ginger-basil sauce, steamed lobster with, 152
lime noodles with vegetables, sesame, and, 230
mussels steamed with lemongrass, dried chile, coconut juice, and, 46
Thai basil oil, 66
Thai chiles, 9. *See also* Chile(s)
Thai fried chicken wings with hot-and-sour sauce and salted mango, 59–60
Thai herbs, lobster with, 156–157
Thai jewels and fruits on crushed coconut ice, 253–254
Thai-style "barbecued" red snapper, 128
Thai sundae, 256–257
Toasts, shrimp, with water chestnuts, 42
Tofu
soft, Shanghai noodles with golden garlic and, 235
spicy ginger tofu, 212

Tofu skin(s), 9–10
salmon in, with green curry lentils, 136–137
Tomato(es)
chutney, monkfish with tandoori spices and, 135
mango salad, cherry tomato, long bean, and tamarind, 93
sauce: "barbecued" red snapper, Thai style, 128; stir-fried shrimp with two flavors, 148
tomato egg drop soup, 73
Tom yum gai (chicken and coconut milk soup), 77
Tropical fruit. *See* Fruit; *specific fruits*
Tuiles, coconut, 86
Tuna
ribbons of, with ginger marinade, 51–52
rice cracker–crusted, with spicy citrus sauce, 49
seared, with Sichuan pepper and soy-mustard sauce, 48
shaved tuna, chile tapioca, Asian pear, and lime, 53–54
Turmeric, 10

V

Vanilla
strawberry, vanilla, and red wine sorbet, 276
Vegetable(s), 212–220. *See also specific types*
Chinese, chicken noodle soup with, 78–79
crispy vegetable rolls, 19–20
green curry vegetables, 219–220
lamb shank braised with green curry and, 200–201
lime noodles with basil, sesame, and, 230
pineapple fried rice with, 225
shredded vegetable salad, 91
spicy egg noodles with, 236–237
spicy ginger tofu, 212
spring, chicken curry with fat noodles and, 176–177
steamed mushrooms with ginger and sticky rice, 213
steamed spicy eggplant, 217
stir-fried corn and broccoli, 216
vegetable fried rice, 228
water chestnuts, sugar snap peas, and shiitakes, 214
Vietnamese coffee
and chocolate tart with condensed milk ice cream, 262–263
ice cream, 271
Vinaigrette. *See also* Dressing
black sesame, 147
browned butter, 122
citrus, 95–96
coconut-anise, mixed lettuces with, 86–87
soy-mustard, seared tuna with Sichuan pepper and, 48
Vindaloo, pork, 206–208
Vinegar gelée, 17–18
Vong, 2–3

W

Walnuts, sweet sesame, chili prawns with, 40–41
Water chestnuts, 10
shrimp toasts with, 42
Thai jewels and fruits on crushed coconut ice, 253–254
water chestnuts, sugar snap peas, and shiitakes, 214
Watercress, poached sole with noodles and, 115–116
White port, 10
Wild mushrooms. *See* Mushroom(s)

Y

Yogurt
cilantro-yogurt dip, chicken samosas with, 27–29
lime frozen yogurt, 244–245
Yuzu juice, 10